Hiking and Backpacking

Outdoor Adventures

Library of Congress Cataloging-in-Publication Data

Hiking and backpacking : outdoor adventures / Wilderness Education Association; editors, Marni Goldenberg, Bruce Martin.

p. cm.

Includes bibliographical references.

ISBN-13: 978-0-7360-6801-7 (soft cover : alk. paper)

ISBN-10: 0-7360-6801-5 (soft cover : alk. paper)

1. Hiking. 2. Backpacking. I. Goldenberg, Marni, 1972- II. Martin, Bruce, 1969- III. Wilderness Education Association (U.S.)

GV199.5.H55 2008

796.51--dc22

2007020356

ISBN-10: 0-7360-6801-5

ISBN-13: 978-0-7360-6801-7

The Web addresses cited in this text were current as of July 18, 2007, unless otherwise noted.

Acquisitions Editor: Gayle Kassing, PhD; **Developmental Editor:** Melissa Feld; **Assistant Editors:** Martha Gullo and Anne Rumery; **Copyeditor:** Alisha Jeddeloh; **Proofreader:** Anne Rogers; **Permission Manager:** Dalene Reeder; **Graphic Designer:** Nancy Rasmus; **Graphic Artist:** Dawn Sills; **Cover Designer:** Keith Blomberg; **Photographer (cover):** Layne Kennedy/Corbis; **Photographer (interior):** see pp. 255-256 for full listing; **Photo Asset Manager:** Laura Fitch; **Visual Production Assistant:** Joyce Brumfield; **Photo Office Assistant:** Jason Allen; **Art Manager:** Kelly Hendren; **Illustrator:** Keri Evans; **Printer:** United Graphics

Printed in the United States of America   10 9 8 7 6 5 4 3

The paper in this book is certified under a sustainable forestry program.

Human Kinetics
Web site: www.HumanKinetics.com

United States: Human Kinetics
P.O. Box 5076
Champaign, IL 61825-5076
800-747-4457
e-mail: humank@hkusa.com

Canada: Human Kinetics
475 Devonshire Road, Unit 100
Windsor, ON N8Y 2L5
800-465-7301 (in Canada only)
e-mail: info@hkcanada.com

Europe: Human Kinetics
107 Bradford Road
Stanningley
Leeds LS28 6AT, United Kingdom
+44 (0)113 255 5665
e-mail: hk@hkeurope.com

Australia: Human Kinetics
57A Price Avenue
Lower Mitcham, South Australia 5062
08 8372 0999
e-mail: info@hkaustralia.com

New Zealand: Human Kinetics
P.O. Box 80
Torrens Park, South Australia 5062
0800 222 062
e-mail: info@hknewzealand.com

Hiking and Backpacking

Outdoor Adventures

Wilderness Education Association

Editors

Marni Goldenberg, PhD
California Polytechnic State University

Bruce Martin, PhD
Ohio University

HUMAN KINETICS

Contents

Preface

Welcome to *Hiking and Backpacking*. Our goal is to provide an introduction to hiking and backpacking for all users of natural areas. This book is a resource for those participating in day hikes, short backpacking trips, and more extended backpacking expeditions. It also functions as a text in introductory hiking and backpacking courses taught at the university level.

This book was written in cooperation with the Wilderness Education Association (WEA). The WEA was founded in 1977 to promote safe and responsible use of backcountry and wilderness areas and to promote the professionalism of outdoor leadership, thereby enhancing the conservation of the wild outdoors. For the past 30 years, the organization has been working to fulfill this mission through a network of affiliate organizations now composed of approximately 50 colleges, universities, and private institutions throughout the United States. The WEA sponsors various educational programs through this affiliate network. These programs use nature's classroom to teach the knowledge and skills required for responsible recreational use of backcountry and wilderness areas.

Human Kinetics looked to the WEA to produce *Hiking and Backpacking* as part of its Outdoor Adventure series. The authors of this text have considerable experience in practicing and teaching hiking and backpacking as well as wilderness living and travel in general. All of the authors share the WEA's commitment to promoting safe, responsible recreational use of backcountry and wilderness areas. This shared commitment is based on a great love and passion for wilderness and the outdoors and a subsequent desire to protect and preserve wilderness and natural areas for future enjoyment.

Hiking and Backpacking contains nine chapters. Chapter 1 presents an overview of hiking and backpacking as well as information on natural areas and the types of trails found in those areas. It also introduces the principles and practices of Leave No Trace. Chapter 2 contains information on becoming fit for hiking and backpacking, including physical fitness, stretches, nutrition, and level of training. Chapter 3 covers footwear, clothing, and other gear needed for hiking and backpacking adventures. Chapter 4 helps you to get trail ready by introducing information on getting to the trailhead, planning a route, and navigating once you are on the trail. Chapter 5 introduces safety considerations related to hiking and backpacking as well as considerations in confronting emergency and survival situations while on the trail. Chapter 6 introduces basic hiking techniques such as the rest-step, rhythmic breathing, hiking on-trail and off-trail, ascending and descending steep terrain, and making stream crossings. Chapter 7 covers day hiking considerations such as hiking with children, hiking with dogs, hiking in various types of terrain, and engaging in various types of hikes. Chapter 8 provides information on preparing for the overnight experience, such as rules and regulations for camping, selecting a campsite, and minimizing impact on a campsite. Chapter 9 describes how to plan safe, enjoyable, and environmentally sound wilderness trips of various lengths.

In each of the chapters you will find chapter-opening quotes and consumer, safety, technique, and trail tips. The chapter-opening quotes reflect the essence of the information covered in each of the chapters. The book concludes with success checks and lists of references directing you to additional sources of information (such as additional readings and Web sites) on each of the topics covered in this book. You can use the success checks to test your retention of the information covered in the chapters.

We hope that you find *Hiking and Backpacking* to be useful and enjoyable. We also wish you safe and happy adventures on the trail!

PART I

Preparing for a Hiking or Backpacking Adventure

CHAPTER 1

Going Hiking and Backpacking

When you have worn out your shoes, the strength of the shoe leather has passed into the fiber of your body. I measure your health by the number of shoes and hats and clothes you have worn out.

Ralph Waldo Emerson

Perfect moments make life worthwhile. They happen when you're in the right place with the right people at the right time. They are moments where time seems to stand still, colors appear more vibrant, you can smell and almost taste the freshness of the earth and air around you, and you feel strong and sure. These moments are essential and are often found in out-of-the-way places that awaken your senses and take emotional and physical effort to reach. Hiking and backpacking can lead to many perfect moments, giving the opportunity to reach those out-of-the-way places. All you need is an adventurous frame of mind, a good pair of hiking shoes, a pack with essentials, and a piece of land large and rugged enough to explore. It doesn't matter where you live; in every region there are a variety of places to search for perfect moments and reap the benefits of a hiking or backpacking adventure.

There are hikes for everyone, depending upon the time you have, the condition you're in, and the challenge you want. On one extreme, you can spend months backpacking the Appalachian Trail; on the other extreme, you can take a 20-minute hike in a large city park for a short nature break. In between these two extremes are endless opportunities. In this chapter, you will learn how to embark on the different options of hiking and backpacking, where you can hike and backpack, and how hiking and backpacking will enrich your life, and you will consider the skills you need to hike and backpack efficiently and safely. To begin this journey, open your imagination and put yourself on the trail. Take a deep breath and imagine yourself in the following scenarios.

We'll begin with a casual day hike along a prairie in the U.S. Midwest. You're on a mowed trail surrounded by tall grasses dancing in the wind. The ground is soft and as you walk you feel sure in your stride and at peace. You're with a good friend and the conversation seems to roll easily with the terrain. The sun is warm, but it's fall so it's not too intense. As you reach the top of a brief ridge, you find yourself slightly out of breath due to your pace but in awe of the sight in front of you—a sea of reds, yellows, and oranges. You are pleased because you came to enjoy the fall colors, and the colors of the deciduous forest are vibrant in contrast to the brown grasses leading up to it. You and your friend stop for lunch to enjoy the view, and then continue on the loop trail back to your car. Along the way you continue to enjoy the dancing grasses, the warm sun, your conversation, and the contrasting fall colors. Falling asleep that night, you feel satisfied with the day. Your body is a little tired from the hike, but you feel rejuvenated, and closer to your friend.

Next, imagine being 6 miles (10 kilometers) into a 7-mile (10-kilometer) hike to a 13,000-foot (3,962-meter) peak in the Rocky Mountains. You're with three of your most adventurous friends, and you've been climbing steadily and steeply toward the treeless peak since leaving your car at the trailhead early in the morning. The group was full of excitement and soon you found yourselves in a consistent pace where you were able to balance breathing, walking on a rugged trail, taking in the scenery, and talking with your friends. Now the conversation has disappeared as the terrain has grown steeper and the air thinner. You are aware of every breath and of your heart pounding, and it takes another hour of having to deliberately continue to put one foot in front of the other before you reach the peak. Once you're at the summit, you share a yell of triumph with your friends. It feels like you're on top of the world. In every direction you see gray mountain peaks and blue-green ridges laid out like waves in the sea. You feel strong and surprisingly energized even though you can feel every muscle in your legs. It's a perfect moment: You're in the right place at the right time with the right people.

Finally, imagine yourself nestled in your sleeping bag under a tarp at the edge of a clearing surrounded by scrub oak on the side of a knoll in the Smoky Mountains. You've been backpacking for 4 days and this is the highest campsite you've had and the first with a view. You're facing east and to your delight the soft light of the sunrise and the chatter of the birds woke you up to see a magnificent sight—endless rolling green ridges supporting a horizon layered with oranges, yellows, and reds. You think about waking up your two snoring friends sleeping next to you, but they seem so peaceful you decide to keep this experience between you, the sun, and the birds.

Going to these places in your imagination will not lead you to perfect moments or the other benefits of hiking, but actually seeking out places to hike and backpack will tone your body, soothe and energize your soul, and connect you with the natural world and the people you choose to take with you.

> The richness I achieve comes from Nature, the source of my inspiration.
>
> *Claude Monet*

HIKING AND BACKPACKING: A HISTORICAL LOOK

Because hiking and backpacking predominantly take place in wild lands, the history of hiking and backpacking in the United States can be traced by viewing the history of the conservation and preservation of wilderness. Hiking and backpacking did not exist as recreation until the 1800s, when society became industrialized and people looked to nature for a place to escape the pressures of urban environments. Before then, hiking and backpacking were simply a means of transportation.

Hiking allows you to explore many places you can't reach unless you're on foot.

What's Hiking All About?

Hiking is a simple activity. It only requires a good pair of hiking boots or shoes and a natural area. Hiking can take 20 minutes or a full day depending upon the terrain and the mileage you choose. It differs from walking in that you are usually on a natural trail with uneven terrain, rocks, and roots. These trail features can slow you down, so most people hike slower than they walk on paved surfaces. Still, like walking, hiking is done by putting one foot in front of the other. As you hike, you will be amazed at the places you can explore with foot power. Hiking can take place in a large city park, county park, regional park, state park, wildlife refuge or area, national forest, national park, provincial park, or other land put aside for conservation and recreation purposes.

What's Backpacking All About?

Backpacking is a multiday hiking trip where you carry everything you need to survive in a large backpack. You can backpack on an overnight trip, or with good planning you can stay out through-hiking for months at a time. Typically, you carry shelter, clothing, cooking supplies, 2 or 3 quarts (2-3 liters) of water, water purification supplies, and food for up to 10 days at a time. The main difference between going out for a weekend and going out for a week is the amount of food that you carry. In addition, you need a good pair of hiking boots to support your ankles, good raingear, and a comfortable backpack to carry your essentials.

A backpacker carries what he needs on his back for an overnight trip or longer.

TRAILS

Even if you are not through-hiking, every backpacker should try a few sections of each of these trails in their lifetime.

U.S. Trails

The Appalachian Trail is 2,175 miles (3,500 kilometers) and goes from Georgia to Maine through South Carolina, North Carolina, Virginia, Maryland, Pennsylvania, New York, Connecticut, Massachusetts, Vermont, and New Hampshire (www.appalachiantrail.org).

The Pacific Crest Trail is 2,650 miles (4,365 kilometers) and goes from the Mexican border to the Canadian border through California, Oregon, and Washington (www.fs.fed.us/pct).

(continued)

(continued)

The Colorado Trail is 500 miles (805 kilometers) and goes from Denver to Durango (www.coloradotrail.org).

The Great Western Trail is more than 3,000 miles (4,828 kilometers), but it is still being developed in many places. It goes from the Mexican border to the Canadian border through Arizona, Utah, Idaho, Wyoming, and Montana (http:// gwt.org/index.html).

The Continental Divide Trail is 3,100 miles (4,989 kilometers) and begins at the Mexican border, follows the Continental Divide through New Mexico, Colorado, Wyoming, Idaho, and Montana, and ends at the Canadian border. In Canada the trail continues as the Great Divide Trail (www.cdtrail.org).

Canadian Trails

The Great Divide Trail is 747 miles (1,200 kilometers) and follows the Continental Divide through Alberta and British Columbia (www.rmbooks.com/gdt/history. htm).

The West Coast Trail is 47 miles (75 kilometers) and is a rugged and strenuous trip along the west coast of Vancouver Island in British Columbia (www. westcoasttrailbc.com).

The National Hiking Trail is 6,214 miles (10,000 kilometers) and takes you from Ontario to western Nova Scotia through southern Quebec (www.canadatrails. ca/hiking/index.html).

Australian Trails

The Bibbulmun Track is 598 miles (963 kilometers) and is in Western Australia. It begins in Kalamunda, near Perth, and continues to Albany on the South Coast. (www.naturebase.net/content/view/27/792/).

The Bicentennial National Trail is 3,312 miles (5,330 kilometers) and begins in Cooktown, North Queensland, and ends in Healesville, Victoria. It is the longest marked trail for self-reliant multiuse trekking in the world (http://home.vicnet. net.au/~bnt/).

The Heysen Trail is 758 miles (1,200 kilometers) and begins at the Parachilna Gorge in the Flinders Range and follows the Mount Lofty Ranges to Cape Jervis on the Fleurieu Peninsula (www.heysentrail.asn.au).

New Zealand Trails

New Zealand offers spectacular backpacking opportunities and scenery on all three of its islands. Begin your search for tramping, as they say in New Zealand, at www. tramper.co.nz.

European Trails

There are endless hiking and backpacking options throughout Europe. Use the trail database to begin your search: www.traildatabase.org.

Car camping allows you to spend time overnight in the outdoors but without the necessity of carrying everything you need on your back.

In Between
Day Hiking and Backpacking

What if you don't want to carry everything you need on your back, but you want to hike for multiple days? The solution is to car camp, or camp in the front country. Front country campsites are sites you can drive to. They can be found in county parks, state parks, national parks, and national forests and vary from walk-in rustic sites to sites with water and electricity hookups for campers. The key to camping in this manner is to find sites that offer good hiking opportunities. Some campgrounds offer ample amenities such as full-functioning bathrooms and showers but only have short hikes that are often crowded. When choosing campsites, look for areas that are also designated trailheads.

Taking Care of Yourself, Your
Companions, and the Environment

Hiking and backpacking can take you into the backcountry, the remaining wild places. These areas are recreational and ecological resources, and their value depends upon the integrity of their natural state. Even though recreation in the form of hiking, backpacking, climbing, skiing, camping, and similar activities is accepted, all of these activities have lasting effects that threaten the health and vitality of wild lands. In response to balancing access with protection of the land, Leave No Trace principles (figure 1.1) were developed in cooperation with

Leave No Trace Principles

1. Plan ahead and prepare.
2. Travel and camp on durable surfaces.
3. Dispose of waste properly.
4. Leave what you find.
5. Minimize campfire impacts.
6. Respect wildlife.
7. Be considerate of other visitors.

Plan Ahead and Prepare

- Know the regulations and special concerns for the area you'll visit.
- Prepare for extreme weather, hazards, and emergencies.
- Schedule your trip to avoid times of high use.
- Visit in small groups. Split larger parties into groups of 4, 5, or 6.
- Repackage food to minimize waste.
- Use a map and compass to eliminate the use of marking paint, rock cairns, or flagging.

Travel and Camp on Durable Surfaces

- Durable surfaces include established trails and campsites, rock, gravel, dry grasses, and snow.
- Protect riparian areas by camping at least 200 feet (61 meters) from lakes and streams.
- Good campsites are found, not made. Altering a site is not necessary.
- In popular areas,
    - concentrate use on existing trails and campsites;
    - walk single file in the middle of the trail, even when wet or muddy; and
    - keep campsites small. Focus activity in areas where vegetation is absent.
- In pristine areas,
    - disperse use to prevent the creation of campsites and trails, and
    - avoid places where the human impact is just beginning.

Dispose of Waste Properly

- Pack it in, pack it out. Inspect your campsite and rest areas for trash or spilled foods. Pack out all trash, leftover food, and litter.
- Deposit solid human waste in catholes dug 6 to 8 inches (15-20 centimeters) deep at least 200 feet (61 meters) from water, camp, and trails. Cover and disguise catholes when finished.

- Pack out toilet paper and hygiene products.
- To wash yourself or your dishes, carry water 200 feet (61 meters) away from streams or lakes and use small amounts of biodegradable soap. Scatter strained dishwater.

Leave What You Find

- Preserve the past: Examine, but do not touch, cultural or historic structures and artifacts.
- Leave rocks, plants, and other natural objects as you find them.
- Avoid introducing or transporting nonnative species.
- Do not build structures or furniture or dig trenches.

Minimize Campfire Impacts

- Campfires can leave lasting effects in the backcountry. Use a lightweight stove for cooking and enjoy a candle lantern for light.
- Where fires are permitted, use established fire rings, fire pans, or mound fires.
- Keep fires small. Only use sticks from the ground that can be broken by hand.
- Burn all wood and coals to ash, put out campfires completely, and then scatter cool ashes.

Respect Wildlife

- Observe wildlife from a distance. Do not follow or approach them.
- Never feed wildlife. Feeding wild animals damages their health, alters natural behaviors, and exposes them to predators and other dangers.
- Protect wildlife and your food by storing rations and trash securely.
- Control pets at all times, or leave them at home.
- Avoid wildlife during sensitive times (i.e., mating, nesting, raising young, winter).

Be Considerate of Other Visitors

- Respect other visitors and protect the quality of their experience.
- Be courteous. Yield to other users on the trail.
- Step to the downhill side of the trail when encountering pack stock.
- Take breaks and camp away from trails and other visitors.
- Let the sounds of nature prevail. Avoid loud voices and noises.

Figure 1.1   The seven principles of outdoor ethics form the framework of Leave No Trace's message.

Reprinted, by permission, from Leave No Trace. The Leave No Trace program is managed by the Leave No Trace Center for Outdoor Ethics. The Center is an international nonprofit organization dedicated to the responsible enjoyment and active stewardship of natural lands by all people. Leave No Trace is a cooperative educational program that helps foster stewardship of public lands through education and training. The Leave No Trace message helps public land visitors understand and practice minimum impact skills and ethics. For more information on Leave No Trace, please visit www.LNT.org or call 800-332-4100.

the National Outdoor Leadership School (NOLS) and the major land agencies in the United States—the National Forest Service (NFS), National Park Service (NPS), and Bureau of Land Management (BLM)—to educate people on using the land in a responsible manner that minimizes human impact on the environment. In addition to protecting the natural environment, Leave No Trace principles also teach people how to protect themselves by being prepared and traveling in a responsible manner. Throughout this book you will learn how to use Leave No Trace principles to enjoy hiking and backpacking in a way that protects the environment, your companions, and yourself.

Leave No Trace principles help users minimize the impact they leave on natural resources so that all visitors can enjoy wilderness experiences. Anytime you are in a wilderness area, it is important to understand the effects you have on the land and ways to minimize or eliminate those effects. For example, if a person picks a flower, then that flower is not there for the next visitor to enjoy. There are seven Leave No Trace principles that help establish a common respect and appreciation for the natural environment. Most of these principles are easy to follow, and many are elaborated in greater depth in various chapters throughout this book. In addition, there are many outside resources for learning about the Leave No Trace principles. Read them, discuss them, and practice them with your companions before or on your next backcountry excursion.

INTERNATIONAL LAND MANAGEMENT AGENCIES

Following are examples of land management agencies from across the globe.

Canada

Canadian Forest Service (www.cfs.nrcan.gc.ca/)

Mission: "To promote the sustainable development of Canada's forests and competitiveness of the Canadian forest sector for the well-being of present and future generations of Canadians."

Parks Canada Agency (www.pc.gc.ca/intro/bienvenue-welcome/index_ E.asp)

Mission: To "protect and present nationally significant examples of Canada's natural and cultural heritage foster public understanding, appreciation and enjoyment in ways that ensure their ecological and commemorative integrity for present and future generations."

Australia

New South Wales National Parks and Wildlife Service (www.nationalparks. nsw.gov.au)

Mission: "Responsible for developing and maintaining the parks and reserve system, and conserving natural and cultural heritage, in the state of New South Wales, Australia."

Parks and Wildlife Service of the Northern Territory's Department of Natural Resources, Environment, and the Arts (www.nt.gov.au/nreta/parks)

Mission: "The Service is responsible for developing and managing a comprehensive system of land and marine protected areas for the Territory."

Queensland Parks and Wildlife Service (www.epa.qld.gov.au/parks_and_forests)

Mission: Part of the Environmental Protection Agency (EPA), which "strives to protect Queensland's natural and cultural heritage, promote sustainable use of its natural capital and ensure a clean environment."

Department of Conservation and Land Management, Government of Western Australia (www.naturebase.net)

Mission: "We have the lead responsibility for conserving the State's rich diversity of native plants, animals and natural ecosystems, and many of its unique landscapes. On behalf of the people of Western Australia, we manage more than 24 million hectares, including more than nine per cent of WA's land area: its national parks, marine parks, conservation parks, regional parks, State forests and timber reserves, nature reserves, and marine nature reserves."

Department of Sustainability and Environment, Victoria (www.dse.vic.gov.au/dse/nrenpr.nsf)

Mission: "Responsible for the conservation of Victoria's natural and cultural heritage on public land."

New Zealand

Department of Conservation (www.doc.govt.nz)

Mission: "To conserve New Zealand's natural and historic heritage for all to enjoy now and in the future."

United Kingdom

Natural England (www.naturalengland.org.uk)

Mission: Natural England joins together English Nature, the Countryside Agency, and the Rural Development Service to "work for people, places and nature, to enhance biodiversity, landscapes and wildlife in rural, urban, coastal and marine areas; promoting access, recreation and public well-being, and contributing to the way natural resources are managed so that they can be enjoyed now and in the future."

Where to Go?

One of the greatest joys of hiking and backpacking is exploring different areas. Looking for hiking areas gives you a different perspective on the area where you live and areas you want to explore. Any area put aside for the purpose of letting nature prevail makes for a potential hiking space, but the presence of trails and the designation as a hiking area keep you from competing for the right of way with motorized vehicles. In many places you may share the trail with mountain bikers and horses, so be aware of their presence and be ready to step aside if need be (see chapter 5). Many trails are accessible to people with disabilities. These trails are at least 4 feet (1.2 meters) wide and have been hardened with gravel or are fully paved.

Following are general categories of hiking spaces to explore. In most places it is apparent where to hike, but in some areas it takes some persistence and creativity. The key is to approach your area like an explorer and be willing to find places with trails that offer the experience you're looking for, whether it's a 20-minute nature break or a multiday backpacking trip.

20-minute to 1-hour nature breaks

1-hour to 2-hour hikes

Half-day hikes

Day hikes or peak challenges

Overnight camping with day hikes

Backpacking opportunities (2-3 days)

Backpacking opportunities (4-7 days)

Backpacking opportunities (8 or more days)

City Parks

When hiking in urban areas, walking through a neighborhood park does not count as a hike. However, some parks have natural areas with great terrain for hiking. The key is to find a place where you can escape pavement. These hikes usually aren't extensive, but they are a great way to escape the busy city, take a nature break, or take a training hike for a more extensive hiking or backpacking adventure. Look for city parks that border lakes and rivers; oftentimes you will find trails along bodies of water.

Many cities are creating greenways, corridors of green space that often follow natural land or water features and are managed for recreation and conservation. Some greenways offer great hiking trails and others offer paved paths that you share with bikers and sometimes horseback riders. Greenways also connect nature reserves, parks, and cultural or historical sites in an area. Most city parks are funded through tax dollars and thus rarely charge fees.

County Parks

Many county parks have great hiking terrain. County parks are often bigger than city parks and offer more extensive hiking opportunities. The terrain will depend upon the location, but often you can spend a few hours exploring a county park and cover many miles if you are creative in how you use a network of trails. The mission of most county parks is to provide leisure activities for families in natural areas, so expect to share the trails with people of all ages who are hiking, biking, bird watching, and going to other activities in the park such as swimming, fishing, or picnicking. Most county parks charge a parking fee, but the yearly fee is often a great bargain if you visit the park on a regular basis. For example, in Stearns County, Minnesota, the daily fee at Quarry Park is $4 and the yearly parking fee is $24.

◐◑ Open Space

In the past few decades as urban areas have grown, open-space initiatives have been successful in preserving tracts of land for low-impact recreation such as hiking and outdoor education and in serving as a buffer between urban areas and wild lands. These areas are most likely managed by cities or counties and often offer exceptional hiking opportunities for urban dwellers. Open spaces are likely to offer more rugged trail systems than county and city parks. Most open spaces restrict the use of motorized vehicles, but regulations are different for each. You can expect to share open-space trails with horseback riders and mountain bikers. Fees are rarely associated with open spaces, but again this varies with locations and management. You may pay a small parking fee.

◐◑◍☾◻ State and Regional Parks

State parks vary in size from a few acres holding historical or cultural sites to expansive parks holding thousands of acres. Most state park mission statements include charges to create ample outdoor recreation opportunities while protecting the natural landscape. State parks offer a wide range of recreation and outdoor education opportunities as well as extensive trail systems and camping opportunities. Most state parks have campgrounds with walk-in tent sites, drive-up tent sites, recreational vehicle (RV) sites, cabins, and even yurts. These campgrounds and rustic housing may offer full-service restrooms and even running water at individual sites. Fees for overnight camping vary, but you can expect to pay $7 to $35 per night. Some state parks also have backpacking opportunities. These sites are usually 1 to 5 miles (1.5-8 kilometers) away from a trailhead and offer a more primitive and isolated experience than the campgrounds. These days, state parks require reservations for camping, and most have Internet sites and toll-free telephone numbers for making reservations.

The great thing about state parks is their extensive trail systems that allow you to explore the different regions of a state. Because of the focus on outdoor education, it's also hard to go to a state park without learning about the area's historical, cultural, or natural resources. As a hiker, state parks are great places to explore. Depending upon the size of the park, you can expect to spend a half-day to 2 or 3 days hiking on a network of trails. Most trails are hiking only, biking only, horseback riding only, or a combination of all three. Most parks do not allow motorized vehicles on trails, but some may. Some state parks were originally set aside for watershed protection, and these parks tend to have the most restrictive regulations. Many of these parks have trails for hiking but do not allow other activities or dogs. For hiking in a state park, you can expect to pay $5 to $10 for a day permit. If you plan to hike in many state parks in a year, buying a year pass is more economical. These passes grant access to all state parks and cost around $45.

◖◗◕◐ ▢ ▢ ▢ National Forests

www.fs.fed.us

The mission of the USDA Forest Service (USFS) is "to sustain the health, diversity, and productivity of the Nation's forests and grasslands to meet the needs of present and future generations." Within this mission is lots of room for hiking. Originally national forests were set aside as reserves for timber, minerals, and water resources. Today those demands on the land are balanced with recreation, wildlife habitat, wilderness, clean water, timber, and forest products. National forests offer extensive trail systems and opportunities ranging from day hikes to backpacking trips that last a few weeks. The USFS manages 192 million acres (777,000 square kilometers) in 175 national forests and grasslands ranging in size from 50,000 to 1 million acres (202-4,047 square kilometers) (Martin et al., 2006).

The terrain of national forests will vary greatly depending upon location. Most national forests in the western and eastern United States are mountainous whereas in the Midwest these reserves are national grasslands. National forests are places for both hikers and backpackers. They offer day hiking with designated campgrounds as well as opportunities for remote car camping. In addition, national forests provide ample opportunities for backpacking. Most hiking can be found by accessing trailheads and then using a map and compass to navigate a trail network. Recreation fees can be expected at some trailheads. Permits are becoming required by many national forests for backpacking. They allow agencies to put limits on the number of people hiking or backpacking in order to offer primitive solitary experiences and protect resources from overuse. Check with the local forest service districts to find out about their policies and fees.

USE A PASS TO SAVE MONEY

America the Beautiful National Park and Federal Recreational Lands Pass (www.nps.gov/fees_passes.htm)

In 2007, the America the Beautiful National Park and Federal Recreational Lands Pass was introduced, replacing the Golden Eagle Passport. The $80 annual pass is honored throughout the United States to cover entrance and day-use fees in areas managed by the USFS, NPS, BLM, Bureau of Reclamation, U.S. Fish and Wildlife Service (USFWS), and U.S. Army Corps of Engineers (USACE).

National Parks of Canada Pass (www.pc.gc.ca)

In 2007, the cost for a National Parks of Canada Pass was $62.40 (Canadian dollars). This pass is honored in 27 national parks throughout Canada to cover entrance and day-use fees.

◐◑◕◉▣▣ National Parks, Monuments, and Reserves

www.nps.gov

The mission statement of the NPS calls for it to preserve "unimpaired the natural and cultural resources and values of the national park system for the enjoyment, education, and inspiration of this and future generations . . . to extend the benefits of natural and cultural resource conservation and outdoor recreation throughout this country" (NPS, 2006). Today the U.S. national park system holds 84 million acres (339,936 square kilometers) in nearly 400 national parks, monuments, recreation areas, seashores, battlefields, and historic sites. Most of these sites provide ample opportunities for hiking and backpacking in areas known for their scenery.

Mount Rainier National Park in Washington state plays host to 1.5 to 2 million visitors each year, many of whom come to enjoy the park's 260 miles of trails.

For generations, national parks have offered many Americans their first experience hiking and backpacking. As you arrive at a national park or monument, you receive a map that marks the hiking and backpacking trails. Most national parks require backpackers to obtain permits and to camp in designated areas in order to protect resources from overuse and to protect the backpacking experience. Most places do not require permits for day hikes. All national parks have an entrance fee ranging from $10 to $25. If you are expecting to visit a few national parks, buying an annual pass can save you money (see pages 16-17). Contact individual sites for their permitting policies and fees.

☽ ☾ ☾ ☾ ▣ ▣ Bureau of Land Management

www.blm.gov

The BLM was established in 1976 to unify more than 2,000 land management laws enacted over the past century. The BLM manages 261 million acres (105,218 square kilometers) of grasslands, forests, mountain areas, deserts, and arctic tundra in 12 western states. The mission of the BLM is "to sustain the health, diversity, and productivity of the public lands for the use and enjoyment of present and future generations" (BLM, 2006). BLM lands offer a wealth of opportunities for hiking and backpacking. Some areas are open only to low-impact activities in wilderness study areas (see the next section), but other areas are shared with mountain bikers, rock climbers, horseback riders, and all-terrain vehicles (ATVs). The policies for each tract of land are unique to meet the needs of the area. Like other national lands, BLM lands are likely to have user fees. Check with the local BLM office for specifics and to find out the best places to hike and backpack.

▲ ▣ ▣ ▣ Wilderness Areas

www.wilderness.net

In 1964 Congress passed the Wilderness Act to preserve large tracts of undeveloped land. The areas are typically larger than 5,000 acres (20 square kilometers) and contain ecological, geological, educational, scenic, or historical legacies. There are currently 662 wilderness areas holding 105 million acres (424,920 square kilometers) across the United States. Most wildernesses are found in the western states, but 13 eastern states have wildernesses within their boundaries (Wilderness Society, 2006). Wilderness areas are managed by the NFS, NPS, BLM, and USFWS. In Canada, wilderness can be found in national and provincial parks.

Because of their primitive character, wilderness areas are perfect places to hike and backpack. Wilderness areas that are within a few hours' drive of a major city, also known as *urban wildernesses,* tend to offer great day hikes. For example, Twin Peaks Wilderness in the Wasatch-Cache National Forest, which is based in Salt Lake City, has many outstanding hikes to peaks for day hikers willing to gain 6,000 feet (1,829 meters) of elevation and hike 5 to 15 miles (8-24 kilometers) in a day. This wilderness area also offers great 2- to 4-day backpacking opportunities. Again, most of these trips focus on reaching peaks, but the trails also allow you to survey a variety of ridges and drainages and take in breathtaking views of the Salt Lake Valley and the mountains beyond.

Typically wilderness areas allow only primitive means of transportation, which means you're either on foot or on a horse—mountain bikes and motorized vehicles are not allowed. Other regulations include group size limits and limits on the number of nights you can camp in one place. Because wildernesses are some of the most remote places you can visit, make sure you're prepared. Even if you are going just for a day hike, be sure you have an emergency stash of food, effective rain gear, extra warm clothing, a means to purify water, and a means to make a fire. Australia, New Zealand, European countries, and Canada also have lands set aside as wilderness.

◑◑ U.S. Fish and Wildlife Service, Bureau of Reclamation, and Army Corps of Engineers

www.fws.gov

These management agencies do not have recreation as their main mission, but they do have some opportunities for hiking and backpacking on their lands. Again, check with local agencies to discuss recreation opportunities, policies, and fees.

◑◑ Nature Preserve Properties

www.nature.org

The first priority of nature preserves is to preserve areas, but they often have hiking opportunities. Most require guests to be accompanied by a guide or to hike in conjunction with volunteer stewardship duties. A good way to begin exploring the opportunities in nature preserves is to contact your state's nature conservancy. Oftentimes nature preserves restrict hiking and recreation opportunities because their focus is to protect nature, not provide recreation.

◐◑◑◍◐⬛⬛⬛ Private Property

There are large (and small) tracts of private land that offer opportunities for hiking and backpacking; the key is to have permission to access them. One example of private property put aside for hiking is Philmont Boy Scout Ranch in northern New Mexico. Each year more than 20,000 Boy Scouts from across the nation and the world take 14-day hiking treks through the backcountry of the ranch. In order to participate on a Philmont trek, you must be part of a troop that has a trek planned.

⏱ ◔ ◑ ◐ ⛰ ☾ 🎒 🎒 🎒 Canadian Parks and Forests

Parks Canada (www.pc.gc.ca)

There are 27 national parks throughout Canada. They are protected for public understanding, appreciation, and enjoyment, while being maintained in an unimpaired state for future generations. National parks have existed in Canada for well over a century and offer a great deal of variety in hiking and backpacking destinations.

Canadian Forest Service (www.cfs.nrcan.gc.ca)

The Canadian Forest Service has a mission similar to the USFS and offers opportunities for hiking and backpacking.

Provincial Parks (best accessed by searching for parks in individual provinces)

Each province in Canada has provincial parks dedicated to preserving the natural environment and offering opportunities for enjoyment, such as hiking and backpacking. These parks are comparable to the United States' state parks.

Conclusion

Hiking and backpacking are relatively simple activities. Besides needing to know how to take care of yourself and your companions, it's good to know what equipment to take, how to pack, and how to walk with a load on your back that may weigh half your body weight (ideally, your backpack should weigh one-quarter of your body weight). This book will inform you how to prepare your body; how to prepare your equipment; and how to choose the right footwear, clothing, and gear. It will also discuss the necessary safety and survival skills. Once you are prepared, you are ready to hit the trail. Using good trail etiquette and proper hiking and camping techniques will help you best enjoy your adventures. There is no single way to hike or backpack; they are unique experiences that can be tailored to meet personal preferences. In reading this book, we hope you go from imagining yourself in different hiking and backpacking scenarios to enjoying the fresh air and scenery as you hone your skills through many adventures. Remember, around each bend in the trail is a potential perfect moment waiting to happen.

CHAPTER 2

Getting Fit for Hiking and Backpacking

> What would you do if you knew you wouldn't fail? One person working toward a dream is worth 99 people just working.
>
> *Lani Kraus*

Most people can become fit enough to backpack. A woman known as Grandma Gatewood walked more than 2,000 miles (3,219 kilometers) on the Appalachian Trail in sneakers, carrying her belongings in a duffle bag slung over her shoulder. She started her hiking career at 65 years old. Search for Grandma Gatewood on the Internet and learn more about her history.

Hiking and backpacking are meant to be fun, not endurance tests. They provide a great way to improve your fitness and become more self-reliant. It is important to be fit enough to be able to enjoy the trip you are on. The more physically fit you are, the more self-confident and less worried about keeping up you are likely to be, and therefore the more relaxed you will be. When you are fit, you can hike while socializing without getting out of breath. Of course there is an old backpacking joke that when you come home from a weeklong backpacking trip, you are now in shape to start a weeklong backpacking trip.

Many people walk for exercise; hiking is just a step beyond and it burns a few more calories than brisk walking. You can start hiking at almost any level of fitness as long as you plan the hike in relation to your fitness. Being fit means different things to different people. For me, being fit means being strong enough and having enough endurance to complete a trip with comfort, so being physically fit for a day trip with little elevation gain or loss is different than being fit for a backpacking trip that includes hiking to the top of a fourteener in Colorado (i.e., a mountain over 14,000 feet, or 4,267 meters).

When hiking in the backcountry, you need to be fit both physically and mentally. These two are related: If you are comfortable with your physical preparedness, it will add to your mental comfort. Likewise if you are concerned about your physical preparedness, you will be less mentally prepared for outdoor or wilderness travel.

In this chapter you will read about the benefits of being fit for a trip, the importance of the match between fitness and trip, how to gauge your present physical condition, and some ways to attain or maintain the level of conditioning you desire. You may find that you are already fit enough for the trips you would like to take. However, if you would like to become fitter, you can establish fitness goals, create an overall fitness plan, and then begin your fitness program.

Fitness Benefits of Hiking and Backpacking

Hiking and backpacking help increase and maintain fitness levels and contribute to health and well-being. One of the great things about hiking is that you can use it to get in shape for backpacking. And of course, regular exercise is necessary just to maintain overall health. Hiking and backpacking are fun ways to burn calories, spend time with other people, and eat well.

There are many documented health benefits from spending time in the natural world. Sunlight offers vitamins D and E, both important for immune functions as well as increased serotonin levels, which elevate mood. Nature has a restorative power and can help alleviate depression (Sanders, Yankou,

& Andrusyszyn, 2005). Contact with nature is correlated with living longer, and actual biochemical changes occur in response to trees, plants, and animals (Frumkin, 2001). As we enjoy the sights and sounds of nature, in addition to learning something about the natural environment, stress levels decrease and endorphins, which also elevate mood, are released.

We experience long-term benefits from improving and maintaining physical fitness through hiking and backpacking both on the trail and at home. Moderate physical activity can result in lower health care costs and increased work performance. Regular exercise improves mental health, providing a holistic sense of wellness, more positive moods and emotions, better mental clarity, and better stress management skills, enabling us to better respond to the demands and joys of life. This leads to higher self-confidence, greater self-competence, and better judgment and decision making.

Many people who suffer from asthma and other chronic diseases feel better and have fewer symptoms when outdoors. Of course, you should not take any chances; always carry fresh prescriptions with you, and depending on your health, check with your health care practitioner about physical activity levels.

By improving cardiorespiratory capacity, muscular strength and endurance, flexibility, body composition, and motor skills, you reduce the risk for many diseases and injuries. The weight-bearing exercise of hiking and backpacking reduces the risk of osteoporosis. Cardiorespiratory fitness and proper body composition help lower blood pressure, decrease the risk of heart disease and diabetes, increase bone density, and contribute to a longer life. Being fit helps reduce the risk of injuries because it allows for greater muscle control and flexibility. Body movements are more efficient and posture improves. Regular exercise reduces stress and increases vitality and energy to achieve everyday tasks. When we are physically active, we set a positive example for children and friends.

BENEFITS OF EXERCISE

Dr. Frederick Kasch saw the benefits of exercise well before medical science and at a time when the general population thought that exercise was for elite athletes and not the average person. From the 1930s through the 1960s, Kasch conducted research and worked to change societal attitudes toward exercise. In a 33-year longitudinal study, Kasch's subjects that exercised to stay fit suffered minimal losses in fitness and no changes in body fat or body composition, and at 69 to 89 years old, these men continued to hunt, ski, mountain climb, and play tennis with their blood pressure remaining within the normal range. Kasch changed researchers' belief that if you had heart disease and exercised, you would kill yourself. Now what he believes is common knowledge: Exercise affects every cell and organ in the body and is necessary for health and well-being. Kasch developed many fitness tests that are used today and included in this chapter. At 93 years old in 2006, Kasch was continuing his fitness program at his home and hunting camp in Wisconsin so he

(continued)

(continued)

could hike, hunt, ski, body surf, and dance. He also was honored in 2006 by San Diego State University's Center for Optimal Health and Performance (COHP) for his profound influence on generations of students, adult fitness participants, colleagues, and researchers around the world, as well as for starting the COHP, being professor emeritus there, and for publishing over 100 scientific papers.

Components of Physical Fitness

There are five components of physical fitness: cardiorespiratory endurance, muscular strength and endurance, flexibility, body composition, and motor skills. Hiking and backpacking develop all five areas. Some people want to engage in fitness programs as part of their daily routine and get into better shape for hiking and backpacking. Others want to use hiking and backpacking to increase their fitness to move on to more challenging trips.

Cardiorespiratory Endurance

Cardiorespiratory endurance, or aerobic fitness, is the ability to perform endurance exercises, including hiking and backpacking. It is a measure of the heart's ability to pump oxygen-rich blood to the working muscles during exercise and the muscles' ability to take up and use the oxygen to produce the energy needed to continue exercising. The heart itself is an important muscle to keep in shape and increase in strength. With higher cardiorespiratory endurance, you can hike and backpack without getting out of breath easily and take on more hilly terrain.

Muscle Strength and Endurance

Both muscle strength and endurance are necessary for hiking and backpacking. Muscular endurance is the ability of a muscle group to generate force over and over again, whereas muscular strength is the maximum ability of a muscle to generate force. Although you need a certain amount of strength for lifting packs and such, you do not need to engage in intense strength training for hiking and backpacking. Instead of looking for the maximum amount of weight you can lift with a muscle, you want your legs to perform multiple lifts or repetitions as you hike. As you train for muscular endurance, you also gain muscle tone and strength. Increased strength and endurance decrease the incidence of low back pain and reduce the risk of injuries on the trail.

Flexibility

Flexibility is the ability to move joints freely through their full range of motion. Improved flexibility increases joint mobility, provides resistance to muscle injury, helps prevent low back problems, and improves efficiency of body movement. Flexibility helps in hiking and backpacking when lifting packs, performing camp tasks, and hiking on uneven terrain where there may be rocky footing and streams to jump.

Body Composition

The term *body composition* refers to the relative amounts of fat, lean tissue (e.g., muscle, organs, bone), and water in your body, as well as your fat distribution. With the proper composition, the body is able to use fuel and water efficiently and reduce joint stress. As discussed later, body composition is a useful and easy measure of overall fitness used by many outdoor programs to determine trip fit.

Motor Skills

Motor skills include movement qualities such as agility and coordination. Because of hiking terrain and other potential obstacles, a certain amount of agility and coordination are needed for hiking and backpacking.

Overall Wellness

Fitness is an integration of mind, body, and spirit. It is easy to see why and how we need to be physically fit, but it is just as important to be mentally, emotionally, and spiritually fit. Hiking and backpacking entail certain risks. Without physical fitness, it is easy to imagine some of the physical risks. Additionally, it is necessary to be capable of making safe decisions, and decision making is more effective if you are fit in all dimensions of health. Making optimal use

CONSUMER TIP

Many books have been written about nutrition and copious information is available. Sift through the abundance of literature to understand nutritional considerations and apply them to your life. Do what works for you, keeping in mind that the goal for weight maintenance is for the number of calories you eat to be the same as the calories used in daily activity. Recently, the United States Department of Agriculture (USDA) came out with a revised food pyramid, and on its Web site (http://mypyramid.gov) you can create an individualized food plan coordinated with your physical fitness plan as well as your caloric needs for trips. Other useful sites are listed in the Web Resources section at the end of the book.

of food, staying hydrated, sleeping well, and making positive and healthy lifestyle choices contribute to mental, spiritual, and physical preparedness. If you practice poor nutrition or have poor sleeping habits, it is hard to increase endurance and to not feel tired. If you smoke, it is harder to increase cardio-respiratory capacity.

Nutrition: Eating for Optimal Health

Heavy exercise such as backpacking uses carbohydrate as a primary fuel source. Diets low in carbohydrate can lead to chronic fatigue because muscle carbohydrate stores are depleted and you are breaking down the very muscles that you want to build up. Good nutrition is essential to achieving physical fitness and wellness and is crucial to health both before and during trips. Diets should provide all of the components of food (called *nutrients)* needed to fuel activity, promote growth, and repair body tissues. We need to pay attention to all six classes of essential nutrients: water, protein, carbohydrate, fat, vitamins, and minerals, including electrolytes.

On and off the trail, breakfast is important. Research shows that people who begin their day with a healthy breakfast live longer and have an easier time losing or maintaining weight. Plan to get a mix of complex carbohydrate, protein, and fat at every meal. Appropriate food combinations maximize power and endurance. Avoid sugary snacks (empty calories), which can spike blood sugar and cause the body to work harder to maintain health (this includes soda).

Men and women have different nutritional needs. Women have more life changes that affect metabolism and nutritional needs, including menstrual cycles, pregnancy and lactation, and menopause. When you use resources on nutrition, check the appropriateness of the information for your sex.

TRAIL TIP

Part of training includes eating the kind of foods that you will eat on the trail while at home. You will see how your body reacts to the foods. If you use pre-packaged dehydrated foods, read the ingredients in case you are allergic to any of them. Some dehydrated foods contain monosodium glutamate (MSG), to which many people are allergic, and some people are allergic to the sulfates that are found in most dried fruit. Get a cookbook for backpacking such as *Lipsmackin' Vegetarian Backpackin'* (Conners, 2004). A Ferris State University student said of the recipes in the book, "I find that I can count on the serving sizes to be big enough to fill me up, even when I'm starving from hiking all day. And they tend to be tasty!"

ACTION PLAN FOR BETTER NUTRITION

Eat 5 servings of fruits and vegetables a day.

Include 3 servings of whole-grain foods a day.

Consume a calcium-rich food at each meal.

Eat a variety of foods.

Read food labels and pick nutrient-dense foods. (Nutrient-dense foods have a high nutrient–calorie ratio. Nutrient-dense foods are the opposite of empty-calorie foods, which are low in nutrition compared with their calorie content.)

Avoid high-fat fast foods.

Avoid too much sugar and soda.

Pick vegetables and fruits with bright colors.

Water

The human body is about 60 to 70 percent water. Blood is made up of approximately 83 percent water, while the lungs are almost 90 percent water and the brain 75 percent. Water circulates nutrients to every cell, lubricates organs and joints, helps with digestion, flushes out toxins, metabolizes fat, and maintains body temperature. No wonder water is so important to our well-being! Even a 1-percent decrease in hydration can impair judgment and decision making as well as physical ability. Many people in the United States are chronically dehydrated, and water needs increase when hiking and backpacking. Both on trail and off, we need to train ourselves to prehydrate before activity begins, hydrate during the activity, and rehydrate at the end of the day.

Individual needs for water vary depending on dietary factors, age, size, environmental temperature and humidity levels, exercise, and the effectiveness of the person's system. People with a higher ratio of fat to muscle need to hydrate more often than people with a lower ratio. This is because people with more muscle mass usually store more water in muscle glycogen, which releases water for the body to use when it's broken down to release energy.

We replenish water through drinking water and eating food. Most people need 6 to 8 glasses of water a day. Water intake needs to increase with heat, altitude, and exercise. After sweating through a couple of hours of activity, a person may need to replace 1 gallon (4 liters) or more of water.

TECHNIQUE TIP

During exercise, frequent breaks to drink small amounts of water help maintain hydration without creating stomach discomfort. Using a hydration system such as a Camelback can help you have water accessible all the time. Dark-yellow urine may indicate inadequate hydration.

IMPORTANCE OF ELECTROLYTES

Electrolytes, including sodium, potassium, magnesium, calcium, chloride, bicarbonate, and sulfate, are used to conduct nerve impulses and activate enzymes, helping to balance the water inside and outside of cells. There has to be enough water flowing inside the cells and electrolytes to help with that transport. If the water gets stuck outside of the cells and there are not enough electrolytes to move it through the cell membrane into the cells, we still feel the effects of dehydration. Electrolyte imbalance, and specifically a lack of magnesium, potassium, and sodium, is thought to cause muscle cramping and more aching after exercise.

For most people, water combined with a proper diet adequately maintains electrolyte levels even when sweating. Sport drinks and powdered additives, which usually contain sugar, can unnecessarily spike blood sugar levels. While hiking and backpacking, use salt when cooking and bring foods that are high in electrolytes.

Sleeping

Most Americans are not getting enough sleep. Sleep needs vary, but most adults need 7 to 9 hours of sleep each night. A sleep deficit of 2 hours a night has detrimental effects on health and increases the risk of accidents. You want to be rested before and during a hiking or backpacking trip.

Without adequate sleep, fitness training is not as effective. Other reductions in functioning include concentration, memory, and coping, as well as motivation, a key component when engaging in a physical fitness program. Sleeping is so necessary to health that a study showed that the protective effects of avoiding smoking, alcohol, and unhealthy foods were lost when people did not get enough sleep. Fortunately, hiking and backpacking or a physical fitness program can help you sleep, though vigorous exercise should cease about 3 hours before sleeping. Physical exercise improves the ability to handle stress, which can interfere with sleep, and it changes your core temperature in a way that helps you sleep. People who are more physically fit are more likely to fall sleep more quickly, wake up less often during the night, have more slow-wave sleep, and feel more rested when they wake up in the morning. On a trip you can have the joy of frustration-free exhaustion at the end of the day and look forward to a solid night's sleep. Be sure to plan your route to allow for adequate sleeping time.

Smoking

Smoking is a lifestyle choice that has huge implications for hiking and backpacking. Smokers are more prone to breathlessness, chronic cough, and excess phlegm production than nonsmokers, and the impact of smoking is felt in a relatively short time. Shortness of breath has a huge effect on pace and endurance. It is best not to smoke, of course, and while getting fit for a hiking or backpacking trip, it is even more important not to smoke. If you don't smoke, then don't start; if you do smoke, try using this new activity as a reason to quit.

Matching Fitness to Trips

Design your trips to fit your fitness and skills. To make sure your physical skills match the trip, research the area well. How fit you need to be depends on the length of the trip, daily mileage, terrain and trail conditions, pace, amount and steepness of the ascent or descent, altitude and acclimatization, and whether the trip involves hiking with daypacks or backpacking with heavier overnight packs. Sometimes trail conditions vary, and when backpacking you may be carrying a pack that is one-third of your weight.

Hiking and backpacking involve aerobic exercise and sustained energy output. A realistic appraisal of your fitness level will help you choose an appropriate trip in length, location, difficulty, and style. It also will help you in designing a training or fitness program for more difficult hiking and backpacking. Remember, you usually can start hiking at your current fitness level (if you are overweight or have some other physical limitation, check with your health care practitioner first). Special considerations such as having physical disabilities or being pregnant will affect fitness and choosing trips, and these are discussed later in this chapter.

Regular medical exams are encouraged for everyone, though most people younger than 30 years do not need a physical exam before engaging in an exercise program that is low to moderate in intensity. Although the risks associated with moderate exercise are thought to be less than those associated with a sedentary lifestyle, if you have any questions about your health, a consultation with your health care provider is a wise investment before initiating a training program. If you answer yes to one or more of the following questions, talk with your health practitioner before you engage in fitness tests or become more physical:

1. Has your health practitioner ever said that you have a heart condition and that you should limit your physical activity?
2. When you engage in physical activity, do you feel pain in your chest?
3. Do you ever become dizzy and lose your balance, or do you ever lose consciousness?
4. Do you have a bone or joint problem that worsens during physical activity?
5. Do you currently take prescription drugs for blood pressure or a heart condition?
6. Can you think of any other reason that you should not engage in physical activity?

Trips in remote locations have limited access to medical care and other resources and therefore require a higher level of physical and mental preparedness. A difficult trip with daily mileage of more than 7 miles (11 kilometers) and daily elevation changes of more than 2,000 feet (610 meters) usually requires a specific conditioning regimen. Embarking on a trip at altitudes above 7,000 feet (2,100 meters) brings additional considerations. We all have physical reactions to altitude; we need to breathe more often and our pulse rate increases. In general, you are hiking uphill as you ascend into altitude, and this will be easier if you have good cardiorespiratory fitness, which also will help you cope with the normal increase in respiration and pulse rate. (See chapter 6 for more details.)

At first, pick a flat trail close to home and work from there. There are greater resources to fall back on in case of problems, which is usually mentally comforting. As your confidence, physical fitness, and mental fitness increase, go on a moderately difficult day or weekend trip close to home. Practice hiking on a variety of trail conditions (rocky, smooth, rough) and varying the amount of weight you are carrying before traveling to remote areas. If you always prefer easier trips, whether close to home or in remote locations, that is fine. Backpacking does not need to be a competition where hikers try harder and harder trails each weekend. Learn your preferences and enjoy yourself.

Start hiking at a pace where you do not get out of breath while carrying on a conversation.

Where to Start

Hiking is a great way to get in shape for backpacking, or it can be a wonderful sport itself. To warm up for a hike, walk slowly for 3 to 5 minutes and lightly stretch for 2 to 5 minutes. To cool down, lightly stretch for 5 to 10 minutes, focusing on the legs and ankles.

The objective is to walk at a steady, unbroken pace. Start at a pace where you do not get out of breath while carrying on a conversation. Your pace will depend on your fitness level, your load, and the terrain. As you hike, regularly take long, deep breaths. This helps get oxygen to the muscles and prevent lactic acid buildup. With each mile (1.6 kilometers) per hour that you increase your speed, you double the amount of energy that you expend.

Know your body. Some people walk at a moderate pace and for a very long time, and others keep a fast pace all the time. Some people overestimate their fitness, and others tend to underestimate their fitness. Additionally, medical conditions affect fitness. Hike at a pace that is comfortable for you and set reasonable goals. Again, in this sport the objective is to walk at a steady, unbroken pace.

Special Considerations

Sometimes there are special considerations during training and on the trail. Women who are pregnant and people with disabilities enjoy the outdoors and often hike and backpack, but they may need modifications in training, water intake, and gear.

Pregnancy

Many women train, hike, and backpack while pregnant. Usually health practitioners tell women to keep their current exercise level but not to begin any higher level of exercise. Additionally, some health practitioners recommend

SAFETY TIP

If you are traveling with friends, it is a good idea to know the fitness level of the other group members. To start with, everyone should fill out a health form and share this information with each other. If you are paying someone else to provide the trip, they may ask for health-related information, but should keep your information confidential. In an informal group, share this information to ensure safety so that you will be better able to help each other if someone has a problem. Understanding what medical conditions you and your group members have and how these conditions may interact with the particular demands of your trip is important.

limiting vigorous activity during the first trimester. For example, you might take only weekend hiking trips with a base camp during the first trimester and avoid any altitude hiking. However, during the second trimester, if you are in shape and are backpacking already, you might continue backpacking. Listen to your body. Base the pace and duration of the activity on how you feel that day and consult your health practitioner.

People With Disabilities

People who have special needs or disabilities often can hike and backpack. A person who is blind climbed to the top of Mount Everest. A woman who had a leg amputated climbed Mount Rainer during a celebration of the 100th anniversary of the first ascent of that mountain by a woman. Many people who have diabetes, asthma, and other diseases find that by improving their health through hiking and backpacking and maintaining a fitness program, the effects of their disease are lessened. Mountains for Active Diabetics (MAD), a worldwide organization of outdoor adventurers who are diabetic, has a mission to inspire and educate people with diabetes about outdoor pursuits. They have hosted several international symposiums on diabetes, mountains, and outdoor sports (www.mountain-mad.org). On the Tip of the Toes (www.pointes-des-pieds.com/nousen.asp) is an organization that offers adventure expeditions for teenagers living with cancer.

Often there are special considerations and workable modifications for hikers and backpackers with certain diseases. For example, people with diabetes or cystic fibrosis lose fluids faster, which makes a larger consumption of water necessary both during training and on the trail. People with asthma need to bring their inhalers (check with your health care practitioner to see if you should use your inhaler before exercise) and use extreme caution if they are training for hiking and backpacking and the air pollution index is orange or red. People who use wheelchairs often have poor leg circulation and may have no sensation, so they need to consider clothing and temperature carefully. People with limited mobility should use clothing that is easy to get on and off. Work with your health care practitioner to understand your personal capabilities for hiking and backpacking and to develop an individualized fitness program for hiking and backpacking, and check the Web resources at the end of this book.

Determining Your Current Level of Fitness

When we are fit, we can sustain the output required for hiking or backpacking and enjoy the trip more. To know if you want to begin a fitness program or if you are fit for the hiking and backpacking you want to do now, you need to understand your personal fitness. Use a combination of the following tests to get an idea of your current fitness level. For example, if your fitness were measured solely on your ability to run 1.5 miles (2.5 kilometers) in a certain amount of time, you may not look very capable. On the other hand, you may be able to run this distance relatively easily, but not be able to stretch very far. If you look at several tests and consider how well you perform on them, you will find the level of hiking and backpacking for which you are fit.

Use the test results to help choose an appropriate trip or to use as a benchmark as you embark on a fitness program. If you want to increase your fitness, retesting every 1 to 3 months provides motivating feedback as you progress. As mentioned previously, you can hike on easy trails close to home at almost any level of fitness. To backpack, you should complete the baseline tests at the average level or better.

The following self-assessments can help you determine your overall fitness. Many may remind you of physical fitness tests in high school. They measure body composition, cardiorespiratory fitness, strength and endurance, and flexibility.

Body Composition

A number of tests are available for assessing body composition, and they are probably the most common baseline fitness tests. A high percentage of body fat is associated with poorer physical condition and an increased risk of disease, and the theory is that there is an optimal ratio of fat, muscle, and water. This optimal ratio is dependant on age. Generally, research suggests that for men, an optimal range is 6 to 17 percent body fat; for women, the range is 14 to 24 percent body fat, while up to 25 and 31 percent respectively is acceptable (see www.bmi-calculator.net/body-fat-calculator/body-fat-chart.php). If your percentage of body fat is in the optional range, then you should be able to complete moderate day hikes and weekend backpacking trips as long as you are moderately aerobically fit. If it is in the acceptable range, then you should be able to complete easy day hikes and weekend backpacking trips. If it is in the obese range, check with your health care practitioner before hiking and backpacking. If you have too little fat, you will need to be especially careful to eat well while hiking and backpacking in order to have enough energy and stamina. Hiking and backpacking will use more calories than normal and can help you lose weight, if you so desire.

Several low-tech tests of body composition are available, such as the body mass index and the waist-to-hip ratio. The accuracy and limitations of each are assessed next.

Body Mass Index

Body mass index (BMI) is a popular test because it is simple to self-administer. It has limitations, but it is generally useful for informing you if you are underweight, normal weight, overweight, or obese. However, if you are fairly muscular or have particularly large or small bones, the BMI likely will be unreliable. BMI is a measure of the ratio of body weight divided by height squared. A BMI of 25 and above is overweight; 30 and above is obese. A score under 20 may indicate that you are underweight. There are many Web sites that will do the calculations for you, such as www.bmi-calculator.net.

Waist-to-Hip Ratio

To calculate your waist-to-hip ratio (WHR), measure your waist and hip circumferences while standing up and without bulky clothes. Place the tape snugly around the body but not pressed into the skin. Measure your waist at the navel and at the end of a normal exhalation, and record measurements to the nearest millimeter or 16th of an inch. Divide the waist circumference by the hip circumference to determine WHR. Aim to keep your WHR (waist size divided by hip size) at .85 or less (women) and .9 (men). For growing children or teens, waist sizes that are less than half their height are healthy. A higher-than-recommended WHR seems to indicate too much fat to be healthy. This test gives you a general idea of the shape you are in.

Cardiorespiratory Endurance

Cardiorespiratory endurance can be measured using the 1.5-mile (2.5-kilometer) run test and the 3-minute step test. You want to be able to breathe comfortably as you hike, and in order to check your progress, it is useful to calculate your target heart rate. Some people like to wear a heart monitor, which displays your current heart rate while you exercise and calculates other values, such as maximum heart rate, average heart rate, $\dot{V}O_2$max, and recovery measurement. To measure heart rate, count your heart beats by taking your pulse either at the neck or wrist. Count the beats for a full minute for the most accurate reading, or count for 30 seconds and double the number, or count for 15 seconds and multiply by 4.

HEART RATE–RELATED DEFINITIONS

active heart rate (AHR)—The number of times the heart beats during exercise or activity.

maximum heart rate (MHR)—The maximum number of times the heart should beat during exercise. MHR is found by subtracting your age from 220.

resting heart rate (RHR)—The number of times the heart beats at rest. RHR is most accurate in the morning just before getting out of bed. It is least accurate directly after eating.

target heart rate (THR)—The number of times the heart should beat per minute during exercise in order to achieve a training effect.

training effect—The changes that take place in the body as a result of exercise.

To find your THR, calculate your MHR. Subtract your RHR from your MHR and multiply this number by .6. This number is the bottom of your range for a training effect. Add your RHR to the bottom of your training-effect range to get the top of your training-effect range. For example, if you are 20 years old with an RHR of 70, your MHR is 220 − 20 = 200. The lower end of your training-effect range is 200 (MHR) − 70 (RHR) = 130. The upper end of your training effect is 130 × .6 + 70 (RHR) = 148. Therefore your heart rate range for a training effect is 130 to 148 beats per minute. Use this as a guide and don't sweat over a few beats here and there.

The 1.5-Mile Run

The 1.5-mile (2.5-kilometer) run test works well for college students and other young adults who are in fairly good shape. It is not well suited for sedentary people over 30 years old, people with joint problems, and obese people. The objective is to complete a 1.5-mile (2.5-kilometer) distance in the shortest amount of time possible. Use a flat track and run in moderate weather. Some people run, others jog, and still others combine running and walking. Accurate timing is crucial. Try to keep a steady pace, and remember, it is okay to practice. Check your results at www.exrx.net/Calculators/OneAndHalf.html.

Step Test

A second cardiorespiratory test is the step test. Use an 18-inch (46-centimeter) step, usually the height of a bleacher. Take your pulse before beginning the test. For 3 minutes, step up on the step with both feet and back to the floor with both feet. (Use a 4-beat cycle: up, up, down, down). Do 24 complete steps each minute. Check your pulse when the 3-minute cycle is done, and again after another minute has gone by, then in 2 minutes, and 3 minutes. Record your results. As an example, if your heart rate is 80 beats per minute after 1-minute rest, you are in excellent shape; if it is 135 beats per minute, you are in poor shape; and average is about 110 beats per minute. Gauge your trips on your results. If you are in excellent shape, then you can start backpacking after you gain the other necessary skills. If you are in poor shape, start with hiking or other activities to get into shape. As you get into better shape, it should take less time for your heart to return to the pretest heart rate.

Muscular Strength and Endurance

As mentioned previously, muscle endurance, or the ability of a muscle group to generate force over and over again, is important for hiking and backpacking. Although hiking and backpacking will increase endurance, you can also train for muscle endurance, and as you do, you will usually gain enough muscle strength for your backpacking and hiking needs. Two common methods of evaluation are the push-up and curl-up tests. If you have poor endurance and little strength, then hiking and backpacking will be hard. Start with easy trips and when you feel improvement, try harder trips.

Push-Up Test

The push-up test evaluates the endurance of shoulder and arm muscles. Begin in the standard push-up or modified push-up position (on the knees). For the standard position, a partner counts the number of correctly performed push-ups in 60 seconds, telling you the time remaining at 15-second intervals. For both positions, warming up with a few push-ups followed by a 2- to 3-minute recovery period is helpful. The modified push-up position test is not timed; it is completed when you cannot do another complete push-up without a rest period. Table 2.1 tells you how to interpret your results.

Table 2.1 Norms for the Push-Up Test for Men and Women (number completed)

Age group (years)	Excellent	Above average	Average	Below average	Poor
Men					
15-19	39+	29-38	23-28	18-22	17-
20-29	36+	29-35	22-28	17-21	16-
30-39	30+	22-29	17-21	12-16	11-
40-49	22+	17-21	13-16	10-12	9-
50-59	21+	13-20	10-12	7-9	6-
60-69	18+	11-17	8-10	5-7	4-
Women					
15-19	33+	25-32	18-24	12-17	11-
20-29	30+	21-29	15-20	10-14	9-
30-39	27+	20-26	13-19	8-12	7-
40-49	24+	15-23	11-14	5-10	4-
50-59	21+	11-20	7-10	2-6	1-
60-69	17+	12-16	5-11	1-4	1-

Reprinted, by permission, from J.R. Morrow et al., 2005, *Measurement and evaluation in human performance*, 3rd ed. (Champaign, IL: Human Kinetics), 250; adapted from Nieman 1995.

Sit-Up and Curl-Up Tests

The sit-up test evaluates abdominal and hip muscle endurance, whereas the curl-up test evaluates only abdominal muscle endurance. The curl-up differs from the sit-up in that the trunk is not raised more than 30 to 40 degrees off the mat or floor, shoulders about 6 to 10 inches (15-25 centimeters) above the mat or floor. Research suggests that the curl-up causes less stress on the lower back than the conventional sit-up, there is less chance of hitting your head hard when you return to the lying position, and it is easier to avoid undue stress on your neck in the up position. To do the curl-up test, lie on your back with knees bent 90 degrees. Extend your arms next to your body and have a partner place a piece of tape about 3 inches (8 centimeters) away from your fingers. Complete the curl-up by raising your trunk until your finger tips touch the tape, and return to the starting position. The test is not timed and is performed at a slow cadence of 20 curl-ups per minute. This cadence can be kept using a metronome set at 40 beats per minute or having a friend keep count (curl up on one beat and down on the next). Perform as many curl-ups as you can without missing a beat, up to a maximum of 75. Use table 2.2 to evaluate your results or use an online calculator, such as the one found at www.preventdisease.com/healthtools/articles/curlup.html.

If you prefer the sit-up test, lie on your back with your knees bent 90 degrees, your arms crossed in front of your chest, and a partner holding your feet firmly on the floor. Do as many sit-ups as you can correctly complete (bring your chest up to your knees and then return to the original lying position) in 60 seconds. A partner counts the number of correctly performed sit-ups, telling you the time remaining at 15-second intervals. Use table 2.3 to evaluate your results.

After comparing your results with the tables, you can establish goals. Your performance should improve within the first 3 to 4 weeks of training and continue to improve thereafter. For example, if you are only able to do a few curl-ups, try to increase the number by five each week. This will increase both your strength and endurance.

Flexibility

Flexibility is joint specific and no single test is representative of total-body flexibility, though general flexibility is often evaluated with the sit-and-reach test and the shoulder flexibility test. Usually, only people who regularly stretch are likely to score above-average levels of flexibility. However, regardless of your current flexibility classification, attaining above-average levels is usually

Table 2.2   Norms for Muscular Endurance Using the Curl-Up Test

Age group (years)	Poor	Average	Good	Excellent	Superior
Men					
< 35	15	30	45	60	75
35-44	10	25	40	50	60
> 44	5	15	25	40	50
Women					
< 35	10	25	40	50	60
35-44	6	14	25	40	50
> 44	4	10	15	30	40

Source: Powers, S.K., Dodd, S.L., Noland, V.J. (2006). *Total Fitness and Wellness*, 2nd edition. San Francisco: Pearson.

Table 2.3   Norms for the 1-Minute Sit-Up Test for Men and Women (number completed)

Age group (years)	Excellent	Good	Above average	Below average	Poor	Very poor
Men						
18-25	60-50	48-45	42-40	34-32	30-26	24-12
26-35	55-46	45-41	38-36	30-29	28-24	21-6
36-45	50-42	40-36	34-30	26-24	22-18	16-4
46-55	50-36	33-29	28-25	21-18	17-13	12-4
56-65	42-32	29-26	24-21	16-13	12-9	8-2
66+	40-29	26-22	21-20	14-12	10-8	6-2
Women						
18-25	55-44	41-37	36-33	28-25	24-20	17-4
26-35	54-40	37-33	32-29	24-21	20-16	12-1
36-45	50-34	30-17	26-24	18-16	14-10	6-1
46-55	42-28	25-22	21-18	13-10	9-6	4-0
56-65	38-25	21-18	17-13	9-7	6-4	2-0
66+	36-24	22-18	16-14	10-6	4-2	1-0

Adapted from L.A. Golding, C.R. Myers, and W.E. Sinning, 1989, *Y's way to physical fitness*, 3rd ed. (Champaign, IL: Human Kinetics), 113.

possible. You can improve your flexibility through a stretching routine, yoga, tai chi, qigong, or similar activities.

Sit-and-Reach Test

The sit-and-reach test measures trunk flexibility, which includes the lower back muscles and hamstrings. After gently stretching the lower back and hamstrings, sit on the floor with legs stretched in front of you and feet about 12 inches (30 centimeters) apart. Place a yard stick or meter stick in front of you with the zero mark toward your body and the 15-inch (38-centimeter) mark at your heels. Place one hand on top of the other with the tips of the fingers aligned, and slowly lean forward by dropping the head toward or between the arms, keeping the knees straight. Record your farthest score out of three tries. A score of 15 for men and 17 for women is average. Don't worry if you are above or below average; just work to improve.

Shoulder Flexibility Test

The range of motion for the shoulders is measured in the shoulder flexibility test. While standing, raise your right hand above your head and reach down your back as far as you can. At the same time, reach your left arm up your back toward your right hand, trying to overlap your fingers as much as possible. Measure the finger overlap, rounding to the nearest inch or centimeter. If you fail to overlap, your flexibility is very poor, and if your fingertips barely touch, your flexibility is poor. A 1-inch (3-centimeter) overlap is average, a 2-inch (5-centimeter) overlap suggests good flexibility, a 3-inch (8-centimeter) overlap indicates excellent flexibility, and a 4-inch (10-centimeter) overlap indicates superior flexibility. Complete the test again with the left hand reaching down your back and the right hand reaching up your back.

Getting Fit for Backpacking

Hopefully by reading this chapter you have begun to think about the positive benefits of getting fit for backpacking and how increasing your fitness will make hiking and backpacking more enjoyable. Now that you have an idea of your baseline fitness as well as the fundamentals of fitness, you can decide what trip to take or design a personalized program to get in the shape you want. As you work through a fitness program, you need commitment, vigilance, and attention to detail, but you also need fun ways to maintain enthusiasm. Without a plan and solid preparation for change, including enlisting the help of others and having realistic goals, less than 20 percent of people succeed in taking action (Prochaska, Norcross, & DiClemente, 1994). Finally, your new behavior becomes so ingrained that it is an essential part of daily living, and your day or weekends would seem incomplete without some energizing physical activity or a simple hike in a natural area. If you decide that you need or want a fitness program to get into shape for backpacking, read on.

TRAIL TIP

Exercise must be performed regularly to keep in shape. If we become sedentary, it takes about 8 weeks to lose 30 to 40 percent of muscle endurance and about 10 percent of muscle strength. Other estimates are that we lose 50 percent of our fitness without exercise for 2 months. This is clearly a case of use it or lose it.

Establish Your Support System

After designing your program, it is a good idea to enlist the support of friends and family. In addition to having a positive attitude about getting in shape, you need social support from family and friends for encouragement and to help you with commitment. It helps to have someone else motivating you and sharing similar goals. Research has shown that when people exercise with partners, they exercise more regularly and attain higher fitness levels. Find people who share your passion for an activity and use the companionship as extra incentive to achieve your goals. If you have been exercising alone, try a class. Join a group of Thursday-night walkers or join a cycling club. Find a hiking buddy or two, look for a hiking club in your area, or start your own.

Everyone has to make time to start a new activity such as backpacking, especially if you also need to get in shape. For the general population, lack of time is cited as the number one reason for not exercising. Think about any other concerns you have about starting to hike or starting a fitness program, such as being bored during exercise, being too embarrassed to exercise in front of others, or being unable to afford a health club membership, and figure out how to remove these obstacles from your path.

I did it. I said I'll do it, and I've done it.

Emma "Grandma" Gatewood, after she summited Katahdin

Identify Your Goals

Establishing a fitness goal can seem overwhelming and arbitrary. People wonder, "How do I know what it will take to be fit enough for my trip?" Your first step is to set realistic goals. To identify your personal goals, ask questions such as, "What kind of trip do I want to take and am I fit enough for the hiking and backpacking I want to do?", "What kind of trip do I want to train for?", and "Do I need weight training, or am I in adequate shape for the hiking I want to do and I just need maintenance?" If you already engage in a fitness program, then you may want to make some adjustments for backpacking.

Listen to your body and use common sense. If exercise is not fun or rewarding in some manner, it will be very hard to maintain. One of the great things about hiking and backpacking is that, as mentioned, hiking can be used to get in shape for backpacking. You can exercise in a gym or you can start outside and stay outside. Each season provides great opportunities for outdoor exercise, from cross-country skiing and snowshoeing in the winter to swimming, kayaking, tennis, hiking, and backpacking in the summer. The key to a successful training program is to pick something that increases your heart rate and that you enjoy enough to perform regularly or to use a combination of activities that you will stick with.

Variety in activities helps us maintain activity levels (Glaros & Janelle, 2001). It helps reduce boredom and dropout rates while broadening physical abilities by helping you develop better motor skills. Pilates, tai chi, yoga, qigong, walking, jogging, step aerobics, ballroom dancing, in-line skating, swimming, stair-climbing, rowing, and cycling all help improve overall fitness. Even a power walk through an outlet mall can provide a different twist on your usual walking circuit. Be creative. Pick the mix that works for your schedule and lifestyle and then enjoy!

Keep the steps toward the goal small and achievable, and stay encouraged even if you have to miss a day or revise your plan—keep moving toward your goal, and reward yourself for meeting intermediary goals. Visualize yourself both working toward your goal and reaching your goal. Imagery is powerful and increases the likelihood of success.

SAFETY TIP

To avoid injuries while training, be sure you have the appropriate clothing, footwear, and equipment. Clothing should dissipate heat and keep you dry. Footwear should be suitable for the activity and fit you well. Packs need to fit properly. If you are cycling for training, wear a helmet.

Training Details

Volumes have been written on how to train. Here are some general recommendations and a couple of specific plans that you can adapt to your needs. When exercising to improve physical fitness, the muscles need to work harder than they currently do; however, exercise sessions do not need to be exhausting. The adage "No pain, no gain" is not true and actually can be dangerous, both on and off the trail. Start slow and progress with manageable increases in workout intensity, usually increasing intensity or duration not more than 10 percent per week. Once you reach the desired fitness level, you no longer increase your workout duration or intensity; you simply maintain the current workout level.

Warm-Ups and Cool-Downs

When training, hiking, or backpacking, plan for a warm-up, a primary conditioning period, and a cool-down. A warm-up entails moving for about 5 minutes in a way that increases your core temperature a couple of degrees and increases blood flow to the muscles that will be engaged in the workout. The nutrient-rich blood warms the muscles and lubricates the joints.

Walking for 5 minutes is a simple warm-up. Other warm-up activities include jumping jacks and jogging in place or around a track once—any light movement that raises your temperature. After you have warmed up, stretch. Muscles and tendons need to be warm before stretching; otherwise there is a greater risk for injury. A warm-up reduces the strain to the heart imposed by rapidly engaging in heavy exercise. When hiking, you can hike a few minutes, stop to stretch, and then continue hiking. You can use this pattern when backpacking, too, as long as you are careful when putting on your pack—or better yet use the buddy system and have a friend help you with your pack, and stop after 5 or 10 minutes to stretch. This 5 or 10 minutes usually corresponds to the time when you are feeling like shedding your outer layer anyway. See figure 2.1 for some sample stretches.

After you have warmed up and stretched, you move into the workout, or primary conditioning period. This is the fitness activity of the day, whether it is hiking, backpacking, jogging, dancing, or cycling. You need to plan the frequency, or how often you will work out; the intensity, or how hard you will work out; and the duration, or how long you will work out each time.

SAFETY TIP

Avoid overuse and traumatic injuries by using the four Rs. *Rest* and *recover* between activities, *rehydrate* during and after activities, and *replenish* your nutrients, including enough carbohydrate for your activity level.

Figure 2.1 Once you have hiked a few minutes, stop to stretch, and then continue hiking. Some sample stretches are *(a)* calf stretch, *(b)* hamstring stretch, and *(c)* quad stretch.

Immediately following the primary conditioning period, begin a cool-down, or a 5- to 15-minute period of low-intensity exercise. Cooling down is important to help prevent blood from pooling in the muscles you have worked and to help disperse lactic acid that has built up, which in turn helps prevent muscle soreness. After vigorous exercise, blood tends to remain in the large blood vessels around the muscles, and this can cause lightheadedness or even fainting. Low-intensity exercise moves the blood back toward the heart. When backpacking, camp chores, such as setting up the tent and purifying water, are good cool-down activities.

Frequency and Duration

To increase physical fitness, most people need to work out three to five times per week for at least 30 minutes to experience gains. Some research suggests that even three 10-minute periods of walking a day contribute to greater health and wellness, but to get in shape for a backpacking trip, complete a 30-minute workout at least three times a week, working up to 60 minutes while increasing the intensity.

Intensity

The intensity of exercise can be measured in terms of heart rate increase for cardiorespiratory training and the degree of tension felt during a stretch for flexibility training. If you are lifting weights, a load that can be lifted only 5 to 8 times before complete muscle fatigue is considered high-intensity training, whereas a load that can be lifted 50 to 60 times without resulting in muscle fatigue is considered low-intensity weight training. Use strength training to keep muscles toned, and use weights that you can lift for 30 repetitions before beginning to feel fatigued. During your workout continue to drink water at regular intervals, and take breaks when you need to.

Enthusiastically doing too much too quickly is a common cause of injury both on and off the trail. Start conservatively and then slowly progress toward maintenance. Avoid overtraining, or increasing the exercise duration or intensity too quickly, because this results in stiff and sore muscles as well as fatigue and injury. Vary your activities to avoid injuries from repetitive movements. Adequate rest of the muscle groups between workouts and adequate nutrition are essential. Light to moderate exercise training boosts the immune system and reduces the risk of infection, whereas intense exercise training or overtraining reduces the body's immunity to disease (Kreider, Fry, & O'Toole, 1998). Fatigue, frequent colds, and frequent injuries can be warning signs of overtraining.

You can also incorporate training into your daily life. Instead of using the elevator or escalator, take the stairs. Walk or bicycle to work. If you drive, park so that you have a 10-minute walk and walk briskly. Don't park as close to the store as possible; park in the back of the lot instead. Begin to consciously think about ways to make your body work every day.

Cardiorespiratory Training

Increasing aerobic ability is a primary objective in getting fit for hiking and backpacking. Most training activities will focus on this aspect of fitness. A cardiorespiratory training log can help you track and analyze your progress. Figure 2.2 shows a sample training log for walking and backpacking.

To use hiking as your cardiorespiratory fitness program, pick a trail that's suitable for your hiking level and that's close to home. You can vary activities even during the same week; for example, you might do a day of walking, a day of swimming, and a day of stair-climbing (especially if it is raining). Use

CONSUMER TIP

Pilates is an excellent technique for strengthening the core muscles of the body because in addition to working the abdominals, it triggers the pelvic floor muscles deep in the core that support the internal organs and are involved in bladder control. Strengthening the core muscles supports the back, leading to better posture, coordination, flexibility, and alignment, and it increases hiking and backpacking abilities. Many gyms and health centers offer Pilates classes, and DVDs are available for home use.

Week	Phase	Exercise	Duration (min./day)	Intensity (min./mi.)	Frequency (days/week)	Comments
1	Startup	Walking	20	15-20 (9-12 min./km)	3	Feels good.
2	Startup	Walking	30	Same	3	20 min. seemed too easy.
3	Slow progression	Walking	30	12-15 (8-9 min./km)	3	Going okay; substituted kayaking with friends one day.
4	Progression	Walking	33	Same	3	Going well.
5	Progression	Walking	37	Same	3	Only went out twice because I didn't feel well.
6	Progression	Trail walking	37	20 (12 min./km)	3	Feels good to be out.
7	Progression	Trail walking	37	Same	3	Did stair-climbing one rainy day.
8	Progression	Trail with 10 lb (4.5 kg) backpack	30	Same	3	Have to readjust pack.
9	Progression	Trail with 15 lb (7 kg) backpack	30	Same	3	Need to vary trails.
10	Progression	Trail with 20 lb (9 kg) backpack	30	Same		Need to get a buddy.
Etc.						Joined a hiking club.
24	Maintenance					Awesome!

Figure 2.2 Sample cardiorespiratory fitness log.

stair-climbing in preparation for trips that will include hills and altitude. Substitute the stair-climbing machine for walking in the log in figure 2.1 and vary the level of intensity on the machine. Every day during your warm-up, listen to your body and then trust what you hear. Base the pace and duration of the activity on how you feel that day, no matter what you have planned.

Strength Training

As you train for cardiorespiratory endurance, you will gain strength. As you walk, use the stair-climbing machine, or jog, your legs (quadriceps, hamstrings, and calf muscles) will become stronger. Additionally, you will be more comfortable backpacking with more strength in your back (low back, latissimus dorsi, trapezius, and rhomboids), shoulders (deltoids), stomach (abdominals), chest (pectoralis major), gluteal muscles, and hip abductors and adductors. To see demonstrations of over two dozen beginning and advanced core strengthening exercises, go to this Web site: www.sparkpeople.com/myspark/ex/all_exercises. asp. If you use kayaking, canoeing, or even cycling as training, you will gain some upper-body strength. See figure 2.3 for a sample log.

Be sure to stretch each time you do any strength training. Certain body weight exercises provide strength training, including toe stands, squats, push-ups, hip abductions, back extensions on the floor, and curl-ups. Try to exercise each of the major muscle groups, starting with the larger muscles. Do the exercise or lift a weight 8 to 12 times, rest, and then repeat another 8 to 12 times. Movements should be smooth and slow, about 2 seconds for lifting and 3 to 4 seconds for lowering. Exhale through your mouth as you lift.

If you use weights or machines, work on technique before adding much weight. Increase the weight by 5 percent or less every 2 to 3 weeks and, unless you want to be a bodybuilder, move to a maintenance phase after a month. You should not strength train every day, and if you are just getting started it is easy to be overwhelmed by all of the recommendations and jargon. Create a routine using the equipment or weights available to you (even cans of soup work).

Training twice a week for less than an hour each time is enough, and remember, you usually can gain adequate strength from cardiorespiratory training. Refer to the strength training log for a sample plan using weight training exercises and a few exercises using weights. As you progress, add more exercises or weights.

Flexibility Training

To gain the flexibility you need for hiking and backpacking, stretch after warm-ups and during cool-downs, and maybe practice yoga, qigong, or tai chi at home or in a class. If it helps, make a training log for flexibility and practice daily. When stretching, gently stretch the muscle and hold for at least 10 seconds and up to 30 seconds. Breathe through the stretch. Stretch after you have warmed up and avoid any bouncing. Common stretches include toe touches; neck, back, and shoulder stretches; hamstring and calf stretches, quadriceps stretches; and chest and arm stretches. To see demonstrations of 10 common stretches, go to this Web site: www.sparkpeople.com/myspark/ex/all_exercises.asp.

Strength Training Log

Week	Exercises	Day 1	Day 2	Comments
		Record weight lifted or check when exercise is completed		
2 sets of 8 repetitions				
1	Squats			Feels good to work out. I am starting slowly.
	Push-ups; modified or wall push-ups			
	Toe stands			
2	Squats			Need to get a work-out buddy. I keep thinking that I'm not going to have time to keep exercising. My cousin said she might like to work out with me.
	Push-ups; modified or wall push-ups			
	Toe stands			
	Hip abductions (side hip raises)			
	Floor back extensions			
	Upright row, 1 lb (.5 kg)			
3	Squats			Got my cousin to do this with me. It really helps to have a friend to work out with. I think I am feeling more energetic. I like that I have stuck with it.
	Push-ups; modified or wall push-ups			
	Toe stands			
	Hip abductions			
	Floor back extensions			
	Upright row, 1 lb (.5 kg)			
	Abdominal curls			
2 sets of 12 repetitions				
4				I'm getting better. I feel stronger and have more energy. Still hard some days.
Add	Overhead presses, 1 lb (.5 kg)			
	Chest presses, 1 lb (.5 kg)			

Figure 2.3 Sample strength training log.

Personal Conditioning Program

Start with light loads and work up to carrying 20 to 25 percent of your body weight. A pack for a weekend trip with food and gear may weigh 25 pounds (11 kilograms) and for a week-long trip, 40 pounds (18 kilograms). For small women, it is hard to fit all the gear in and keep the weight to 25 percent. When you are in good shape, carrying 30 percent of your body weight usually works.

When hiking with a backpack, walk erect with a shorter stride than your normal walking stride. This helps keep the back and neck from becoming strained by increased pressure. Use a walking stick or trekking poles to avoid slumping over and to aid in stability. When going uphill, shorten your stride even more. When backpacking, with each mile per hour that you increase your speed, you double the amount of energy you expend. You might work up to 2.5 to 3 miles (4-5 kilometers) per hour during training hikes, even carrying a backpack. However, when actually on the trail, you might hike at a slower pace, taking time to enjoy the scenery and smell the flowers.

A sample 3-month outdoor training regime is found in figure 2.4. The training gradually increases in intensity and duration. When adding hills, do fast uphill and downhill walking for 15 minutes and repeat this three times during a week. In each of the months, one day can be a longer hike, keeping the pace at your rate for the month. In the second and third months you may enjoy hiking in areas that have gullies and ridges, boulders, and uneven paths, which will challenge your dynamic balance.

Conclusion

Hiking and backpacking have many mental, physical, and spiritual fitness benefits; however, to gain these benefits and be safe, you need to know your fitness level so that you can pick trails best suited for you. After reading this chapter and understanding what it means to be in shape for hiking and backpacking, you can decide what works for you, whether that means hiking on an easy trail close to home to get in shape or spending time getting in shape before hiking

Month	Times/ week	Terrain	Intensity (min./mi.)	Duration (min.)
1	3	Level	20 (12 min./km)	25-30
2	3	Level and 15 min. on hills	15-18 (11 min./km)	25-50
3	3-6	Level and 15 min. fast on hills	15 (9 min./km)	50

Figure 2.4 Sample 3-month outdoor training regime.

on a trail. Knowing some of the reasons to be fit and how to become fitter will make you a safer hiker. Being fit for hiking and backpacking makes you better able to handle the inherent challenges of these sports. You can come back to the information in this chapter time and again as you progress from hiking to backpacking or when you want to reach a higher fitness level.

Some people approach backpacking as a competitive challenge—each weekend has to be harder than the one before, or anything less than grueling is boring. However, others prefer to cover less ground and soak up the details. If you're in shape, you can make choices about your pace and enjoy the details without sacrificing safety. The joys of stepping light and steady under a pack and seeing amazing countryside are immeasurable.

Footwear, Clothing, and Gear

It is better to be
prepared for an
opportunity and
not have one,
than to have an
opportunity and
not be prepared.

Whitney Young Jr.

The idea that the clothes make the person is often associated with outdoor pursuits. In the field, clothes are the items that keep us warm, the gear we use, and the boots we travel in. The sideshow of bright fabrics and fancy logos at local gear shops draws neophytes into the store, and the result is the spending of your hard-earned money toward something you supposedly can't live without. The goal of this chapter is to provide a basic understanding of common gear to help you decide what you truly can and cannot live without.

Basic Rules for Purchasing Gear

It has yet to be proven that someone who spends a bundle of money on gear and clothing has a better time hiking and backpacking than someone who is thrifty when purchasing these items. A general rule when buying footwear and clothing for the trail is to look at three aspects: expense, durability, and weight. Beyond footwear and clothing, there is gear (e.g., backpack, stove, sleeping bag). When analyzing gear, you might consider multiple uses for the same item, while still examining expense, durability, and weight. A simple explanation of these rules (expense, durability, and weight) will assist you in developing an outdoor arsenal.

- **Expense.** Always consider the expense of any single item of footwear, clothing, or gear. Before purchasing an item, reflect on needing it versus wanting it. Do you have something that would substitute for the item (e.g., you have a tarp but not a tent; do you really need a tent)? Can you rent or borrow that piece of equipment? Is the need for the item enough to justify the expense (e.g., why purchase a four-season tent when all that is needed is a three-season tent)? Can you purchase something less expensive that would fulfill that need (i.e., a tarp instead of a tent)?

- **Durability.** The second rule to consider when procuring outdoor items is durability. Expense and durability are often associated; however, do not assume that the more expensive an item is, the better it is. This is not always true, so it pays to be a wise and informed consumer of outdoor equipment. Instead of getting caught up in fashion trends, focus on function instead. Having gear that works is good, but it is even better if the gear works and is durable. Increased cost does not always equate to increased durability. Many times increased cost is defined as the same object but made with lighter materials. The more lightweight materials may not be as durable as the traditional materials, but they could lighten your pack. With increased technology also comes increased care and upkeep. When dealing with stoves, many agencies use either a Coleman Peak 1 or Whisperlite. This is due to their durability since many new outdoor participants are rough on gear.

- **Weight.** At first, weight is an issue that most people do not think about on a piece-by-piece basis. Instead, new hikers tend to view weight using a full-pack mentality. Weight and durability often conflict: The lighter an item is, the less durable it may be. The reduction of materials or the use of lightweight materials in the production of an item may require that the purchaser have more experience using the lightweight item. As mentioned, the reduction of weight at times increases the level of care required to keep the equipment in proper working order. An example of this is a down sleeping bag compared with a synthetic sleeping bag. The down sleeping bag is warmer and lighter, but when wet it is not useful and becomes very heavy. A synthetic bag is heavier overall, but it still works if wet. A down sleeping bag, which is warmer and lighter by weight than a synthetic sleeping bag with the same temperature rating, will require more care, in that you must prevent it from getting wet.

Feet First

Boots are the single most important investment that you will make. Every trip comes down to how comfortable you are with your footwear. Boots are the equipment that physically link you to the trail.

Selecting the Right Boot

Boot selection needs to be based on anticipated terrain, pack weight, and size and weight of the backpacker (Drury & Bonney, 1992). Try on as many different brands as possible and compare positives and negatives of each. When trying on boots, wear them around the store and shop for other items to assist in establishing how well the boots fit beyond standing in a single spot. If the retailer has an incline board, stand on the board and walk down it to ensure that your toes do not touch the end of the toe box when walking downhill. If your toes touch, you may incur black toe during a long downhill section of a trail. Black toe is caused by a bruising or blistering of the toenail bed when the toe is repeatedly jammed against the end of the boot. Different boot types include lightweight, medium-weight, and heavyweight boots. See figure 3.1 for a photo comparison. When purchasing boots, as the durability of the boot increases, the price and many times the weight will increase. This is due to the increased materials and products used in the construction of the boot to make it more durable.

- **Lightweight boots.** Lightweight boots are useful for day hikes, when carrying little weight, and when the terrain will be easy to moderate (Drury, Bonney, Berman, & Wagstaff, 2005). They are generally constructed with some synthetic panels to reduce the weight of the boot and break-in time. Lightweight boots are often lower in cost; they also are less durable, waterproof, and stable (Graydon & Hanson, 1997). Before purchasing any boot, reflect on what type of hiking you are going to be doing; if you are going to be moving between moderate terrain and easy terrain, you will probably want to purchase a boot that is more durable.

- **Medium-weight boots.** Medium-weight boots are useful for loads of 20 to 40 pounds (9-18 kilograms) moving over moderate terrain (Drury et al.,

2005). Soles on medium-weight boots are more durable, and a solid leather upper often provides more support to the ankle than lightweight boots. Depending on the construction of the boot, medium-weight boots may be a mixture of leather and synthetic panels or all leather.

• **Heavyweight boots.** Heavyweight boots are useful for heavy loads over moderate to rough terrain (Drury et al., 2005). These boots are generally constructed of leather, with the sole cemented or stitched to provide durability. Other items to consider when looking at heavyweight boots are a gusseted tongue to prevent water from entering the boot easily and minimal seams to decrease points of entry for water. The heavyweight boot will also have a shank

Figure 3.1 Examples of (a) medium-weight and (b) heavyweight hiking boots.

in the sole to create a more rigid structure and assist in prevention of injuries to the feet from jagged points poking through the soles.

Feet, Socks, and More

The previous standard for socks in the outdoors was that each person must always wear two pairs of wool or synthetic socks to prevent blisters. However, with advances in boots, shoes, and sock fibers, this rule is now obsolete. For the majority of outdoor experiences you will want to wear socks that are wool, synthetic, or a wool–synthetic blend; use what works for you. Try a multitude of socks before deciding what is right for you. (See chapter 5 for information on blister prevention and care.)

Gaiters are another piece of equipment that may be valuable (figure 3.2). Gaiters provide protection by sealing the boundary between the pant leg and the boot. They can be valuable in keeping socks and pants dry, preventing debris from entering the boot over the cuff, and providing protection from biting insects. Gaiters can be used for both on- and off-trail travel. Full gaiters, extending to approximately calf height, provide extra protection in snow, water, and rough terrain. A half gaiter, which extends just past the top of the boot, does an excellent job of keeping small stones and trail material from getting into your shoes or boots and causing problems.

Figure 3.2 Gaiters provide extra protection from snow, water, rough terrain, biting bugs, and unwanted items that might accidentally slip into your boots.

Breaking in Boots

Never purchase shoes or boots and expect to take them directly into the field. Just one person in a group doing this can cause an entire trip to be evacuated due to foot problems. The break-in time for boots varies, but a good rule is to walk approximately 50 miles (80 kilometers) in the boots before wearing them on an extended trip. The boots will need to be used in a variety of settings for you to understand how the boots and your feet match up. Wear the boots to places where you can change shoes if a blister arises or your feet begin to hurt. Better to have this happen at the mall instead of on mile 4 of a 12-mile (19-kilometer) day. This break-in time allows you to soften the boots for a better feel across rugged terrain. It also allows you to identify potential hotspots before wearing the boots for an extended amount of time. During the break-in time you might consider using the double-sock method to reduce potential hot spots.

Camp Shoes

Camp shoes, which are worn at the end of the day, are a valuable part of any backpacking trip. They allow swollen and heavy feet to relax and breathe. In addition, camp shoes are friendly for the environment. The softer soles of a camp shoe do not grab soil and thereby decrease possible impacts on the environment. Camp shoes do not have to cost a fortune, either; old running shoes, day hikers, or other comfortable shoes work well. The main thing to look for in camp shoes is comfort. If your boots fail, they could be an alternative shoe to hike in. A primary safety concern in a camp shoe is that it should have a closed toe. The enclosure allows for extra protection against puncture wounds to the toes. Any participant who stubs a toe has the possibility of puncturing a toe. This could be a trip-ending scenario based on the degree of the injury.

Hiking Poles

Hiking poles, also known as *trekking poles,* have come a long way from that stick you carried while walking in the woods as a kid. Hiking poles are now made of light, durable materials that telescope to a variety of lengths. Most poles now have some sort of antishock system that helps reduce the abuse to your body. Even though poles add extra weight, they greatly reduce the strain to your knees. This may not be a big deal in the beginning, but after 8 days straight, the strain will add up. In addition, your knees will thank you 30 years from now when you are still going strong. Plus, it can be very helpful to have that third or fourth appendage on the ground in certain situations. Hiking poles are very much like boots in that there are as many types as there are mountains to climb. To find the right hiking poles, test-drive as many as you can, and then buy some in your price range that you like and that meet all your needs. Hiking poles can range in price from $15 to $150. As always, make a wise investment with your money.

Use of hiking poles can provide added balance and help reduce knee strain.

Dressing for Outdoors

Dressing for the outdoors means providing protection from the elements. This protection may come in the form of fabrics created to breathe, or let moisture and heat out. Other fabrics provide protection by preventing heat loss and keeping the cold wind from getting to the skin. Heat is transferred or lost from the body to the environment in four ways (see table 3.1). Climate will determine what type of transference you want to occur. You can accentuate the transference by choosing certain types of clothing.

Clothing selection for the outdoors has to do with two main things: maintaining your body temperature and protecting yourself from the elements. Maintaining a normal core body temperature, around 98.6 degrees (37 degrees Celsius), is necessary to keep from getting too cold (hypothermia) or too hot (hyperthermia); both are uncomfortable and can become deadly. Therefore, having the proper clothing and gear is essential for any trip to be safe.

Table 3.1 Ways the Body Loses Heat

Method of heat loss	How it occurs
Evaporation and respiration	Occurs when the body sweats and the sweat evaporates, creating a cooling effect on the skin.
Conduction	Occurs when heat from an external source adds or takes heat to or from the body. When sitting on snow, body heat is transferred to the snow in an attempt to warm (melt) the snow. The opposite is true if your hands are cold and you grab a warm cup; the heat of the cup is transferred to your hands in an attempt to warm them, which in turn cools the cup.
Convection	Occurs when air moves across the body to dissipate heat.
Radiation	Occurs when the body radiates heat without coming into contact with another surface due to blood vessels moving blood close to the skin.

Adapted from Drury, Bonney, Berman, and Wagstaff 2005; Drury, Bonney, and Cockrell 1991.

Fabric Choices

Cotton, silk, and wool have been the fabric standards for backpacking. Advancements in technology have not been limited to just computers, however, but have found their way into fabrics as well. The traditional standards are still used today, but there are also new fabrics that assist the body in staying cooler and warmer when needed. Some of the fabrics that are currently available include Capilene, polypropylene, Supplex, Gore-Tex, fleece, polyester, Thermax, and nylon. Keep in mind that this is not an all-encompassing list, but just a few to show the abundance of fabric development. Table 3.2 groups the fabrics into three types: natural fibers, synthetics, and blends.

Laws of Layering

Dressing in layers is essential to participating in outdoor pursuits. You must be able to maintain your body temperature without overheating (hyperthermia) or becoming too cold (hypothermia). There are three essential layers to enjoying the outdoors effectively and safely: the base layer, the insulating layer, and the wind and rain layer. Each has a significant purpose for protection in the field. The base layer is next to the skin. This layer should have the ability to wick moisture away from the body, providing a cooling or warming effect. Quite often it is composed of a synthetic fabric with the aforementioned capabilities. The next layer of clothing should be an insulating layer. The purpose of this layer is to trap body heat, allowing the body to heat the space between the base and insulating layers. The outermost layer is the wind and rain layer.

Table 3.2   Fabric Comparison Chart

Fabric type	Advantages	Disadvantages
Natural fibers		
Cotton	Comfortable	Holds moisture and dries slowly
	Breathes in warm weather	Loses warmth when wet
	Low cost	
Wool	Insulates when wet	Scratchy to skin
	Low cost when bought used	Heavy and bulky
Silk	Insulates when wet	High cost
	Odor resistant	
	Holds shape and does not pill	
	Strongest natural fiber	
	Wicking capability	
Synthetics (e.g., acrylic, polypropylene, polyester, nylon, Gore-Tex)		
	Quick drying	High cost
	Comfortable	May retain body odor
	Wicking capability	Not effective against wind
	Wide variety available	Proper care needed for long life
Blends (e.g., polyester and cotton, acrylic and wool)		
	Best elements of both fabrics	Worst elements of both fabrics

Adapted from Drury, Bonney, Berman, and Wagstaff 2005.

This layer is what first protects you against harsh environmental conditions. It prevents wind and water from getting to the insulating and base layers. The wind and rain layer is generally waterproof (i.e., Gore-Tex) or windproof (i.e., Windstopper), depending on the outdoor conditions. For safety, make certain that you have at least two out of the three layers (see figure 3.3).

Figure 3.3 Every season requires an altered wardrobe. Here are a few ways that you might adjust for the various seasons.

SAFETY TIP

Whenever you are embarking on a trip, always expect the worst conditions and prepare for them. It is better to be prepared for any condition rather than chancing it. Do not place yourself in a dangerous situation. Weight gained by carrying rain gear or other typical weather items is minimal when compared with the weight of concern related to a poor decision to not carry needed items.

What to Wear on the Trail

As previously mentioned, dressing in layers is key to success on the trail. Some things to consider when dressing for the trail include comfort, durability, and functionality. Choose clothes that allow free movement but do not bunch due to being too loose. Ask yourself the following questions when selecting clothing for the trail. How durable is the selected clothing? Will the clothes hold up to several days of constant use? Does the clothing have more than one possible function? An example of clothing with several functions would be a pair of lightweight pants with removable zippered legs that allow the pants to be converted into shorts during hotter times of the day. Clothing functions should generally tie into the layering system, allowing for fewer items in the pack.

What to Wear in Camp

After a long day on the trail, your only thought may be to change into some clean and dry clothes. Make certain to dress warmer for camp than for the trail since you will be less active. Your body will be radiating heat, which may cause clothing to feel warm when you first put it on. Keep in mind that as your body cools, you will want to add layers. Clothing in camp should be comfortable and breathable, allowing the hot zones of the body to cool down.

Head Coverings and Other Items

Covering your head provides several functions, including reduction of heat loss and protection from the sun. "If your feet are cold, put on a hat," is a trail saying that provides insight into how much heat is lost through the head. Head coverings for cold weather might include a balaclava (ski mask), stocking hat, beanie, or fleece hat, just to name a few. Protection from the sun can be accomplished through a variety of hats, but the two most common are baseball caps and wide-brimmed hats. Baseball caps provide shade for the eyes and protection from the sun directly on the head. A wide-brimmed hat will provide the same protection as a baseball cap with the added benefit of sun protection for the ears and neck.

Selecting and Using
Day Packs and Backpacks

When you finally make the decision to step into the outdoors, you have to decide for how long you are going: an afternoon, a day, several days, or even weeks. Based on trip length, you have to make gear decisions. How big of a pack do you need, what items need to go in the pack, and how do you pack all of your stuff into such a small space?

Day Packs

The choices of day packs are as plentiful as days in a year. The majority of day packs are a form of internal-frame packs. The most important question to ask when selecting any pack is, "Will it hold everything I need for my outing?" The size needed will vary from person to person and will depend upon weather conditions, terrain, time of year, and so on. The reason for using a day pack instead of a backpack is that you don't always need the extra room. For many people, the more room they have in their pack, the more likely they will take items they do not need.

The hydration system consists of a bladder, or storage tank, with a hose connected to the tank that allows a hands-free approach to hydration while on the move.

Once again, a good day pack does not need to cost a fortune to be effective. Many beginners already own a pack or book bag that meets the needs of most day trips. Some packs have holster-like pockets designed for water bottles. Some manufacturers have also integrated water systems into day packs, and there are backpacks that consist of a Mylar bladder inside a nylon cover with a long plastic tube to drink from. These water bags may also be purchased separately and placed in the top pocket of your pack. Water bags provide easier access and promote more consistent water intake. To stay on the safe side, if you use a water bladder you should also carry a water bottle such as Nalgene as a backup in case your water bladder is punctured, causing it to leak. Many budding outdoor enthusiasts start with a day pack for their hiking trips and then use the knowledge they gain from hiking when selecting and buying a backpack.

Backpacks

The two main types of backpacks on the market are internal frame and external frame (see figure 3.4). People often advocate for the style of backpack they use. Most provide dramatic stories of how either an external- or internal-frame pack is the greatest or the worst pack to purchase. A general consideration in pack selection is the type of traveling done (i.e., on-trail versus off-trail). External-frame packs are excellent when traveling on-trail. They allow the weight of the pack to be more evenly distributed to the hips and provide better ventilation between the pack and the body. Internal-frame packs are better for traveling off-trail. The low profile of internal-frame packs allows them to sit closer to the body, reducing the grabbing effect of shrubs and other foliage in typical

CONSUMER TIP

How to Pack Your Backpack

Pack according to the rooms of your house.

Living room—games, books, checkers, things you will use in your down-time

Kitchen—stove, cooking gear, eating gear, food

Bedroom—sleeping pad, sleeping bag, extra clothes

Bathroom—personal items, hygiene items (e.g., toilet paper, toothbrush, soap)

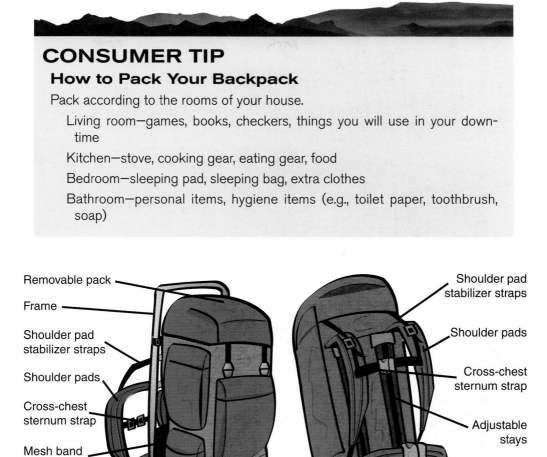

Figure 3.4 Backpacks come in various sizes and shapes, but the two major classifications are (a) external frame (note that you can see the metal or composite frame) and (b) internal frame (you cannot see the frame).

off-trail travel. On-trail or off-trail travel can be done with either pack; just be aware of the pros and cons with each.

Packing Properly

When packing, use the conveniently balanced system (CBS). *Convenience* means having close at hand the items that will need to be accessed often or quickly. Examples of these items include the trail map, compass, rain gear, and first

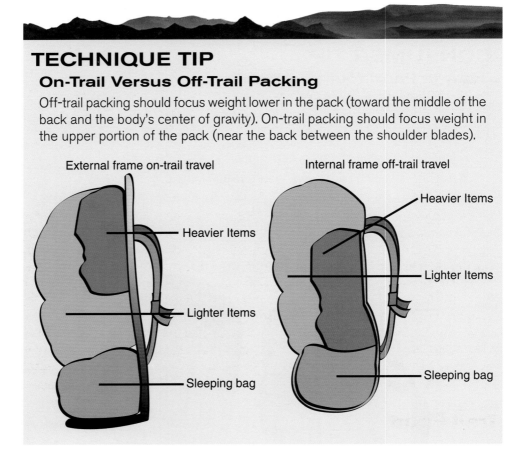

TECHNIQUE TIP
On-Trail Versus Off-Trail Packing

Off-trail packing should focus weight lower in the pack (toward the middle of the back and the body's center of gravity). On-trail packing should focus weight in the upper portion of the pack (near the back between the shoulder blades).

External frame on-trail travel

Heavier Items

Lighter Items

Sleeping bag

Internal frame off-trail travel

Heavier Items

Lighter Items

Sleeping bag

aid kit. Having a *balanced* pack can allow for longer and stronger days on the trail. When packing, attempt to balance items side to side and top to bottom. Lighter items (e.g., the sleeping bag) should be at the bottom of the pack, while heavier items (e.g., food) should be near the top of the back, close to the body. Packing in a systematic way allows for easier recall when items are needed. It also allows for efficient timing if items are packed the same way each time. Organize stuff sacks or ditty bags (nylon or cloth bags of various sizes that are used to store gear or clothing) by color or use see-through mesh to make things easier to locate (Drury & Bonney, 1992).

Food and Water: Eating on the Trail

For many, the concept of eating in the outdoors is seen as a negative aspect of backcountry settings since the comforts of fast food, huge grocery stores, and 24-hour convenience markets are far away. Many new hikers who venture out

CONSUMER TIP

Always pack at least one comfort food in case you do not want to eat what someone else has fixed. This will work well for one day or night, but it is not a plan for nightly outings. For this reason, it is a good idea to play an active part in menu planning and food preparation.

of civilization are surprised to discover that eating well is a huge component of most outdoor adventures. Food and water consumption on the trail are directly related to attitude, enjoyment, and safety. Not only are they a vital part of every trip, but they are probably one of the areas where creativity is most valued and encouraged. Furthermore, more than one major expedition has been ruined due to the poor quality or lack of food and water. Plan to eat and drink heartily on any trip you participate in because that will be your source of energy for the trip. Backcountry outings are no time to go on a diet or skimp on food. You will need to eat a great deal on a trip to get yourself going; make certain you are aware of what is and is not available to be eaten on a trip. Finally, allow plenty of time and variety for cooking.

Trail Food

During both summer and winter you should maintain a balanced diet. As long as you are eating a balanced diet, supplemental vitamins and minerals are probably not necessary. Carbohydrate should make up around 60 percent of your diet. This should give you the short-term energy you need. Examples are starches and sugars that come from pastas, rice, drink mixes, and fruit. Fat should be about 20 to 25 percent of your diet and provide long-term energy. Cheeses, nuts, meats, and margarine are good sources of fat. Protein will make up the rest of your diet at 15 to 20 percent. Protein assists in the building and repairing of body tissue. Examples include meat, cereal, vegetables, legumes, soy products, and wheat products.

In addition, remember to drink adequate amounts of water while on a trip. The minimum water consumption for most people during the summer is 2 to 4 quarts (2-4 liters) per day. Hydration level is not only important for comfort and mental alertness, but water consumption also aids in regulating body temperature, digestion, and waste disposal (Pearson, 2004). Bringing powdered sport drinks that contain carbohydrate and electrolytes to mix with water may help replace sodium lost in sweat. Also lightly salt your food before the outing and carry along some salt for meals while you are on the trail.

Menu Planning

Planning the proper meals for a trip is directly related to the outcome of that trip. Consult every member of the group to make sure you are meeting the dietary needs as well as the likes and dislikes of everyone. Make certain you know about any food allergies before hitting the trail. Some people will eat anything whereas others are very picky; make sure you know the preferences of everyone on the trip.

Food Planning Questions

- ☐ Will your meal be hot or cold?
- ☐ Will the food spoil or freeze?
- ☐ How far are you going?
- ☐ What type of activity will be done?
- ☐ What level of activity (mild, moderate, or strenuous) will be done?
- ☐ How many people are going?
- ☐ What are the group members' likes, dislikes, and allergies?

The options for proper nutrition in the outdoors are not contained merely at the outdoor store in freeze-dried packets; they are as close as your refrigerator

TECHNIQUE TIP
Cooking Outdoors

- Variety is the spice of life; make a spice kit.
- Cook with a group of 2, 3, or 4 people in order to save time, pots, and fuel and to limit leftovers.
- Take turns being the chef.
- Divide the food, stove, utensils, and pots equally within the cooking group, so that one person is not carrying all the weight. Furthermore, if one person's gear is lost, you will not lose your entire kitchen.
- Plan with your group many days ahead of the trip.
- Reuse the boiling water for tea, coffee, soup, and so on.
- Try to keep all food in one or two large stuff sacks.

CONSUMER TIP
Food Packing

- Use film canisters to hold spices. Be sure to label them!
- When packing food, place it above any items that could ruin it (e.g., gas, soap, sunscreen).
- Double bag everything.
- Assume the worst-case scenario for spillage.
- Mark bags with permanent marker.
- Put all bags for one meal in larger bags (if using the menu-planning system).
- Keep frequently used condiments or utensils in a separate bag.
- Minimize space by taking prepackaged foods out of boxes (make sure to cut out and bring cooking directions).
- Bring heavy-duty garbage bags to carry out your garbage.

and kitchen cabinet. Generally, only the wealthy or those new to backpacking will purchase their food at a gear store. The better choice is your local supermarket or natural-food grocery. The two basic types of food planning for trips are bulk rations and menu planning. The bulk-ration system is when you have a variety of items to cook and decide what your meals will consist of one meal at a time. The menu-planning system is when you plan out what you are having for each meal before the trip and purchase and pack accordingly. Following are a variety of tips and tricks to make cooking outdoors easier and more effective.

Water Treatment

When using water in the backcountry, a simple rule to remember is, "What you cannot see will hurt you." Bacteria and viruses in the water can ruin a trip if a few simple precautions are not followed. There are four typical ways to treat water before ingesting it. See also table 3.3 for a treatment comparison chart.

1. Boil the water. The first and most effective method of treating water is to boil it. Once the water has come to a rolling boil it is considered safe to drink. It is suggested that it have a continuous boiling time of at least 1 minute. The benefit of boiling is that the water is safe to drink as soon as it cools down enough to handle. The disadvantages of this method include the consumption of stove fuel and inefficient use of travel time on the trail.

2. Filter the water. The second treatment method is filtration. The filtration of water may be effective against bacteria based on the filter design, but it is not effective against viruses. The advantage of a manufactured filter is that it is relatively quick to use; however, the cost and weight of a filtering unit is a notable disadvantage.

3. Treat the water with chemicals. The third water treatment method is chemical. Chemical treatments (iodine and chlorine) are extremely effective against bacteria and viruses. The benefit of chemical treatments is expense; both iodine tablets and crystalline iodine products are inexpensive. The cost of chemical treatments is the wait time (generally 30 minutes or more). In addition, extended exposure to any chemical can create health problems later on.

4. New technologies to treat water. The fourth type of water treatment uses state-of-the-art technology to purify water. One of the newer technologies is the SteriPEN, which uses ultraviolet light (UV) to sterilize the water. It is designed to kill viruses and bacteria such as giardia and cryptosporidium, and it may be one of the quickest and easiest methods on the market for purifying water. The user simply has to press a button and place the device in the water container to purify the water. This is a clear advantage; however, the battery requirement, the initial high cost, and the question of durability may be more of a disadvantage for novice backcountry users. The next cutting-edge method in which to create potable water quickly and effortlessly is the MIOX purifier. The MIOX uses a combination of mixed oxidants and an electrical charge to eliminate viruses and bacteria such as giardia and cryptosporidium, making water safe to drink. Just as with the SteriPEN, the MIOX system is expensive, delicate, and requires batteries.

Table 3.3 Water Treatment Comparison Chart

Method	Advantages	Disadvantages
Boiling	Most effective method	Slow and inconvenient
	Effective against all pathogens	Uses fuel
Filtering	Relatively quick	Expensive to purchase unit
	Effective against most bacteria	May break or clog
		Not effective against viruses
Chemical	Effective against bacteria and viruses	Unpleasant taste
	Can combine with filtering	Requires exposure to chemicals
New technology	Quick and easy to use	Uses batteries
	Effective against most pathogens	Delicate
		Expensive to purchase unit

Adapted from Cox and Fulsaas, 2003.

First Aid Kit

A first aid kit is essential for any trip in the outdoors. The supplies needed for a first aid kit vary greatly depending on the type of trip, location, participants, terrain, time of year, and so on. There are two main concerns related to the first aid kit. The first is having one and making sure to bring it on every trip. The second is having the appropriate knowledge and training to use it correctly. Adequate training in wilderness-related first aid techniques is a crucial component of your first aid kit. A variety of ready-made first aid kits are on the market that are designed for everything from day trips to 3-week expeditions. Most people use ready-made kits but also include tried-and-true items from their own experience (see table 3.4). Many experts agree that the most effective part of a first aid kit is the training and judgment of the person using it.

Table 3.4   Items to Include in a First Aid Kit

Medical items

_____	1	Sunscreen	_____	5	2 × 2 in. (5 × 5 cm) gauze sponges
_____	1	Box mixed bandages	_____	5	4 × 4 in. (10 × 10 cm) gauze sponges
_____	1	8 oz (237 ml) tincture of benzoic	_____	10	Exam gloves
_____	1	50 in.² (323 cm²) moleskin	_____	10	Alcohol swabs
_____	1	20 in.² (129 cm²) mole foam	_____	1	Trauma scissors
_____	1	Adhesive tape	_____	1	Tweezers
_____	2	2 in. (5 cm) roller gauze	_____	1	3 in. (8 cm) elastic bandage
_____	1	Microshield rescue mask	_____	1	Iodine tablets

Medication

_____	20	Acetaminophen tablets	_____	20	Betadine ointment packets
_____	20	Ibuprofen tablets	_____	10	Sting relief pads

Adapted from Cox and Fulsaas, 2003.

Essentials for Day Hiking

There are numerous essential items that every day hiker should have when day hiking. Some people refer to these items as the 10 essentials. However, if you ask 10 different outdoor experts, most likely you will receive 10 different lists. The main purpose of the essentials is to prepare you for all situations, both seen and unseen. The essentials help you avoid survival situations rather than help you try to make it through one. They differ depending on climate, terrain, time of year, activity, and geographical location, so the following list of essentials is only a guide. Do not limit yourself to just 10; add what you think you will need to address any situation that can occur in the backcountry.

The Essentials

- [ ] Clothing (see the clothing list at the end of the chapter)
- [ ] Topographical maps of the area and compass (know how to use them)
- [ ] Tarp (emergency shelter)
- [ ] Stove, fuel, and fuel bottle
- [ ] Cooking gear (pot grippers, serving spoon, and pot)
- [ ] Water purifier (filter, iodine tablets or iodine crystals)
- [ ] Eating utensils (bowl, cup, spoon and fork or spork)
- [ ] First aid kit (including duct tape)
- [ ] Food
- [ ] Flashlight and extra batteries (headlamps or headbands for hands-free use)
- [ ] Knife (small, multipurpose with locking blades, such as a Swiss Army knife)
- [ ] Shovel or trowel
- [ ] Stuff sacks or dry bags
- [ ] Water bottles or hydration system
- [ ] Whistle (safety)

You need special shoes for hiking— and a bit of a special soul as well.

Emme
Woodhull-Bäche

Gear Considerations
for Overnight and Longer Trips

You now have your trip planned and ready to go except for gear. How cold will it be? Will there be snow? Do you need a tent or tarp? These are just a few questions that will help determine what you need to bring. As you read through the following information, keep these questions in mind to assist with decisions on what to pack.

Sleeping Bag

Currently there are two basic fill options for sleeping bags: synthetic insulation fill or goose down. See figure 3.5 for a cross section of a sleeping bag. Each type of fill has advantages and disadvantages that must be addressed before purchase and usage in the field. One of the primary concerns is the amount of warmth the bag will provide. Sleeping bags are rated from 30 to 40 degrees Fahrenheit (–1-4 degrees Celsius) to less than 0 degrees (–18 degrees Celsius). This means that if the ambient air temperature is at 30 degrees Fahrenheit (–1 degree Celsius) and you're sleeping in a 30-degree Fahrenheit bag, you will be warm. Make sure that you check what temperature rating you are looking

Pockets of fill

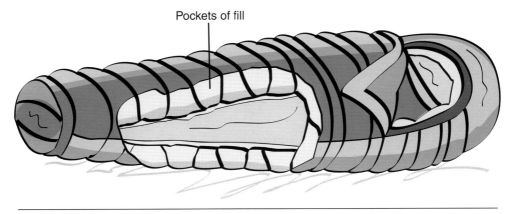

Figure 3.5 In this cross-section of a sleeping bag, notice how the pockets of fill (synthetic or down) create pockets of air to keep you warm.

at, Fahrenheit or Celsius (32 degrees Fahrenheit = 0 degrees Celsius). Also note that this is just a suggestive rating. If you tend to feel cold at night, you might consider getting a bag that is rated for 10 degrees (12 degrees Celsius) colder than what you need. If you tend to feel warm, you might consider going warmer by 10 degrees.

The primary benefit of synthetic-filled bags is the retention of warmth even when wet. They also dry more quickly than goose-down bags. Another benefit of the synthetic fill is the lower cost compared with goose down. The concern regarding a synthetic fill is the bulkier size and additional weight. Size and weight per bag will vary by manufacturer. The materials that constitute a synthetic sleeping bag will also vary from manufacturer to manufacturer. Synthetic bags are especially beneficial on canoeing trips or trips in areas with poor weather or bountiful water crossings.

The primary benefit of goose-down bags is the ability to compress them to a smaller size than synthetic sleeping bags. They also weigh substantially less for the same warmth as their synthetic counterparts. Fill ratings range from 550 (lowest) to 900 (highest). Most well-known manufacturers are now starting bags at 750. Higher fill ratings generally equate to greater warmth, weight, and compressibility. Currently, most manufacturers have bags in the 30- to 40-degrees Fahrenheit (−1-4 degrees Celsius) range that weigh less than 2 pounds (1 kilogram). Concerns regarding down-fill bags are the increased cost and easy absorption of water. A wet down bag will lose its loft and ability to warm, and it can take an extended amount of time to dry in wet conditions. When traveling in a wet climate, extra care needs to be taken if using a down bag (i.e., double bagging, using a waterproof stuff sack).

Typically, a 20-degree Fahrenheit (−7-degree Celsius) bag (synthetic or goose down) should fulfill the requirements for most people who backpack or hike throughout spring, summer, and fall. As with all outdoor activities, be aware of the climate of the season when you will be visiting an area.

Sleeping Pads

A sleeping pad is critical for a good night's sleep. The pad provides a barrier between your body and the ground, reducing conduction of body heat into the ground. The two basic options for a sleeping pad are closed-cell foam and a self-inflating mattress (see figure 3.6 for examples). Each type of sleeping pad has benefits and disadvantages. A closed-cell pad is lighter, more durable, and costs less, but it is less comfortable than a self-inflating mattress. A self-inflating mattress provides increased comfort and greater barrier distance from the ground, but it can absorb water and is susceptible to deflation due to puncturing. If traveling without a pad, use items within your pack to create a barrier between the ground and the sleeping bag.

Figure 3.6 The two basic options for sleeping pads are *(a)* closed-cell foam and *(b)* self-inflating mattresses.

Tent

The type of tent that you choose should be based on personal preference as well as how the tent will be used. Some considerations when deciding what tent to use include how much the tent weighs, what time of year the tent will be used, how much room is needed, the size and number of the people using the tent, and cost.

Tent Categories

There are two categories of tents: three-season tents (all seasons except winter) or four-season tents. Three-season tents are generally lighter and less expensive. They are usually made with mesh top panels that allow for better ventilation during hotter weather, whereas four-season tents have solid paneling that reduces the ability of cold winds to enter. The upper solid panels of a four-season tent can be zippered open, allowing for ventilation as needed. There are also four-season tents that can be converted into three-season tents by zipping out the solid upper panels. Regardless of the style, each tent should come with a covering called a *rain fly* to provide protection in case of inclement weather.

Tent Sizes

The size of the tent will dictate several factors, such as how much space will be available while inside the tent. A good test before purchasing is to set up a sleeping pad and bag and lie down in the tent to establish touch points along the walls. Points of contact can create areas of condensation inside the tent. If possible, have someone lie inside the tent with a sleeping pad and bag at the same time as you to determine whether the tent is spacious enough for you. The number of people that the tent will sleep also dictates the weight—the greater the sleeping capacity, the heavier the tent. The most common tent designs are for two and three people. When analyzing tent weight, keep in mind that the weight (e.g., poles, tent, and fly) can be divided among and carried by everyone who will be sleeping in the tent.

Tent Styles

A tent that requires no stakes to build or pitch is called a *free-standing tent*. A dome tent will generally have two or more poles that are flexible and that provide support for the tent to stand up on its own. Although the tent does not require stakes, it is a good idea to stake the tent out to provide greater stability. Another style is the tunnel tent. A tunnel tent will generally have two or three poles that create an upside down *U* at each end of the tent. This style must be staked out on each end to create support for the tent to stand. See figure 3.7, *a* and *b*, for a comparison.

Figure 3.7 a Example of a dome-style tent (free standing) shown with and without the rain fly.

Figure 3.7 b Example of a tunnel tent without a rain fly (requires stakes to remain standing).

Stoves

Stoves are a necessity in the backcountry since the use of wood fires has become a safety and environmental concern in many areas. When used properly, stoves have minimal impact on the backcountry. Before rushing out and purchasing a stove, a few questions have to be answered. See also figure 3.8 for a comparison of various stoves.

1. What is the weight of the stove? Weight can range between 1 and 2 pounds (.5-1 kilogram) without fuel. Butane stoves are well under a pound (.5 kilogram), and liquid gas stoves weigh in the aforementioned range.

2. What type of cooking will you be doing (e.g., boiling water and stirring, or creating backcountry gourmet dishes)? The type of cooking you will be doing will affect your stove choice. If your backcountry cooking skills are limited to boiling water, then a stove that simmers well might not be necessary. If you are a self-proclaimed backcountry gourmet, then a stove that simmers well will be beneficial.

3. What type of fuel will you be using? Many stoves on the market today use liquid gases, which have the ability to burn many different styles of fuels: white gas, kerosene, automobile gas, diesel, and jet fuel. When purchasing a stove, identify whether it is a multifuel or single-fuel stove. See table 3.5 for a fuel comparison chart.

4. How easy is the stove to use? Ease of use is directly related to the amount of time you spend learning about your new stove. Read the directions

Figure 3.8 From left to right, a white gas stove, external fuel bottle, butane stove (in foreground), and fuel canister.

beforehand, and learn how to tear down, build, and repair your stove. This educational process should take place before entering the field. Cook a meal in your backyard before heading out on the trail and learn how to make the stove work for you.

5. How reliable is the stove? Reliability most often depends on maintenance, not manufacturing. Simple maintenance and preventive measures will ensure that your stove will last for years of use.

Table 3.5   Fuel Type Comparison

Fuel type	Advantages	Disadvantages
White gas	High heat output	Priming required to light
	Spilled fuel evaporates quickly	Spilled fuel highly flammable
	Easy to find and inexpensive	
Butane	Instantly has high heat output	Lower heat output
	No spilling	Canister disposal required
	No priming required	Higher cost of fuel
Kerosene	Not as unpredictable as white gas	Produces sooty smoke if not set up correctly
	High heat output	Must be primed by something other than kerosene
Propane	Easy to use	Limited availability
	Temperature not a large factor	Canister disposal required
	Larger tanks can be refilled	Higher cost of fuel
Denatured alcohol	Quiet	Lower heat output
	Lightweight	Increased cooking time
	Burns clean	

Graydon & Hanson, 1997; Drury, Bonney, Berman, & Wagstaff, 2005

CONSUMER TIP

Think about all the factors of a stove, not just weight, before purchasing. One versatile stove is cheaper and better than purchasing three different stoves that are only good in certain situations.

Cooking Gear

When traveling in a group, it is common for the group to have shared items, including the cooking equipment. Depending on the length of the trip, cooking equipment includes a stove, fuel, a pot set, pot grips, a frying pan, and a spatula. The cooking gear needs to be durable and able to withstand abuse from several different users. The cook set will generally be a nested pot set where pots fit inside one other to maximize space when packing. Depending on the group size, it is a good idea to carry a minimum of a 1.5- or 2-liter pot, a smaller 1-liter or .5-liter pot, and a lid for both (which may double as a fry pan). Another item that may be carried is a bake pan for making backcountry goodies such as brownies, breads, and other baked goods. Each person should bring eating utensils such as a bowl (unbreakable), cup (insulated), spoon and fork (or spork), and bowl or plate (unbreakable). An additional item that is nice to have but not mandatory is a spice kit with your favorite spices (e.g., salt, pepper, sugar, allspice, hot sauce).

Gear Function and Maintenance

After a fun week on the trail, you arrive home. Walking into your house, you toss the backpack and gear into the closet until your next adventure. This is a common mistake made by many, and you will wonder why you have to do field repairs on gear during the next trip. Simply put, you have spent your hard-earned money on items that you want to last. Simple maintenance will extend its lifespan for years so that it will become like an old friend that you rely on while on the trail.

Caring for Boots

After leaving the trail, wash boots inside and out to reduce mildew buildup. Once the wash is complete, fill the boots with newspaper and then place them in a warm, ventilated area to dry. Following the washing of your boots, you may want to reapply a waterproof agent. Never dry boots over a campfire or in a household dryer; this will lessen the integrity of the boot material. For questions regarding the care of your specific boots, review the manufacturer's care instructions.

Cleaning and Storage

Count the posttrip maintenance as part of your trip. You will become more familiar with your equipment and it will receive the tender loving care that it needs and deserves.

Store gear in an area that is dry and does not receive direct sunlight. Damp areas and locations with direct sunlight have the potential to break down the materials in outdoor gear. There are several common storage issues to consider.

For example, rather than storing your sleeping bag in a compression sack, place it in a larger bag where the fill material can fluff out and relax. Before packing up from a trip, set up your tent to allow it to fully dry out; failing to follow this step can lead to mildew, wreaking havoc on tent fabric. Water filters need to be taken apart and aired out in order to prevent mildew, bacteria, and other unwanted items from developing in the lines. Stoves should be emptied of fuel and put into a storage container when the trip is completed. If in doubt about a piece of gear, clean it, allow it to air dry, and store it in a dry area away from direct sunlight.

Conclusion

Before you head out onto the trail, it is good to know that you have made the correct decisions regarding your safety. As Robert J. Ringer said, "If you are prepared you are able to feel confident." The gear you carry and knowing how to use it can make all the difference between a safe trip and one that may give you nightmares. Having the correct equipment during the most adverse conditions can make for some memorable experiences. So keep a few things in mind before you head out on your next adventure:

- Consider expense, durability, and weight when buying equipment.
- Be kind to your feet since they are what you travel on. Break in your boots.
- Be like an onion and have layers: base, insulating, and wind–rain layer.
- Do not sleep on the ground; sleep on a pad.
- Clean and maintain your equipment.
- Pack using the CBS (conveniently balanced system).
- Know when to drink water (boiled, filtered, or chemically treated) and when not to (untreated).
- Know your essentials.
- Know what you're getting into (i.e., day trip or overnight).

These basic ideas will allow you to have outdoor experiences that will create memories for a lifetime. Many people think of going into the outdoors as a way to rough it. However, always keep your safety and the safety of others in mind. Outdoor experiences will give you enough challenges when you have the right equipment for the right place. Do not make things more difficult and less enjoyable by not using the information provided in this chapter. This information is here for you to learn from our mistakes in the hope you do not repeat some of the poor decisions we have made from time to time. Go prepared, feeling confident in your newly acquired information. On the following pages, there are lists that will help you decide what to take with you.

Hiking Gear

- ☐ Clothing (see the following clothing list)
- ☐ Backpack
- ☐ Topographical maps of the area (know how to use them)
- ☐ Compass
- ☐ Stove, fuel, and fuel bottle
- ☐ Cooking gear (pot grippers, serving spoon, pot)
- ☐ Water purifier (filter or iodine tablets or iodine crystals)
- ☐ Tarps (emergency shelter)
- ☐ Eating utensils (bowl, cup, spoon and fork or spork)
- ☐ First aid kit
- ☐ Food (repackage food to minimize waste and space)
- ☐ Flashlight and extra batteries (headlamps or headbands for hands-free use)
- ☐ Knife (small, multipurpose with locking blades, such as a Swiss Army knife)
- ☐ Matches and lighter
- ☐ Shovel or trowel
- ☐ Stuff sacks or dry bags
- ☐ Water bottles or hydration system
- ☐ Whistle (safety)
- ☐ Soap (biodegradable and phosphate free)
- ☐ Multiple bandannas (several uses)

Backpacking Gear

- ☐ Clothing (see the following clothing list)
- ☐ Backpack
- ☐ Topographical maps of the area (know how to use them)
- ☐ Compass
- ☐ Tent (or tarp)
- ☐ Stove, fuel, and fuel bottle
- ☐ Cooking gear (skillet, pot set, pot grippers, spatula, serving spoon)
- ☐ Water purifier (filter, chemical, or extra fuel for boiling)
- ☐ Sleeping bag
- ☐ Tarps
- ☐ Ground cloth
- ☐ Sleeping pad
- ☐ Eating utensils (bowl, cup, spoon and fork or spork)
- ☐ First aid kit
- ☐ Food bag (medium-size stuff sack)
- ☐ Food (repackage food to minimize waste and space)
- ☐ *NOLS Cookery* (Pearson, 2004) or recipes
- ☐ Flashlight and extra batteries (headlamps or headbands for hands-free use)
- ☐ Knife (small, multipurpose with locking blades, such as a Swiss Army knife)
- ☐ Lash straps at least 4 feet (1.2 meters) long (metal buckles if possible) and 20-foot (6-meter) multipurpose 1/8-inch (.3-centimeter) cord; if in bear country, 40 feet (12 meters) of 1/4-inch (.5-centimeter) rope

☐ Matches and lighter

☐ Repair kit (sewing kit, rip-stop repair tape, air-mattress repair kit, spare stove parts, duct tape, small pliers)

☐ Shovel or trowel

☐ Stuff sacks or dry bags

☐ Water bottles or hydration system

☐ Whistle (safety)

☐ Personal care items

☐ Soap (biodegradable and phosphate free)

☐ Multiple bandannas (several uses)

Optional Items

☐ Camera and film (padded, waterproof case is also a good idea)

☐ Candles, candle lantern, or oil lamp

☐ Chair or hammock (e.g., Crazy Creek or Therm-a-Rest)

☐ Sunglasses

☐ Hiking poles

☐ Games (e.g., Hacky Sack, playing cards, Frisbee)

☐ Collapsible water sack or jug

☐ Comb or brush

☐ Hand cream, insect repellant, lip protection, powder (to prevent chafing or blisters from friction), sunblock

☐ Toenail clippers

☐ Toilet paper packed in waterproof bag (consider natural alternatives)

☐ Bathroom disposal bag (sealable bag covered with duct tape for discarded feminine hygiene products and toilet paper)

☐ Toothbrush and toothpaste

☐ Towel (a bandanna works well for this purpose)

Backpacking Clothing

The hiking list can be the same except reduce everything by half.

Underwear

- [ ] Quick drying if possible; silk or a poly-based fabric
- [ ] Boxer shorts for ventilation and prevention of chafing: 2 pairs
- [ ] Thermal top (synthetic or synthetic–wool blend): 1 or 2
- [ ] Long underwear bottom (synthetic or synthetic–wool blend): 1 or 2

Middlewear

- [ ] Long-sleeve, light-weave polyester shirt: 1
- [ ] Wool or fleece trousers with belt: 1
- [ ] Shorts (quick drying): 1 or 2
- [ ] Heavy wool or fleece jacket: 1

Outerwear

- [ ] Rain or wind parka (coated nylon or waterproof, breathable): 1
- [ ] Rain and wind pants: 1

Head and Hands

- [ ] Stocking cap that covers ears and back of neck (wool, fleece, or blend): 1
- [ ] Brimmed cap for sun protection: 1
- [ ] Gloves (wool or synthetic): 1 pair
- [ ] Bandannas: 2 or more

Socks

- [ ] Lightweight wool or synthetic liners (optional): 2 pairs
- [ ] Mid- or heavyweight wool or synthetic: 2 to 4 pairs

Shoes and Boots

- [ ] Boots: 1 pair
- [ ] Sneakers or closed-toe sandals (lightweight nylon or canvas): 1 pair

CHAPTER 4

Getting Trail Ready: Finding Your Way

Good fortune is
what happens when
opportunity meets
with planning.

Thomas Alva Edison

Planning for a day hike or backpacking expedition is a crucial part of the trip. Proper planning can take as little as a few hours or as much as a year or more and will have an impact on the safety and enjoyment of the trip. The preparation phase is the artistic part of the adventure. Anticipation of the trip matches the time available and skill of the participants, and everyone has the chance to explore all the possibilities for the experience. This chapter discusses the logistical components that must be considered for an enjoyable outdoor adventure. The components include planning where to go; specific selection of routes; using trail guides; using maps, compasses, and global positioning systems (GPS); obtaining permits; getting to the trailhead; and preparing for terrain, weather, and altitude.

Planning the Route

Determining where to go is the first step in planning a day hike or backpacking trip. Who the participants are and their fitness level, the time of year, the amount of time available, the desired activities for the trip, and the amount of money that can be spent all influence where you can go for an adventure. Each person must be honest about the desired outcomes of the trip. If even one person has a different goal, the expedition can be a failure. The desired outcomes of any trip are of utmost importance, but planning also requires specific knowledge about terrain, distance to be traveled, altitude, and other factors. Each factor in planning can use a similar decision-making process, funneling information into practical and manageable bits that provide a satisfying experience when combined.

Think about trip planning as a big funnel. The widest part contains all of the possibilities for a trip. Then planning is narrowed down to fit the available resources. There is a great deal of important information to gather in getting ready for the trail. Considerations include general location, planned routes, trail conditions, weather conditions, and who manages the land on which you will travel. Start with the group and the intent of the trip. The trip goals determine what is to be accomplished by the end of the journey. If you have limited time, day hikes may be a good choice. However, if you intend to carry out an expedition over several days or weeks, the planning is quite different. Starting with goals will keep the planning on track. Local outdoor stores, park visitor centers and information kiosks, guidebooks, magazines, and the Internet all contain valuable information about destinations. When you keep the outcomes (goals) in mind, determining a good plan is easy. For instance, if you are interested in scenic views and wildflowers, you can choose a route that offers such opportunities.

Chapter 1 has already explained the many land management agencies that can be involved with trip planning. Each destination is managed by someone, and that person or agency should be contacted as the first step in planning. That source of information will guide you through subsequent steps for successful planning.

Terrain

There are many places to explore! Some have sandy beaches, others have high mountaintops, and still others have gentle slopes. The terrain must be considered in the planning stage. Terrain dictates the equipment, physical conditioning, and technical skills needed for a trip. For example, the Grand Canyon may conjure up images of dry, hot conditions. However, spring in the Grand Canyon may require bringing an 8-millimeter climbing rope and a pair of crampons for traction, because trails on the southern side of the canyon often maintain snow through early summer. In mountainous terrains, trails are steep and require a level of climbing knowledge. Physical conditioning is always something to be considered when hiking or backpacking, because the more difficult terrain you travel through, the more demanding it will be on your body. Additionally, members of your group—for example, children—may not be able to successfully hike long, steep trails. Staying low on well-maintained paths could provide a more positive experience for children who are not physically strong enough to attempt mountain trails.

Terrain will also determine the availability of water sources, tree cover to protect travelers from the sun, and the likelihood of spotting wildlife. And terrains change with the seasons. The winter route up a canyon is likely to be more direct than a summer route. In springtime, rivers may run high and swift, making some trails dangerous or impassable.

Maps, conversations with area rangers, and trail guides provide information about the terrain and climate of an area. Necessary equipment and where you can travel depend on the conditions at the selected location. Proper planning can make the excursion more comfortable in any conditions.

When you choose to stay on-trail, walking and navigation are easier and human impact is controlled. Some choose to travel off-trail for a variety of reasons, such as to experience a more pristine location. Off-trail travel should be planned. Take map bearings and maintain a route plan. Unlike trail hiking, where single-file walking causes less compaction, in off-trail locations it is better to spread out so that a path is not created. Walking on resistant surfaces like rocks or snow also maintains pristine areas. Keep visual contact with all party members and only travel in small groups.

Altitude

Elevation is important to note for several reasons. When traveling to altitudes greater than 8,000 feet (2,438 meters) above sea level, hikers are susceptible to altitude-related sicknesses (Nicolazzo, 1997). Also, it takes more energy to hike uphill, and the steeper the grade, the more difficult it will be. The contour lines on the map can provide insight into the difficulty of a hike. Contour lines are spaced on a map in relationship to the actual lay of the land. The distance between the lines is noted in the map key as the contour interval. The contour interval will vary on different maps depending on the elevation changes of that section of land. On U.S. Geologic Survey (USGS) maps, every fifth contour line is darker and is labeled with the actual elevation. This line is referred to as an *index contour.*

When planning a trip, the contour lines can be counted and then added to or subtracted from the index contour to determine the change in elevation while on the trail. The contour lines also assist in time estimation of a hike. At trailheads and along the trail, signs might indicate linear miles, but they do not address change in elevation. It is easy to stand at a sign to Surprise Lake that says 1 mile (1.5 kilometers) thinking that the whole family can easily hike that far and return to the parking lot before lunch. The surprise is that the lake is also 1,000 feet (305 meters) higher than where the sign is! (See the Time and Energy section for more details on determining how elevation affects time.)

Acclimatization is when the body adjusts to the environment, including elevation, temperature, and general landscape. If a person gains too much altitude too quickly, illness can result. No more than 2,000 feet (610 meters) per day should be gained once you are higher than 10,000 feet (3,048 meters). The body also needs time to adjust to extreme temperature changes as well. A hiker from Oklahoma may have difficulty with the cold and wet conditions in the Rocky Mountains. Similarly, a person from Alaska would probably have difficulty navigating the Grand Canyon in Arizona.

Distance

The distance traveled is important when planning a trip. You need to consider the distance on the trail versus the direct distance between various points. Look at the maps to figure out trail distance before setting out on your adventure. Take into consideration the time and energy needed to travel various distances.

Time and Energy

A system has been developed and used by the Wilderness Education Association (WEA) for years. It includes planning time and energy outputs based on elevation gains and losses. In summary, each increase in 1,000 feet (2,134 meters) equates to 3 to 4 miles (5-6.5 kilometers) on the flat ground (depending on fitness and pack weight). If 1,000 feet equals 3 miles, that changes the estimated time to hike to Surprise Lake to 4 miles—1 linear mile plus 3 miles for the 1,000-foot elevation change. Instead of a 20-minute jaunt to the lake, now 1.5 hours is a more likely scenario. Returning from the lake is trickier since some people go very fast downhill and others are slower. Using the linear estimate is safe, however. The total roundtrip for the family is 5 energy miles (8 kilometers)—4 miles up and 1 mile down. Can your children really walk that far without water, snacks, and good shoes?

Deciding the length of time that you are going to hike can be tricky at first, but these tips can be helpful. It takes a bit of trial and error. At first, give yourself more than enough time to reach the destination before your intended turnaround time, or, if you are spending a full day on the trail, well before dark. Mountains, canyons, and heavily forested areas can get dark well before the sun goes down.

Other Factors

In addition to the terrain, altitude, and distance to be traveled, people in the group are key factors for a successful outing. Knowing your abilities and limitations and being realistic about the outcomes of the trip prepare everyone for the adventure. The assessment of each group member includes fitness levels, experience, skills for the specific activities on the trip, and motivation for being in the outdoors. Many trips are ruined when the group does not take the time to agree on the plans and desired outcomes. For example, if one person does all of the planning, that person's needs will be addressed but no one else's will be. If the leader decides to try to summit several mountains in a weekend and no one else has ever backpacked before, chances are the trip will fail.

Many people like to think that they want to hike and summit peaks. Their physical preparation may be sufficient; however, the mental or psychological part of preparation can be overlooked. It is difficult to imagine how hard it is to do anything at high altitude. Putting one foot in front of the other for hours on end takes persistence and motivation. Also, the weather is not always agreeable. Arriving at a campsite wet, cold, and knowing that the weather will not change for awhile can be discouraging. Thinking about worst-case scenarios can help you prepare for the mental challenges required. (See chapter 2 for more on mental fitness for hiking and backpacking.)

Using a Map, Compass, and More

Using a map and compass takes practice. Before you set off into the wilderness, make sure you understand how to read a map and use a compass. Using these together is important for knowing where you are in the wilderness and feeling comfortable exploring new areas. If you stay on a well-marked trail, you probably won't have a problem if you don't have in-depth knowledge of using a map and compass. Before you set off, it is recommended that you learn how to use these tools to help you be successful on your adventures. GPS can also help you know your location in the wilderness.

Selecting Maps and Other Guides

People have yearned for adventure since the beginning of time. Early adventurers would describe their trip with pictures and words so others could follow the same path. Such is the history of maps and trail guides. Road maps, computer-generated maps, and topographical maps are examples of the tools used when starting on an independent adventure. Following are some tips for selecting maps and other guides.

Maps

Maps help in traveling to a starting point or trailhead. Topographical maps provide a detailed description of the lay of the land from elevation gains to water resources and buildings. Understanding how to use a topographical map can make your journey safer by helping you determine your location, and it can make the journey more enjoyable because the map describes what can be expected during the trek.

Maps are pictures of the topography on which you will be traveling, "a two-dimensional representation of a three-dimensional world" (Drury & Bonney, 1992). They can be found at a variety of locations. Some libraries have map rooms or maps available for use. Maps can also be found on the Internet; however, often when maps are downloaded or copied on a printer, some distortion takes place. They remain a source of information but they are not always reliable for land navigation. The agency that manages the land will often have maps available. These maps range from hand-drawn versions of the landscape to detailed topographical maps made by cartographers.

All you need is the plan, the road map, and the courage to press on to your destination.

Earl Nightingale

Maps are drawn to different scales, from large to small. Maps will be scaled in a ratio form, such as 1:24,000, in which 1 inch (2 centimeters) on the map equals 24,000 inches (60,960 centimeters) on the earth's surface and 1 foot (.3 meter) on the map equals 24,000 feet (7,315 meters) of the earth's surface. The scale can be found at the bottom of the map. Large-scale maps display a large amount of land area in a small amount of space, much like the highway maps used for traveling from town to town. Large-scale maps can give information about general direction, but detail can be lost. Small-scale maps will show a small amount of the earth's surface in great detail.

National Geographic makes maps on a scale of around 1:50,000, which can be found at www.nationalgeographic.com/maps. These maps provide some detail and are very useful for beginning trip planning. The USFS makes maps of the areas that they manage on a scale of 1:48,000. The USGS has made maps at a scale of 1:24,000. USGS maps show more detail and are more commonly used by hikers (see figure 4.1 for an example). An individual USGS map is referred to as a *quadrangle* or *topographic map*. The east and west sides of each quadrangle are based on lines of longitude and the north and south boundaries are latitude lines. This enables you to accurately pinpoint a real location to a map location. Names of the quadrangles are on each side and corner of a map so that you can fit maps together. There is a USGS quadrangle for most points in the

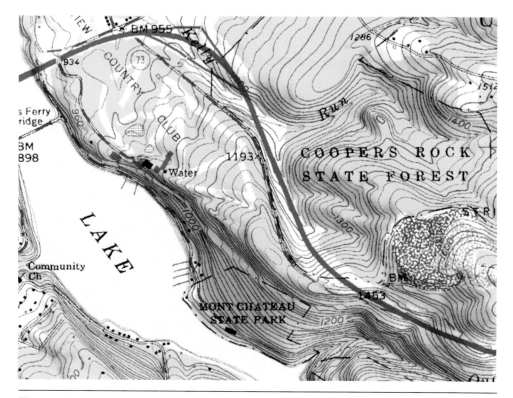

Figure 4.1 This figure shows the detailed information you can get from a USGS quadrangle.

United States. Every state has an index map showing where each quadrangle is located and its name. USGS maps are an essential tool for planning a trip in the United States and can be purchased at www.usgs.gov.

Maps from these three organizations describe details that are universal from map to map. These details are described in the key of the map (see figure 4.2). When planning a trip, you can go from one type of map to another without

Map Legend

The map legend contains a number of important details. The figures below display a standard USGS map legend. In addition, a USGS map includes latitude and longitude as well as the names of the adjacent maps (depicted on the top, bottom, left side, right side, and the four corners of the map). The major features on the map legend are shown in figure 4.2 and labeled below.

1. Map name
2. Year of production and revision
3. General location in state
4. Next adjacent quadrangle map
5. Map scale
6. Distance scale
7. Contour interval
8. Magnetic declination
9. Latitude and longitude

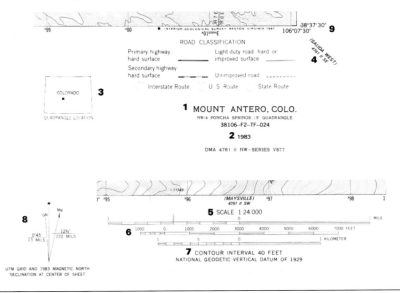

Figure 4.2 The symbols shown at the base of a USGS quadrangle give the user information about what the quadrangle represents.

getting confused. On all types of maps mentioned here, trails are noted by dotted lines, water sources are marked in blue, vegetation that is growing at a height greater than 3 feet (1 meter) is represented by green, and elevation is noted by brown lines. As discussed in the section on altitude, the elevation lines are called *contour lines* and combine to show the contour of the land and present a third dimension.

Trail Guides

Trail guides are also an excellent resource for planning a trip. They vary in detail and quality from published texts to small local guides produced on a copy machine. The information provided by these guides differs from the information that you get from a map. Trail guides often give the author's personal perspective on areas and trails. They also may give hints about where to find water on the trail or how to locate a hidden trailhead, where to locate scenic views, good places to see sunsets, or where to view wildlife. Contact the agency that manages the property where you will be hiking for recommendations. Outdoor equipment stores also have book sections that provide a variety of trail guides. The best trail guides are current and have been authored by a local person or someone who has spent significant time in a location. Finally, ask others for help; over time, people acquire libraries of information about specific locations.

Using a Compass

A compass allows you to determine your exact location and to maintain your bearings or direction while traveling in the backcountry. After exploring the area on a map, it is important to become familiar with a compass. Without a map, a compass tells you where other things are in relationship to where you are standing by using angles. A direction is a line of travel from one point to a destination and is based on angles that create a circle of 360 degrees (Drury, Bonney, Berman, & Wagstaff, 2005). From that direction, a circle can be imagined and divided into four equal parts relating to a cardinal direction: north (0 or 360 degrees), south (180 degrees), west (270 degrees), and east (90 degrees).

In the center of a compass is a floating needle of two colors with one end always pointing to magnetic north. See figure 4.3 for the parts of a compass. The map, however, is oriented to true north (the North Pole). Magnetic north lies approximately 1,000 miles (1,609 kilometers) northwest of Hudson Bay. Therefore, when using maps and compasses together, adjustments need to be made (see the next section).

Taking a bearing refers to using the compass to determine the direction that point B is from the person taking the bearing. When taking a bearing, which is sometimes called *shooting a bearing* (see figure 4.4), it is important to hold the compass flat by holding it at your waist with both hands. The direction-of-travel arrow must remain perpendicular to your waist. Point the direction-of-travel arrow at point B. Your body should be facing the same direction.

- base plate—The rectangular piece that the other parts of the compass rest on.
- direction-of-travel arrow—The arrow on the base plate that points from the compass housing to the front of the compass. This arrow guides hikers while navigating.
- compass housing—The part of the compass that houses the 360-degree circle mentioned earlier. It is attached to the base plate but will rotate when turned. The degrees and the cardinal directions are written on the compass housing.
- magnetic needle—The magnetized needle that points to magnetic north.

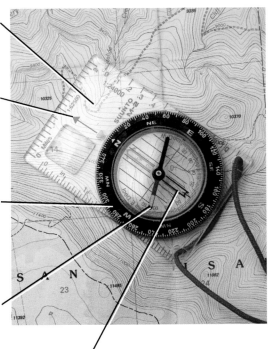

- orienteering arrow—Outline of an arrow that the points toward the 360-degree mark on the compass housing. The orienteering needle rotates with the compass housing.

Figure 4.3 Parts of a compass.

Figure 4.4 When taking a bearing, the compass is held level and steady.

The needle will point to magnetic north as long as metal objects do not interfere. Keeping the base plate flat, rotate the compass housing until the magnetic needle is within the outline of the orienteering arrow. The degree shown on the mark where the direction-of-travel arrow meets the compass housing is your bearing.

Using a Compass With a Map

Hikers use both maps and compasses to help choose and navigate specific routes. A map and compass can also be used, however, to gain specific information about where you will be traveling. To do this, you must first orient your map, or point the map where north on the map corresponds to north on the compass. There are a couple of arrows in the map key—one arrow points to true north and another points to magnetic north. Remember that the magnetic needle on the compass will point to magnetic north, and magnetic north differs from true north depending on your location (refer to figure 4.5). This is called *declination*

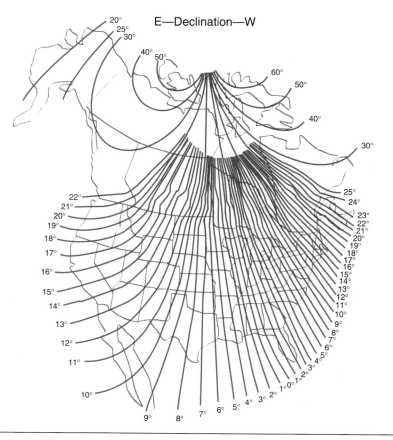

Figure 4.5 Differences between true north and magnetic north can be viewed on this diagram.

TECHNIQUE TIP

1. Place the orienteering arrow on the compass in line with the direction-of-travel arrow.
2. Place the side edge of the base plate in alignment with the magnetic north line located in the bottom portion of the map legend.
3. Rotate the map until the magnetic needle is in line with the orienteering needle.

Voilà—the map is oriented!

or the *difference of degree* between true north and magnetic north. Declination is important because your intended course can be completely wrong if you only use a compass bearing from a map without accounting for difference of declination.

Once the map is oriented, you can find the direction that you need to travel in by placing the compass on the map. The starting point of the hike is point A and the first distinct bend in the trail is point B. With the compass, a general direction can be obtained and distances can be measured with a piece of string and then compared to the scale. These statistics are then noted and stored for navigation when you are on the trail. Experienced hikers keep these records in journals or log books to use when they return to locations.

There are times when hikers know in which direction they need to go, but are unsure about their current location. Knowing exactly where you are has several advantages: it gives you feedback on the progress of the hike, it provides a feeling of comfort, and it's critical if an emergency rescue is required. To find one's exact location, take bearings from two obvious landmarks that can be identified on the map. By drawing a line on the map from one of the landmarks to a point that's 180 degrees from it, and then drawing another line from the second landmark using the same method, you have triangulated your position. Where the two lines intersect is your location! Following are the steps involved with triangulation using a map and compass. Orient the map as described in the Technique Tip on this page.

1. Take a bearing to a point that you can identify on the map.
2. From the point on the map, subtract 180 degrees from the bearing.
3. Using the base plate of the compass, draw a line from the point on the map referenced in step one to the reverse bearing.
4. Repeat steps 2 through 4 using another point.
5. Your location should be where the two lines intersect.

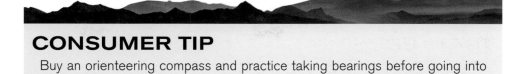

CONSUMER TIP

Buy an orienteering compass and practice taking bearings before going into the field.

Global Positioning System

The global positioning system (GPS) is another useful tool for planning a hike or a backpacking trip (see figure 4.6). GPS was originally developed in the 1970s by the U.S. Department of Defense for navigation, and it is now managed by several agencies and the GPS executive board (Berman et al., 2005). GPS also refers to the handheld device that uses the signals from satellites to determine location. The accuracy of GPS is very high and surpasses the resolution of USGS topographic maps (Berman et al., 2005). GPS provides the latitude and longitude of a location, the altitude of the location, and the speed at which the hiker is traveling. When planning a trip, map quadrants can be stored in the GPS and used in the field to navigate. Many outdoor destinations are designated with GPS data. This is often useful in finding trailheads or roads that are difficult to find in remote locations.

GPS is a useful navigation tool but should not replace knowledge of maps and a compass. Technology breaks, needs batteries, or can be rendered useless in some locations, and GPS is limited to areas where it can receive satellite signals. Maps, compasses, and GPS are three separate navigation systems. Used correctly, each system will back up the information of the others, decreasing the chance that you will become lost.

Figure 4.6 A GPS is easy to use and can supplement your other navigation skills.

TRAIL TIP

Do not rely solely on trail signs. They are correct most of the time but sometimes may have been maintained poorly or turned in the wrong direction. Trail signs are no substitute for navigation skills.

Figure 4.7 Trail signs often point travelers in the correct direction, but you should always double check using your own navigation skills.

Other Navigation Aids

During the planning phase, you have planned your route. On marked trails, signs are often present to verify where you are. At the trailhead is the most important trail sign—a kiosk or board that has up-to-date information about the trail (see figure 4.7). Along the trail, small signs with distance and destination are posted. Sometimes blazes are marked on trees or rock piles (cairns) are built to distinguish the trail location. Markers such as blazes or cairns help a hiker when the path is indistinct. Hikers should regroup at all trail intersections whether there is a sign or not.

Permits and Paperwork

When planning a trip, it is important to be aware of regulations related to land use. You should contact the land management agency during the planning phase to obtain any permission needed before departure. The federal government, states, and cities manage public lands. Management of specific properties is broken down into regional or local offices. For example, people who want to hike in the Grand Canyon would not contact the NPS; instead, they would call the backcountry office at the Grand Canyon for information and permission to use the land.

CONSUMER TIP

If you haven't inquired about permits or fees, this stage of the trip would be the time to do so. Not having appropriate permission may result in fines and being asked to leave the area.

A permit is often required to use public lands. Permits typically state conditions for land use (e.g., number of people in the party, where to camp). There are two categories of permits: private and commercial. Private use and commercial use are interpreted differently by agencies and local districts. In general, in a party that has been awarded a private permit, no person in that party has paid others in the party to be part of the trip. Party members may pay to cover their own expenses, but no member can profit from the trip. Commercial permits are awarded to individuals and companies that are profiting from the trip. These groups include outfitters, guides, photographers, and anyone making money from the use of the land.

Application for permits varies from place to place. Private-use permits often have no required fee and little or no paperwork requirements. Some areas require hikers to simply register by signing in at a trailhead. In many locations, day use does not require a permit. Popular destinations require a permit to be obtained months in advance of the trip and have a user fee. Commercial-use permits are more difficult to obtain. They are often limited and can require a study on environmental impact.

Permitting is important. It provides information that land managers can use for making land management decisions, such as who is using the property and for what purpose. It helps to minimize conflicts among different types of users, such as mountain bikers, hikers, hunters, and bird watchers. It also generates revenue for the land management agency. Land managers can use permits to limit human impact on the environment by restricting where hikers and backpackers may camp or travel. Permits also serve as traffic control by allowing only a specified number of hikers and backpackers to travel in a particular area at a given time.

Getting to the Trailhead

Getting to your backpacking or hiking destination and returning home can be more dangerous than being in the backcountry. Plan ahead for how you will get to your destination and how you will secure your vehicle once you are there.

Driving Safety

While traveling in a vehicle in rural and mountainous areas, be careful and travel at controlled speeds around curves. A large percentage of auto accidents in the mountains involve a vehicle crossing the centerline in the road. Also be aware that people who are not accustomed to curvy roads may be susceptible to motion sickness, so you might want to carry motion-sickness medication in the vehicle. Road shoulders may be soft along steep roads and give way when parked on. Examine the shoulder carefully before driving on it and consider leaving one wheel on the road if it will not impede traffic. Often the side roads that lead to trailheads are rough and are not maintained. Sharp rocks may necessitate changing a flat tire. Finally, due to short but steep inclines and short curves, visibility may be impaired. Get out of the vehicle and check sections of the road that are not visible to the driver before going forward.

Parking

At the trailhead, park in an orderly way in designated areas (figure 4.8). At many trailheads there are no designated individual parking spaces and the lot is not used efficiently. When parking your vehicle, keep others in mind

Figure 4.8 Parking at the trailhead. Before heading out on the trail, make sure that your vehicle is locked and your keys are in a secure location.

SAFETY TIP

In addition to normal emergency supplies, a few things other things are helpful to have in your vehicle when traveling in rural areas:

- Tow rope
- Small fire extinguisher
- Windshield sunshade
- Cigarette lighter
- Jumper cables
- Spare key
- First aid kit

Depending on the location of your destination and the season, there may be other useful items to bring. Some forested areas request that you keep a shovel and a bucket of sand in your car to help extinguish forest fires.

and realize that those traveling with trailers or in recreational vehicles may require extra space to park. Before heading out on the trail, make sure that your vehicle is locked and your keys are in a secure location. Another member of the party should carry a second set of keys. If parked on an incline, engage the emergency brake and consider blocking the tires with a rock or a log. Place all valuable items in a discreet location in the locked vehicle. Bicycles or other items that are on racks should be stored inside the vehicle if possible or locked in some way. Refrain from leaving food in the vehicle, but if you must leave food in it, try to seal the packaging so that there is minimal odor. Food odors in a vehicle will attract animals, and they may damage the vehicle trying to get to the food.

Shuttles

Sometimes you can loop around to your starting point; other times your ending point is different from where you started. In that case, a shuttle system of some sort will have to be factored into your plans. A group member's car may be placed at the end point so that other vehicles can be retrieved after the trip. Or, the group can split into two, pass one another in opposite directions, and swap keys for vehicles at the end points. A friend can pick up the group on a designated day, time, and place. Finally, local commercial outfitters are often willing to set up a shuttle for a fee. Note that any type of shuttle system can take several hours, and this time needs to be factored into the planning.

Managing Risk

Backpackers and hikers often develop a risk management plan while preparing for the trail. There is no a standard format for a risk management plan, but certain information should be documented and shared with others in case of an accident. Risk management forms document the trip itinerary, including trails used and campsites. Contact numbers also need to be listed on these forms, including the numbers of the local land management office, the search and rescue unit closest to your destination, a nearby hospital or health clinic, the local sheriff's office, and a nearby auto repair shop with towing service. A copy of this risk management form should be given to a contact person who will not be going on the trip, and a copy should be kept with the group in the field. Groups also routinely leave itineraries with a nonparticipant. (For more information on managing risks, see chapters 5 and 9.)

Conclusion

When preparing for a hike or a backpacking trip, there are many things to consider. Shortcuts at home can lead to shortfalls in the field, so take the time necessary to ensure a safe and enjoyable trip that will have little impact on the area. Preparing for the adventure should be an enjoyable part of the trip that allows you to explore all the possibilities.

CHAPTER 5

Trail Safety and Survival Skills

Avoidance of a survival situation is more important than learning how to get out of a survival situation.

Paul Petzoldt

We venture into the woods for enjoyment, spiritual enrichment, physical and emotional challenges, and various other reasons. To ensure that we experience the positives in nature, we must make sure that we are being safe while on the trail. Nothing defeats the value of a hiking or backpacking experience more than getting injured or possibly killed as a result of an accident in the backcountry. This chapter introduces basic information that will help you to make good decisions regarding safety in the backcountry. It introduces trail safety, wilderness first aid, rescues, and basic information on how to handle survival situations in the backcountry.

Trail Safety

Dangers arise from two sources in the backcountry: from within the environment and from within individuals using the environment. Dangers that arise from within the environment are called *environmental* or *objective dangers.* These dangers include such things as severe weather, hazardous terrain, and hazardous plants and wildlife. Dangers that arise from within you and your group are called *human* or *subjective dangers.* These dangers are based on your level of preparation for the experience and the way in which you conduct yourselves in the woods. *Level of preparation* refers to having the skills needed to successfully engage in the activity, having the proper equipment for the experience, being physically and emotionally up to the challenges associated with the experience, and being prepared for contingencies that might arise during the experience.

The interaction of environmental dangers and human dangers creates *accident potential* (Hale, 1984; Martin, Cashel, Wagstaff, & Breunig, 2006; Priest & Gass, 2005). The less prepared you are for the environment into which you are hiking, plus the more prevalent the environmental dangers in the area, the greater the potential of an emergency or an accident. The more aware you are of hazards and safety considerations, the more likely you are to avoid trouble in the outdoors.

This section discusses considerations that every hiker and backpacker should keep in mind to ensure a safe and enjoyable experience on the trail. These considerations include terrain, weather, interactions with flora and fauna, and interactions with others while on the trail. The aim of this section is to make you aware of various hazards that you might encounter in the backcountry so that you can work to minimize the potential for accidents.

Terrain

Terrain is not covered extensively in this chapter because it is covered in chapters 6 and 7. Suffice it to say, terrain is a significant safety consideration. Learning to identify terrain-related hazards is essential to traveling safely in the backcountry. Examples of terrain-related hazards include the threat of avalanche when traveling in the mountains in winter, spring, and early summer; the threat of being caught in a flash flood when hiking in desert canyons; and the threat of slipping and falling on loose or icy trail surfaces. Falls often result in nothing more than scrapes and bruises; however, they can also result in deadly slides down steep slopes or over precipices. When traveling off-trail, you may encounter additional terrain-related hazards, including possibly having to climb over downed trees where sprained ankles might result from missteps, having to walk through boulder fields where falling rocks and boulders are a risk, and having to ford streams where being swept off your feet and carried away by the current is a risk. Glacier travel presents the risk of falling into crevasses or sliding down the face of the glacier into rock outcroppings or over cliffs.

Before venturing onto the trail, analyze the various risks associated with the terrain on which you will be traveling and prepare accordingly for those risks. For instance, if you intend to hike in an area where there is a risk of avalanches, be prepared for that risk by seeking training and developing competency in avalanche safety and rescue before venturing into the area. Purchase the needed safety equipment, carry it with you, and know how to use it when you go hiking.

Weather-Related Dangers

An old mountaineer once said, "Only fools and dudes attempt to predict the weather." This is because the weather is so unpredictable, especially in the backcountry. Nonetheless, in the backcountry you must pay attention to weather patterns, and you must be able to cope with varying weather conditions. Before heading out for a backcountry experience, become familiar with the weather patterns in the region. The U.S. National Weather Service can provide an enormous amount of information about the climate of a specific area. Average temperatures and rainfall and snowfall for each month of the year are easily accessible. Become aware of the climatic history of the area in which you intend to travel and prepare for the worst.

You may face a number of weather-related dangers if you are unprepared to deal with variations in the weather. Following are several key weather-related dangers that you should consider as you plan your hike.

Thunderstorms and Lightning

Lightning is a real danger during backcountry travel. Lightning can strike hikers and backpackers in three ways: a direct lightning strike, induced currents near a strike, and ground currents. There are several things that you can do to minimize your exposure to lightning during a storm. First, be observant of the weather. You can typically see and hear approaching storms. If a storm appears to be closing in on you and your group, take measures to protect yourself. When you see lightning and hear thunder, use the flash–bang method to determine how far away the lightning is—count the number of seconds between the lightning flash and the following thunder and divide by 5. Every 5 seconds equals 1 mile (1.5 kilometers). You can determine whether a storm is closing in on you or moving away by repeatedly using this method to gauge the distance of the lightning from your location. When there are 25 seconds

SAFETY TIP

Remember the Leave No Trace principle about respecting wildlife, which proposes the following guidelines:

- Observe wildlife from a distance.
- Do not feed wildlife.
- Be aware of wildlife behavioral patterns and habitat.
- Avoid attracting animals; dispose of waste properly and store food and trash properly.
- Control your pets.

animals' natural patterns. Additional considerations are to secure food so animals do not learn to depend on humans for their meals. There is a saying that a fed bear is a dead bear; animals become more assertive or aggressive when your food source becomes their food source. Anything that has odor attracts animals. Checking with local agencies will provide appropriate information about local animal conditions. See chapter 8 for more information on animals.

Bears

Black bears and grizzly bears are two types of bears that you might encounter when hiking in the woods. It is important to understand the difference between them, both in terms of appearance and behavior. Black bears have a tall rump and straight nose and can be black or brown (see figure 5.3a). Grizzly bears are larger than black bears and have a shoulder hump, low rump, and scoop nose (see figure 5.3b). Grizzly bears that live in the coastal regions of the Pacific Northwest and Alaska are called *brown bears* and are typically larger than inland grizzlies because of a protein-rich diet provided by salmon. All bears can be aggressive, defensive, unpredictable, and dangerous; however, grizzly and brown bears are typically more unpredictable and confrontational than black bears.

When Meriwether Lewis and William Clark first encountered grizzly bears on their expedition through the Louisiana Territory in the early 1800s, they were amazed at the effort required to kill a grizzly bear. Clark describes one such encounter with a grizzly bear in his expedition journal:

> The river rising & current Strong & in the evening we saw a Brown or Grisley beare on a sand beech, I went out with one man Geo Drewyer & Killed the bear, which was verry large and a turrible looking animal, which we found verry hard to kill we Shot ten Balls into him before we killed him, & 5 of those Balls through his lights [lungs]. This animal is the largest of the carnivorous kind I ever saw. (Devoto, 1953, p. 105)

Figure 5.3 Black bears (a) have distinctive rumps, straight noses, and can be black or brown. Grizzly bears (b) have distinctive shoulder humps, low rumps, and scoop noses.

Lewis describes the encounter in his expedition journal as well:

> It was a most tremendious looking animal, and extremely hard to kill notwithstanding he had five balls through his lungs and five others in various parts he swam more than half the distance across the river to a sandbar, & it was at least twenty minutes before he died; he did not attempt to attack, but fled and made the most tremendous roaring from the moment he was shot. (Devoto, 1953, p. 105)

The bear measured 8 feet and 7.5 inches (263 centimeters) tall. Lewis and Clark estimated that it weighed 500 to 600 pounds (227-272 kilograms). The point is that humans are typically no match for bears unless equipped with a gun.

If you encounter a bear on the trail, stay calm and quickly evaluate the situation. Determine what type of bear it is and why your paths have crossed. If the bear is simply passing by, keep it in sight and calmly move away from it. Although bears have poor eyesight, they have an excellent sense of smell; they are unable to see you unless you are nearby, but they can smell you from a great distance. Working your way upwind of a bear so that the wind is blowing your scent toward the bear is a good way to tell the bear that you are around. In most instances, bears will leave the area if they detect your presence. Special caution is required if you encounter a mother bear and her cubs. Mother bears are protective and will let you know that they mean business if they perceive you as a threat. If you encounter a mother bear and her cubs, you should leave the area immediately.

If confronted directly by a bear, talk to it in a low, deep voice, saying "Hey, bear. Hey, bear. . ." Make yourself large, holding your pack, rain parka, or any other item overhead. Slowly back away from the bear. Often bears will charge and stop just short of you in an effort to intimidate you. Do not turn and run. If you do, the bear will perceive you as prey and the chase will be on.

In the unlikely event of an attack by a bear, you should respond differently to black bears and grizzly bears. During an attack, black bears are typically more aggressive than grizzly bears. If attacked by a black bear, fight back. Attempt to hit the bear in the nose and do everything you can to get away from the bear. If attacked by a grizzly bear, on the other hand, it is best to huddle in the fetal position with your knees to your chest and your hands and arms covering your neck and face. In both cases, bear spray can be used as a deterrent.

When traveling in bear country, your best defense is what the WEA refers to as *animal encounter prevention*. Understand the behavioral patterns of bears and become familiar with bear habitat. Such knowledge can help you to avoid encounters with bears altogether. For instance, knowing that bears feed on salmon along streams and rivers in the Pacific Northwest at certain times of year will help you to determine when it is best not to hike and camp along streams and rivers in that region.

SAFETY TIP
Hiking in Bear Country

- Make noise or sing songs, especially when hiking through thick brush and when coming around corners.
- Travel in groups of four or more.
- Include pepper spray in your equipment.

Mountain Lions

Mountain lions are another large predatory animal that you might encounter while hiking or backpacking in certain parts of the country. Mountain lions are also sometimes called *pumas, panthers,* or *cougars.* Mature mountain lions grow to more than 6 feet (2 meters) in length, can weigh more than 130 pounds (59 kilograms), and are reddish in color with a sleek black-tipped tail (see figure 5.4). They are common in the western United States and can be found where deer are plentiful.

Figure 5.4   Mountain lions are also sometimes called pumas, panthers, or cougars.

Encounters with mountain lions are rare, but interactions between humans and mountain lions are becoming more frequent as urban development spreads into prime habitat, especially in places like Colorado and California that have experienced rapid growth in human populations during the past 30 years. Not only are homes being built in areas where mountain lions are common, but cities and counties are also developing parks and open spaces that give citizens recreational access to these areas.

Mountain lions are elusive animals that typically remain hidden from their prey. If you encounter a mountain lion, chances are it has been stalking you for some time. If you are attacked by a mountain lion, fight. In April 2006, a 7-year-old boy was attacked by a mountain lion while hiking with his family along a trail in an open space in Boulder, Colorado. The boy was last in a line of eight hikers when the mountain lion unexpectedly attacked. His family turned around to see the boy's head clenched in the mountain lion's jaws and the mountain lion dragging the boy away. The family fought the mountain lion, wrestling the boy free of its grip. Fortunately, the boy survived the attack, though he suffered severe lacerations and a broken jaw.

If you come face to face with a mountain lion, react to it in the same way that you would to a bear. Make yourself large, talk in a deep voice, hold sticks or other objects over your head, and slowly back away. Do not turn your back on the lion, and do not run.

Always keep a healthy distance between you and any animal you encounter in the backcountry, not just large predatory animals such as bears and mountain lions. There are many misconceptions about the threat posed by animals such as deer, elk, moose, and bison. These animals can harm or even kill when threatened. Never approach animals from the rear, because this is the direction from which predators—stalkers, in particular—often attack. Even smaller animals carry risks. Skunks and raccoons, for instance—common campsite visitors between dusk and dawn—can transmit rabies.

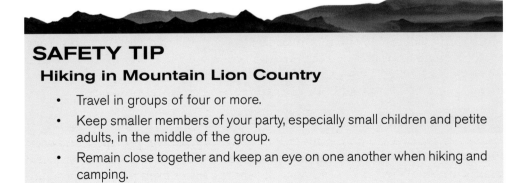

SAFETY TIP
Hiking in Mountain Lion Country

- Travel in groups of four or more.
- Keep smaller members of your party, especially small children and petite adults, in the middle of the group.
- Remain close together and keep an eye on one another when hiking and camping.

Insects and Arachnids

Scott was teaching a lesson on packing backpacks at a trailhead along the Appalachian trail in North Carolina. He was really into the demonstration, hamming it up a bit when suddenly he felt a terrible pain in his feet. He looked down to see hundreds of red ants all over his feet. Some were moving fast while others seemed to be digging in and eating him alive. He yelled and jumped as his students looked on, some laughing, some trying to help. He jumped into a puddle, frantically removing his sandals and rubbing his feet in the muddy water and sand. It felt great for a moment, but his feet soon began to swell, itch, and throb in pain. Scott turned to another instructor to finish the lesson while he went for the first aid kit. He found some soap and water and thoroughly cleaned his feet. He then applied a coating of hydrocortisone to his feet. Within 30 minutes, the swelling was going away, the itch was gone, and his feet were beginning to return to normal.

There are a number of stinging and biting insects to watch out for when hiking and backpacking. In addition to fire ants, beware of ticks, mosquitoes, biting flies, bees, and wasps. Stings and bites by these insects can cause localized skin irritation. They can also cause more serious illnesses: Lyme disease and Rocky Mountain spotted fever in the case of ticks, and West Nile virus and encephalitis, among other diseases, in the case of mosquitoes. Insect repellent can be useful in warding off these types of insects.

If you are stung by a bee or a wasp, treat the area by removing the poison sack and stinger, cleaning the affected area, and applying meat tenderizer or baking soda. Also, beware of developing a systemic reaction to stings that may result in anaphylactic shock. This can be a life-threatening situation that requires immediate treatment with epinephrine and antihistamines. If you are allergic to bee stings, include an epinephrine kit in your first aid kit, and know how to use it.

Two poisonous spiders that you may encounter while hiking and backpacking are brown recluses and black widows. Brown recluses are approximately the size of a U.S. quarter and have a violin shape on their backs. Black widows are about the same size as brown recluses. They are black with a red hourglass on the underside of their abdomens. Black widows are considered the most poisonous spider in North America, though bites are seldom fatal. They can be found throughout the 48 contiguous states. Brown recluses are found in the central United States, from the Gulf Coast through the midwestern states. They prefer living in cool, dark places, such as beneath debris piles, fallen trees and logs, and rock ledges. If you are bitten by one of these spiders, seek advanced medical care in a hospital. Both can cause serious medical problems.

Snakes

There are two types of poisonous snakes in North America: pit vipers and coral snakes. Pit vipers include rattlesnakes, copperheads, and cottonmouths. Coral snakes are small and reclusive, typically shying away from people. See figure 5.5, *a* through *d*, for photos of these snakes.

Figure 5.5 Poisonous snakes you may encounter on the trail or in the backcountry include the *(a)* rattlesnake, *(b)* copperhead, *(c)* cottonmouth, and *(d)* coral snake.

Snake habitats are very diverse. Snakes can reside in rocky areas, trees, bushes, grasslands, streams, and riversides. Most are nocturnal and, due to their low tolerance for temperature extremes, will position themselves in areas that provide effective warming and defensive positioning. If you encounter a snake on the trail or in the backwoods, remain calm and move to a safe position. A coiled snake can lunge at least the length of its body. If you are ever bitten by a snake, the treatment is the same regardless of the type of snake: Remain calm, evacuate, and transport to the closest medical facility. Do not try to catch the snake, and do not use such traditional remedies as applying a tourniquet, swigging whiskey, or cutting the bite and attempting to suck out the venom.

Figure 5.5 *(continued)*

Hunters, Mountain Bikers, and Equestrian Users

Threats to personal safety are presented not only by plants and animals but also by other humans using the same area as you. It is important to be aware of others who are in the area, and it is also important to be aware of basic techniques that can be used to minimize the chance of negative encounters with others in the woods. We will address three primary types of recreationists you might encounter while in the backcountry: hunters, mountain bikers, and equestrian users.

Hunters

At certain times of year, a significant potential threat to your safety in the backcountry is hunting. Always contact the land management agency responsible for the area where you intend to hike or backpack to find out if hunting is permitted in the area. Ask for the schedule of hunting seasons and what is being hunted during each season. If you choose to hike in an area that is a designated hunting zone, always wear blaze orange and make sure that the orange is visible from all directions. However, it is probably best to avoid hiking and backpacking in areas where hunting is going on. Plan to hike in areas where hunting is restricted, or plan to hike when hunting is out of season.

Mountain Bikers

When selecting your hiking trail, find out whether the trail is designated as a multiple-use or a single-use trail. Many trails are designated for hiking only. Numerous others, however, are designated as multiple-use trails, allowing for other modes of travel along the trails, such as mountain bikes. As a hiker, you will be glad to know ahead of time what might be coming around the next corner. Trail etiquette dictates that mountain bikers yield to hikers. Do not take it for granted that all mountain bikers will yield to you, though. Not all mountain bikers practice good trail etiquette. Beware of mountain bikers traveling too fast to come to a controlled stop when traveling downhill and around blind turns.

Equestrian Users

Another mode of travel in the backcountry is on horseback. Again, plan ahead and discover whether you are likely to encounter horseback riders or pack animals during your trip by finding out if they are permitted on trails that you intend to hike. If you do encounter these animals on the trail, you must always yield the right of way. Step to the downhill side of the trail and leave plenty of room to pass. You should move to the downhill side of the trail because horses and other livestock tend to run uphill when spooked. Avoid making sudden movements and loud noises that might spook them. Spooked livestock can jeopardize not only your safety but also the safety of the rider. Do not approach livestock from behind without first making your presence known; most riders and horses do not like surprises. Also, avoid getting too close to or touching horses and other livestock unless invited by the rider.

Wilderness First Aid

In discussing various environmental dangers that you may encounter on the trail, we have addressed several different kinds of injuries that may result from each of these dangers, but there are a variety of other possible injuries and ailments that you may encounter on the trail. This section introduces some of these common ailments and injuries. It also introduces opportunities to become trained to help treat these injuries while on the trail. We will start with blister prevention and care.

Blister Prevention and Care

Chapter 3 discusses the importance of proper footwear, the different categories of footwear for different kinds of hiking and backpacking, and various other considerations that you should address before hitting the trail. Proper footwear for some people is easy—any boot will do. For others it takes many tries and many blisters to calculate the perfect combination of boot, sock, and foot bed. Proper footwear is essential for preventing blisters. It can make the difference between a safe, enjoyable hike in the woods and a hike that results in painful, even debilitating, injuries to your feet.

You can often tell when a blister is beginning to develop. The skin on your feet will begin to feel hot as a result of the friction caused by your socks and boots rubbing against the skin. This area is called a *hot spot.* If you feel a hot spot developing on your foot, stop immediately and find ways to reduce the friction of the sock and boot against your skin. This can be done by applying smooth tape or moleskin to the hot spot. Changing your socks or readjusting the lacing of your boots often helps. In some cases, a new pair of boots may be in order. The key is to stop hiking until the problem is resolved.

Should you fail to recognize and treat hot spots, with continued walking they will likely turn into blisters. If possible, avoid breaking a blister. This will minimize the risk of infection. If the blister must be broken in order to continue walking, clean the area with soap and water, drain the blister with a sterilized pin, apply topical antibiotic ointment, apply second skin dressing (which is a cool, moist, membrane-type bandage), build a raised border around the blister to stop direct contact, and cover with sticky tape.

Roll your sock back on. Loosely lace your shoe or boot and keep on hiking. When possible, remove the dressing, clean the area and allow it to air dry, and apply topical antibiotic ointment covered with a bandage to promote healing.

Common Injuries and Ailments on the Trail

Strains and sprains are two common trail ailments, and they have a variety of causes. To distinguish between the two in the field is helpful but not imperative. A strain is a tear in muscle tissue, and a sprain is the result of an injury to the ligaments. Both are painful and have similar treatments in the field. Treatment in the field follows a medical acronym called *RICE:* rest, ice, compression, and elevation. Rest is helpful because the body is injured and needs time to recover. Ice constricts the blood vessels, decreases swelling, and promotes healing. Since ice is typically unavailable when hiking and backpacking, rely on cold water from streams or lakes as a substitute. Compression can be administered using an elastic bandage, tape, or your boot. Compression also controls swelling and provides support. Elevation promotes blood flow away from the injured area, which decreases swelling. Remember to place a barrier between the ice and your skin, and do not wrap the injured area too tightly.

Intestinal ailments are also commonly experienced in the backcountry. Possible sources of intestinal ailments include food allergies, intolerances to dehydrated food, bacteria, and viruses. Intestinal ailments in the backcountry are no fun and can be difficult to treat. Symptoms that warrant an evacuation include a fever above 102 degrees Fahrenheit (39 degrees Celsius), persistent vomiting or diarrhea, pain, and lack of appetite. When leaving the backcountry, be cautious and gentle with yourself or your companion. The important thing is to evacuate safely and seek medical attention if symptoms persist or worsen.

Training for Medical Emergencies

Every hiker and backpacker should be prepared to treat common injuries and illnesses that arise on the trail. Every hiker and backpacker should also be prepared to respond to medical emergencies. This does not mean that you should be able to provide treatment in every instance. Often it means recognizing when you are unable to provide adequate medical assistance and need to evacuate a victim from the backcountry to get advanced medical care. Three levels of training can be obtained to help prepare you to respond to medical situations in the backcountry: wilderness first aid training, wilderness first responder training, and wilderness emergency medical technician (WEMT) training. Wilderness first aid training is probably enough for the casual backpacker or day hiker. Those who are more avid in their pursuit of hiking and backpacking should consider additional training as either a wilderness first responder or a WEMT.

There are a number of injuries not addressed in this chapter that you might encounter when traveling in the backcountry, including shoulder dislocations, broken bones, spinal injuries, and burns. There are also a number of medical conditions not addressed in this chapter that merit special consideration when traveling in the backcountry, such as asthma, heart disease, diabetes, and chronic joint injuries. We encourage you to seek further information and training in wilderness medicine so that you will be prepared to address medical emergencies should they arise during your hiking or backpacking adventure.

CONSUMER TIP

Several organizations provide training in wilderness medicine. Four prominent examples include the following:

- Wilderness Medicine Associates (WMA)
- Wilderness Medicine Institute (WMI)
- Stonehearth Open Learning Opportunities (SOLO)
- Wilderness Medical Training Center (WMTC)

Emergencies and Survival Situations

To avoid emergency and survival situations, we must first anticipate them. When traveling into the backcountry, even for only a day hike, it is important to consider possible contingencies before your trip. This involves asking what-if questions related to the weather, terrain, and other potential hazards.

- What if the trail that you plan to hike is impassible? Are there alternative routes that you might hike?
- What if the weather is not as expected? Are you equipped for cold, miserable conditions?
- What if you fail to reach your destination at the designated time? If day hiking, are you prepared for a night in the woods? If backpacking, are there alternative campsites along your route? If attempting to summit a peak, is there a time at which you and your group should turn back to avoid having to bivouac along the trail for a night?
- What if your return is delayed? Do you have enough food and water in case you are forced into an extended stay in the woods?

In asking various what-if questions, also determine no-go conditions for your trip. When is the terrain too hazardous for hiking? When is the weather too severe for your trip? When do other hazards, such as the presence of wildfires or wildlife, constitute no-go conditions? Preparing for these contingencies can help you avoid emergency and survival situations in the first place.

Rescue

Despite our best efforts, sometimes things happen. No matter how well prepared we are or how well planned our trip is, there is always the possibility that we will find ourselves in an emergency or survival situation. When such a situation arises, we must be prepared to remedy the situation.

In emergency survival situations, there are three basic sources of help: you, members of your group, and help from an outside party (Kaufmann & Carlson, 1992; Martin et al., 2006). A general rule of thumb when venturing into the wild outdoors is to always travel within groups of at least four people so that if one person is injured or incapacitated, others are present to provide assistance. If an evacuation is required and the group is unable to perform the evacuation, one person can remain with the injured person while the remaining two go for help.

The need for rescue or an evacuation should also be considered in the planning phase of trip. Along with planning for contingencies that may affect your trip, you should plan for the possibility of an evacuation or rescue.

SAFETY TIP

Create an evacuation plan when planning your trip.

- Where is the nearest trailhead to each point along the trail?
- What sources of transportation are available along the trail and once you reach the trailhead?
- Where is the nearest hospital should someone in the group need advanced medical care?
- Whom should you contact in case you need assistance from an outside party? How will you contact your local or regional search and rescue group? How do you contact the agency responsible for the lands on which you are hiking or backpacking?

Six Steps to Survival

The following six steps to survival—recognition, inventory, shelter, signaling, food and water, and the will to survive—are based on the Seven Steps to Survival in *Beating the Odds on the North Pacific* (Jensen, 1998).

Recognition

Recognition of the fact that you are in an emergency or survival situation is the first step to resolving the situation. How do you know if you are in such a situation? In short, you are in an emergency or survival situation when you are in imminent danger and rescue is needed. Sometimes the danger is obvious, and sometimes it is not. Sometimes situations are easy to remedy, and sometimes they are much more complex and require a great deal of time and effort to resolve.

Obvious and easily resolvable situations include such cases as being caught hiking along a ridgeline during a thunderstorm. Lightning is an obvious danger in this situation. Getting off the ridgeline to a lower, more protected area as quickly as possible is the desired course of action. Oftentimes, however, dangers are less obvious. Maybe you are hiking in late spring high in the Rocky Mountains. Trails are typically covered in snow high in the Rockies at this time of year. It is easy to wander off-trail without knowing it. When do you realize that you have lost your trail? When do you decide to backtrack rather than continuing in a direction that you are unsure of?

If you find yourself beginning to ask questions about your location or to have doubts about the safety of a situation, stop and take stock. Determine whether you are faced with some source of imminent danger. If you are, begin to make a plan to resolve the situation.

Inventory

Developing a plan to resolve a survival situation involves conducting an inventory of the resources that are available in the situation. What items do you have that can help you in a survival situation? What items can be found in the surrounding environment that can help you?

Every hiker and backpacker should carry a basic survival kit. *Tom Brown's Field Guide: Wilderness Survival* (Brown, 1983) recommends the following items for a survival kit:

- Pocketknife
- Waterproof matches
- Candle
- 50 feet (15 meters) of strong cordage (parachute cord is a good choice)
- Compass
- 50 feet (15 meters) of monofilament fish line
- Solar-still equipment (5- × 5-inch [13- × 13-centimeter] clear plastic sheet, plastic or surgical tubing, and a collapsible water container)

This list represents a minimal amount of survival equipment. A more extensive list of items that might be included can be found in chapter 3. You should attempt to minimize the bulk and weight of your survival kit, but it should include items that you will need to survive an extended stay in the woods and to call for help: shelter, water, food, and signaling devices. The contents of your survival kit may vary depending on the character of the environment in which you are traveling. For instance, a cold weather survival kit will likely vary a great deal from a survival kit designed for desert travel in the warmer months. You must design the kit to meet your basic physiological and survival needs while in the wilderness.

When developing your survival kit, designate a particular pack as the survival kit. A hip pack is a good choice because it is small and lightweight. Keep the kit in an easily accessible location, and always remember to take it with you as you head out for a hike. A survival kit will do you no good if you leave it at home.

Shelter

Resolution of an emergency situation often will be relatively easy. Sometimes, however, resolution is not so easy and the length of time required to solve the emergency might be rather extensive. In such cases you may face the prospect of spending the night or several nights in the woods, and finding or creating a shelter becomes a primary concern. One of the greatest dangers when stranded in the outdoors, especially during fall, winter, and spring, is exposure to cold. Preventing the onset of hypothermia requires shelter.

Two basic types of shelter are available in an emergency situation: primary shelter and secondary shelter. Primary shelter includes clothing, which has been addressed in chapter 3. Be sure to bring extra clothing in your pack when you go out for a day hike, including such things as wool hats, rain gear, and gloves. Though you may be expecting the best, prepare for the worst. You should be dressed to spend the night in the woods if necessary. Secondary shelter can include such things as tents, wooden shelters or cabins, snow caves, natural caves and rock overhangs, and emergency shelters constructed from materials in the environment. See figure 5.6 for illustrations of survival shelters.

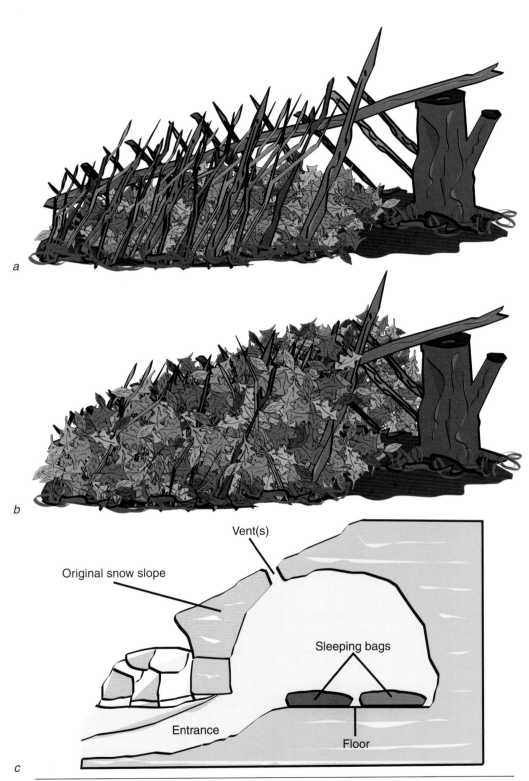

Figure 5.6 Survival shelters. *(a, b)* A basic shelter constructed from wood, leaves, and other natural materials, before and after covering the structure. *(c)* Of the various kinds of snow shelters, the snow cave is the most common and easiest to construct.

General principles in developing a shelter include the following points.

• **Choose a suitable site.** Take advantage of natural features that will help in constructing a shelter, such as rock ledges or overhangs and fallen trees. Choose a location that will not flood or collect water and that is not exposed to wind, rain, and lightning. A place that is close to water is a good place to signal for help. In desert environments during the summer months when hyperthermia is the primary concern, shelter should provide protection from the sun. In more temperate and colder environments, shelter should be on south-facing slopes that provide exposure to the sun for warmth.

• **Insulation from the ground.** Ensolite pads are the most effective form of insulation from the ground. Otherwise, use sticks, tree branches, duff (i.e., organic matter such as leaves and moss), and other materials to build a platform that will serve as a barrier between you and the ground. Build this bed of materials as high as you can because it will become compressed once you are on it. You will later construct your shelter around this bed.

• **Weatherproof your shelter.** Weatherproofing is easy if you happen to have a tent, find a wooden shelter or cabin, or build a snow cave or dig a snow trench for shelter. It is more difficult if you are constructing a shelter using tree limbs and other materials from the surrounding environment. Building a shelter that protects against wind and rain is essential. Wind not only makes you feel colder than the actual surrounding air temperature, it continually steals any warm air that your body is generating. Rain and other sources of moisture also put you at risk because, as mentioned, water conducts heat away from the body at 25 times the rate of air. Use plastic sheeting from garbage bags or tarps for weatherproofing when constructing a shelter. Finally, build a door or hatch that you can close tightly once you are in the shelter.

• **Keep your shelter small and well insulated.** It is easier to warm a small space with body heat than it is to warm a large space. Make the shelter just large enough to fit you and any fellow survivors. Fill the interior with pine boughs, leaves, and duff for added insulation.

Signaling

Although cell phones and VHF (very high frequency) radios may be useful devices for communicating in urban and front-country areas, they are less reliable in many rural and most remote wilderness areas. Satellite phones and personal emergency position indicator radio beacons (PEPIRBs) are more reliable, though also more expensive, devices for signaling distress when in the backcountry. Satellite phones provide a greater range of reception than cell phones, but they too have limitations. PEBIRBs have been adapted from EPIRBs (emergency position indicator radio beacons) for use in the backcountry. Ships at sea rely on EPIRBs to send distress signals when radio communication fails. These beacons communicate the location of the ship in distress and are used only when a ship is sinking. PEBIRBs are smaller devices that function in much the same way. When your proverbial ship is sinking in the backcountry, they can be used to signal that you are in a survival situation, and they can indicate your location to rescuers.

When advanced technology fails or is unavailable, there are a variety of other ways to signal that you are in distress. Noise is one effective way. Your essentials should include a whistle. Blowing on a whistle is much more effective than shouting. Or, if you are hiking with a gun, you can use it to signal distress. With both whistles and guns, three distinct blasts in quick succession indicate distress. Visual communication devices provide another effective way to signal distress. Flares and signal mirrors are devices that you should include in a survival kit. Flares should be saved for when aircraft are in sight and flying at a low altitude. Fires can also be used to attract attention, though in many areas you should be careful not to ignite a wildfire in the process of trying to attract help. Rather than building just one fire, which passersby might view as nothing more than a campfire, build three fires in a line. Most passersby would see this as a request for help.

In creating signals, whether you are using materials that you have with you or materials from the environment around you, make sure that they are visible from the air as well as land. Also be sure to create signals that contrast sharply with the landscape. Bright fabrics stand out from the natural landscape and can be used to attract attention. If you are using logs and other debris to create SOS signals, the U.S. Coast Guard recommends making each letter at least 18 feet (5 meters) long and 3 feet (1 meter) wide to be visible from the air.

Food and Water

Food and water are both needed for human survival. Of the two, however, water is the most important. Without water, humans can typically survive for no more than a week, but we can survive for approximately a month and often longer without food. If you have food but no water, you should avoid eating because fluid that could be better used for other bodily functions gets absorbed in the digestive process.

Your essentials include water, but you should be prepared to replenish your water supply while on the trail. Hikers and backpackers typically carry no more than 2 quarts (2 liters) of water while on the trail. As noted earlier, the human body requires an average of 2 to 4 quarts (2-4 liters) of water per day to function normally. Availability of water is a standard consideration when planning an extended backpacking trip. Backpackers often make decisions regarding route selection, campsite selection, and menu planning based on the availability of water, especially when hiking in arid or desert regions. Backpackers also come equipped to replenish their water supply with water found in the natural environment. Even on a day hike people should be prepared to replenish their water supply while on the trail in case they are caught in a survival situation.

In replenishing your water, you should have some way to treat water taken from the natural environment. There are other alternatives (see chapter 3), but probably the most efficient way to ensure that you will be able to treat your water is to include a bottle of iodine tablets or drops in your survival kit.

They are small, inexpensive, and easy to carry. As mentioned earlier, do not drink water from the natural environment that is untreated because this can further aggravate a survival situation by introducing illnesses resulting from waterborne pathogens such as giardia. Also, do not drink urine or seawater; these can cause vomiting and further dehydration.

Your essentials also include food, but you should be prepared to supplement your diet with food from the natural environment in a survival situation. Food provides the body with the energy needed to stay warm, helps us to stay mentally alert, and helps us to maintain morale. Backpackers typically come prepared with food, but it is important to plan for contingencies. For hikers and backpackers, this means packing additional food in case their return is delayed. In a survival situation, you may find yourself looking to the environment for food. Concentrate on gathering food that is easily accessible, such as fish, plants, berries, and other edibles. Trying to capture or kill larger animals often requires more energy than it is worth. It is better to economize your time and energy by focusing on food that is easy to gather. Learn to identify edible plants and animals in the region. This can enhance the enjoyment that you gain from your hiking and backpacking experiences by making you more familiar with the environment around you. It can also be crucial in a survival situation.

Most important, learn to identify plants and animals that are toxic or poisonous and should be avoided. Edibles that are found in the natural environment can be a wonderful source of nutrition. Just be sure that what you are eating is actually helping you, not hurting you. When in doubt about the edibility of particular items found in the wild, avoid them.

The rhythm of life is intricate but orderly, tenacious but fragile. To keep that in mind is to build the key to survival.

Shirley Hufstedler

The Will to Survive

One of the most important things you can do in a survival situation is maintain your will to survive. In other words, you should avoid giving in to feelings of despair, helplessness, and depression that can result from being caught in a survival situation. One of the best ways to do this is by staying mentally alert and keeping busy trying to improve your situation. This may involve continually working to improve your shelter, gathering food and water, signaling for help, and telling stories and jokes with fellow group members. You may even include a pack of cards in your survival kit as a way to pass the time if caught in a survival situation. By maintaining a positive attitude—by being a survivor—you increase your odds of survival. Refuse to give up. Decide that you will survive, regardless of your circumstances.

We have not discussed building a fire because fire is not considered essential to survival. Finding or creating a suitable shelter is the best way to stay warm in a survival situation. Time and energy spent trying to build a fire is better spent finding or creating a shelter. Once you have created a shelter, you can concentrate on building a fire as a way to signal for help. You can also focus on building a fire as a form of play to lift your morale in a survival situation.

Conclusion

Paul Petzoldt (1984) asserted that avoiding a survival situation is more important than learning how to get out of survival situation, because those who have allowed themselves to get into such a situation typically lack the judgment to get themselves out of it. This chapter has outlined a number of risks that you are likely to encounter should you venture into the woods. It has also provided illustrations of the consequences of being ill prepared for these risks as well as suggestions on what you should do to be prepared. Those who have taken the time to anticipate and prepare for the consequences of potential accidents and injuries in the woods will be much better equipped to resolve these situations should they arise than those who have not bothered to do the same.

PART II

On the Trail

CHAPTER 6

Hiking Basics

I only went out for a walk and finally concluded to stay out till sundown, for going out, I found, was really going in.

John Muir

As John Muir observed, the decision to go out for a walk, regardless of the duration of the journey or distance traveled, opens an adventure of self-discovery. Perhaps you are drawn to hiking because, like Muir, you find nature to be conducive to introspection and meditation or you gain a sense of accomplishment from engaging in the challenges of physical exertion. Your reasons for going out may be as varied as the earth beneath your boots, the clouds above your head, and the creatures flying, crawling, or swimming around you. No matter what draws you to lace up your hiking boots and begin walking down the trail, acquiring the necessary skills associated with hiking will enhance your outing.

The purpose of this chapter is to help you develop basic skills that will enable you to have a more enriching, more enjoyable, and safer hiking experience. The skills examined in this chapter include walking techniques, methods for maintaining energy levels, strategies for various terrains and environments, procedures for climbing and descending, and safe practices for crossing streams and rivers.

Walking Techniques

With the exception of your first year or so when you relied on crawling around on all fours to explore the world, you have probably spent a significant amount of time walking over the course of your life. Walking in urban environments requires some street smarts to safely negotiate the challenges of the asphalt jungle. In a similar manner, possession of trail smarts will help you to more safely navigate the challenges of the trails you venture upon.

The specific walking techniques examined in this section include stretching, rhythmic breathing, and pace. Acquisition of these fundamental walking techniques designed for trail hiking will enable you to walk with greater range of motion, comfort, and efficiency.

Stretching

The weekend has finally arrived. You and a friend have planned a 3-day backpacking trip. Before you jump out of the car at the trailhead and begin pounding out the miles with your gear on your back, consider taking a few minutes to prepare yourself mentally and physically for your trip. A few minutes spent stretching can help to make your hike more enjoyable while reducing the chance of injury (see figure 6.1). Important muscles to stretch include the calves, thighs, arms, shoulders, and lower back.

Whether backpacking overnight or longer, be sure to stretch each morning before breaking camp. On cool mornings, you may choose to hike for 15 or 20 minutes to warm up your body before stepping off the trail in a safe area that will accommodate your stretching routine. If you are anxious to get on the trail because you have a lot of miles to cover, consider incorporating stretching into your routine as you break camp. As you roll up your sleeping pad or tent, try

Figure 6.1 Incorporate stretching into your routine as you break camp by using your trekking poles.

kneeling on the ground as you slowly arch your back and then move your head downward as you straighten your back. To stretch your arms and shoulders, try grasping your trekking poles with arms slightly bent and slowly move side to side and then slowly lean forward and back. As with all stretching, focus on smooth movement and avoid bouncing. Review chapter 2 for a discussion of the benefits of stretching and suggestions for additional stretches.

Rhythmic Breathing

Rhythmic breathing is intentionally walking in synchronization with each breath. Establish a rhythm by coordinating a predetermined number of steps with each complete breathing cycle (i.e., inhalation and exhalation). Slow, deep breaths will draw more oxygen into the lungs with less effort. On level terrain with a moderate load, try three steps as you inhale and three more as you exhale. Being able to carry on a conversation while walking is a sign that your walking and breathing are in rhythm.

When the terrain becomes steeper or you are carrying a heavier load, you can downshift by reducing the number of steps between breaths. By taking two steps as you inhale and two as you exhale, you have decreased the number of steps taken to compensate for the increased energy expended with each step, allowing your breathing rate to remain constant. Extremely steep terrain may require you to take one step as you inhale and one step as you exhale in order to maintain a constant breathing rate. You may also consider shortening the length of your steps to accommodate changing conditions.

If your body is not accustomed to physical activity at higher altitudes where oxygen levels are lower, you will need to adjust your rhythmic breathing to compensate until you have a chance to acclimatize to the environment. Just as you reduced the number of steps between breaths when hiking steeper terrain, you may need to adjust your steps in the same way in response to lower levels of oxygen.

Coordinating the swinging of your arms or the placing of your trekking pole or walking stick with rhythmic breathing will add to your overall efficiency and sense of pace, which is the next technique we will examine.

Pace

Though seemingly counterintuitive, steady, long strides are generally more efficient than numerous quick, short steps. The rate and length of your stride constitutes your pace. Choosing a sustainable rate using an intentionally measured stride will enable you to conserve energy as you travel. The goal is to establish a pace that requires minimal effort to achieve optimal efficiency and well-being. You should select a pace that is sustainable for the long haul. Taking each step slowly and deliberately allows you to go fast by being more efficient, which can result in requiring fewer rest stops. As with rhythmic breathing, this involves adjusting your pace in response to the environmental changes that you encounter. As the terrain gets steeper, the load heavier, or the oxygen thinner, you may choose to shorten each stride or reduce the rate of your pace. Additional factors that may affect pace include natural length of stride, physical condition, heat, humidity, pollen count, hydration, and energy level.

Rest Step

The rest step is a technique that will help you to maintain your pace when traveling over steep trails, snow-covered trails, and trails at higher elevations. Use the rest step when your legs or lungs need a little pause to recover between steps (see figure 6.2). The rest step allows the leg muscles to take a brief break while you are traveling. As you swing your leg forward to take a step, shift your full weight to the rear leg while relaxing the muscles of the forward leg. Locking the knee of the rear leg for a moment allows your body weight to be supported by the skeletal system of the leg. Repeat this procedure with your other leg. This technique allows the thigh muscles to relax completely for the moment as your bones bear the load. Like putting your body's transmission into low gear, the rest step helps you slowly but steadily progress up steep terrain while reducing muscle fatigue. Remember to continue the rhythmic breathing described earlier in this section.

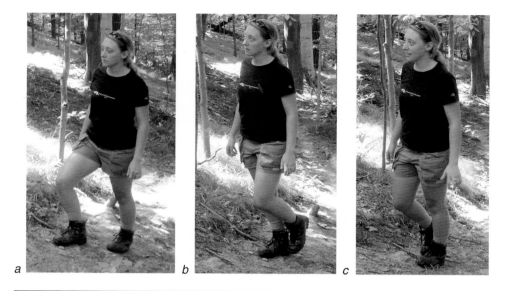

Figure 6.2 The rest step gives your thigh muscles a moment to relax. Shifting your weight to the rear leg allows your body to be supported by the bones of that leg.

The rest step requires practice and a conscious effort to walk in a manner that your body is not accustomed to. You will likely find yourself hiking halfway up a step trail before you remember to use the rest step. The rest step combined with rhythmic breathing can help you conserve energy and hike more efficiently when climbing steep terrain as well as snow-covered trails and at higher elevations.

Trail Manners

Just as there is etiquette at the dinner table, there are expectations for trail use. Etiquette is a system of behavioral expectations that aids in safety and enjoyment and decreases human impact in the backcountry. Think of human interactions as social impacts on other people. Backpackers and hikers are obligated to take care of themselves as well as other visitors to the area. They are also expected to be good stewards of the land that they are visiting. This is an outdoor ethic. Taking steps to care for people and the place will help sustain lands for recreational use.

Avoid walking through other visitors' campsites or resting locations. When crossing the paths of others, be polite but not overly friendly. Moving a little farther down the trail to rest is preferred to stopping right next to another group. Most people go to the great outdoors to get away, so give them their space. Keeping voices low on the trail and in campsites decreases noise in the outdoors and allows everyone to enjoy the sounds of nature.

A feature of many established trails in hilly or mountainous terrain is the switchback, where the trail is designed to minimize the steepness of the climb

Take only photo-
graphs; leave
only footprints.
Sierra Club dictum

by zigzagging back and forth. You should avoid cutting across the switchbacks. Repeated shortcuts can promote erosion, scar the natural setting, and introduce rival trails that may inadvertently be followed by subsequent hikers.

When traveling as a group, consider stepping off the trail, preferably on the downhill side if it is safe to do so, to allow oncoming hikers to pass by. As discussed earlier, coming to a complete stop and stepping off on the downhill side is especially important when traveling on a multi-use trail because horses can easily be spooked by the unnatural appearance of humans wearing backpacks. By stepping downhill you are able to minimize your perceived size, reducing the risk of startling the horses. Mountain bikes, motorcycles, and four-wheelers, on the other hand, should yield to hikers.

Use good judgment when you encounter other hikers while traveling uphill and downhill. If you are hiking uphill and could use a quick breather, stepping off the trail so that those coming downhill are able to pass by makes sense. If you are hiking downhill and see someone struggling up the trail trying to maintain a rhythm, stepping aside so that they can keep on trucking may be the most appropriate thing to do. Always select break sites and campsites well away from the trail. See chapter 8 for more information on campsite selection.

Maintaining Energy Levels

Hiking and backpacking are physical activities that require significant energy reserves from the entire body over extended periods of time. The techniques described thus far are designed to help you conserve energy through efficient breathing and hiking practices. This section will introduce practices designed to help you maintain energy levels by ensuring that you take in adequate nutrition to fuel your body and appropriate amounts of fluid to hydrate your body. Rest breaks are also addressed in this section as a way to avoid exhausting your body while hiking.

Nutrition on the Trail

As your body works, food and water are expended and must be replaced. Food also keeps the body warm when temperatures drop outdoors. Some people are grazers and nibble snacks like trail mix or dried fruit all day long. Others prefer to stop for a more substantial meal in the late morning or early afternoon. During normal hiking conditions, following your appetite will guide you on what and when to eat. Refer to chapter 3 for additional suggestions of types and amounts of foods to bring when hiking or backpacking.

CONSUMER TIP

Commercial trail foods are expensive. Fortunately, you can prepare your own food for less. One healthy, inexpensive trail food is GORP, which stands for "granola, oats, raisins, and peanuts" or "good old raisins and peanuts." Mix equal parts of each ingredient in a resealable bag to create your trail mix. These quick mixtures keep well and are good sources of carbohydrate, protein, and salt.

You can add zip to your mix by including some alternative ingredients:

- Cashews (high in nutrients)
- Dried fruit
- Hot Tamales candies
- Shelled sunflower seeds
- M&Ms

The possibilities are endless! Avoid using too many sugary ingredients. Instead, choose ingredients that are lasting sources of energy.

Staying Hydrated

When hiking, you will need to be intentional about fluid replenishment. The body can lose as much as a quart (1 liter) of water overnight as you sleep, so get into the habit of drinking a quart of water in the morning before you begin hiking to compensate for this nocturnal loss. Always bring at least two full water bottles on the trail, and keep one bottle within easy reach while hiking or during breaks. Drink small amounts of water frequently throughout the day. Avoid sugary drinks that make it more difficult for the body to absorb fluids. Refer to chapter 5 for more information on staying hydrated.

Rest Breaks

Rest breaks briefly relieve your body to avoid exhaustion. If anyone needs to stop for a rest, the pace is too fast. Seek to achieve a balance between group pace and personal pace. One way to achieve this balance is to invite hiking companions with a slower personal pace to hike toward the front. Although some slow hikers might say they prefer to hike in the back because they do not want to slow the rest of the group down, hiking in the front can provide a psychological boost to slower hikers that will enable them to attain a faster personal pace than normal. Should your pace be slower than the rest of the group, the distance between you and the rest of the group increases and your energy level can decrease, resulting in a downward spiral. Hiking in the front can result in an energizing experience that often will enable the entire group to maintain a faster pace. Another option is to divide a large group into two smaller groups.

Sharing words of encouragement with slower hikers by reminding them that as they become more accustomed to hiking they will become stronger or by praising their effort can be helpful. Engaging in conversation or other activity while hiking can also help take their minds off the physical exertion. A practical strategy to assist slower hikers, but one that should be done with sensitivity, is to offer to redistribute some of the weight they are carrying. Since group gear is brought for use by the entire group, invite others to carry this gear rather than an individual's personal gear, which can make it awkward for the slower hiker to ask for it when needed along the trail.

The entire group should stay within sight of each other, with one person serving as a sweep to ensure that no one is left behind. The sweep is the last person in the group, bringing up the rear. The sweep makes sure no one falls behind, alerts the group if the pace is not appropriate for all members, and makes sure that the group does not get too spread out along the trail where visual contact is lost. This helps to prevent the group from inadvertently getting separated, which increases the risk of individuals or smaller groups of hikers mistakenly taking the wrong turns at intersections because they do not have a map.

Just as you want to establish a rhythm with each step, you also want to establish a rhythm for the day by scheduling breaks to occur at regular intervals.

Try traveling for 30 minutes and then resting for 5 minutes. Confer with your companions and modify if necessary. Announce how long a break will be and stick with the stated time. A 5-minute break that stretches into 20 minutes, if repeated at each rest stop, will extend your total time on the trail and delay your arrival at the campsite.

Five-minute breaks are generally preferred because they minimize lactic acid buildup. Lactic acid is a waste by-product of muscular activity. The body burns off the lactic acid when it is active. When you suddenly stop, the body continues to produce the lactic acid for a period of time. If you break for 5 minutes, the lactic acid in your system is minimal and should not cause any problems. Stops of 20 or 30 minutes, as with a lunch break, will allow the lactic acid to clear out of your system. Breaks that fall between 5 and 20 minutes, however, can be problematic because more residual lactic acid may remain in your system for a longer time. Stretching and elevating your feet can help to minimize the effects of lactic acid buildup.

When your judgment suggests that a longer break is appropriate or when you stop for a lunch break, consider removing your socks and boots to let your feet breathe. Inspect your feet and treat any blisters and hotspots (see chapter 5). Elevating your feet will also help to reduce swelling.

In addition to refreshing the body and providing time to drink water and eat snacks, breaks also provide an opportunity for taking photos, adjusting shoulder straps and hip belts, stretching sore muscles, and responding to the call of nature. Breaks are also a good time to adjust clothing layers to maintain appropriate body temperature.

Break location and timing should also be taken into consideration as you hike. Selecting a site with water for a break will prevent extra stops later and will help ensure that you and your party stay hydrated. A site with a view, such as a scenic overlook, enhances the overall experience. Trail etiquette requires that breaks be taken well off to one side of the trail, including packs and other personal gear, to avoid creating obstacles for other hikers (see figure 6.3).

Consider starting the break only after the entire group has arrived. There are few experiences on the trail as demoralizing as finally catching up with the rest of the group only to discover that they have finished their break and are preparing to depart. This can be avoided by providing all party members arriving at the rest spot with an appropriate amount of time to relax. Make an announcement a couple of minutes before the end of the break so that everyone can gather their personal items and prepare to leave.

Trekking Poles

Another technique to maintain energy incorporates the use of trekking poles. Hikers and backpackers fall into several distinct groups: those who use a walking stick, those who use one or two trekking poles, and those who use neither. Although trekking poles are not for everyone, they do offer benefits: They increase stability, reduce knee and low back strain, and increase efficiency by engaging the upper body more directly in the hiking process.

Figure 6.3 When taking a break, be sure to move all your personal gear well off-trail.

TRAIL TIP
Trekking Pole Benefits

- Enhanced endurance
- Reduced spine, hip, knee, and ankle strain
- Increased efficiency in climbing steep trails
- Improved stability when traversing rugged terrain
- Improved breathing through improved posture

Trekking poles have a high-tech appearance compared with the traditional walking stave. They now boast telescoping composite designs with ergonomic grips and carbide tips. They are useful for hiking but provide even greater value to backpackers because some of the weight is distributed to the arms. However, note the environmental impact of trekking poles: graphite tips scratch rock surfaces, leaving visible scars on rocks, and they can damage vegetation and soil surfaces, which can lead to trail creep and erosion. See chapter 3 for more on choosing trekking poles.

When preparing to hike with trekking poles, adjust each pole so that a 90-degree angle is formed from elbow to hand when gripping the pole. Most trekking poles include an adjustable tether that allows the poles to dangle during a break and to be tightened when you want a firmer grip. With a medium grip on each trekking pole, simply plant one pole about 6 inches (15 centimeters) beyond your normal stride. Begin to take a step with the corresponding leg a split second after you have initiated movement of the trekking pole (figure 6.4). Repeat the process with the opposite pole and leg. Most hikers are able to integrate the use of trekking poles with their own rhythm after a short initial attempt.

Trekking poles are especially helpful when ascending and descending. When climbing, firmly grip the handles and plant one pole at a time, pulling yourself forward as you climb. Use the poles to steady your descent when going downhill so that you maintain balance and control. Some hikers prefer to adjust the

Figure 6.4 After a little practice, you'll be able to integrate the use of trekking poles with your own walking rhythm.

poles with changes in the terrain, making the poles shorter when climbing and longer when descending. An alternative is to change hand position, placing your weight on the straps or on top of the hand grips when descending and gripping lower on the handles when climbing.

Strategies for Various Terrains and Environments

Part of the attraction of hiking and backpacking is the diversity of terrain encountered, ranging from the sandy beaches of coastal areas to boulder fields. This section will introduce three specific settings for hiking: trails, off-trail, and boulder fields.

YOSEMITE DECIMAL SYSTEM

The Yosemite Decimal System rates various levels of terrains.

Class 1	Hike is on a designated trail.
Class 2	Hike requires route finding on cross-country terrain.
Class 3	Hike needs the assistance of hands to scramble, but rope is not needed.
Class 4	Hike is on steep terrain and needs a roped belay.
Class 5	Hike is advanced in technical moves and needs protective hardware. Scale is expanded in this class from 5.0-5.13.

Trails

Established trails are the easiest entry point to hiking and backpacking. They often have one or more of the following: established trailheads that provide parking, trail-specific maps and field guides, trail markings, and established campsites. There are many other trails that have none of these amenities. Each type of trail has its own appeal, but in any case, you should be mindful of the dynamic nature of trails. A winter ice storm can down trees that will make a section of trail impassible. Trail signs can become unidentifiable. Spur trails can be established after the printing of your map, luring you in a direction other than your intended destination. Trails can provide a false sense of security, so avoid taking anything for granted.

Always bring a map of the trail you are hiking and consult it often, especially when you are making turns or walking up to intersecting trails. Many trails have signs in the form of a painted blaze or other symbol on trees (figure 6.5). Rules of the trail differ slightly from place to place. When gathering information from the local land manager, the expected behavior will be described. Signs at the trailhead will also have this information.

Figure 6.5 *(a)* A painted blaze, usually rectangular and in white or a primary color, is often used to mark the trail. *(b)* In areas where trees are scarce or there are extended rocky sections, the trail may be marked by cairns.

Off Trail

Hiking or backpacking off trail provides a unique opportunity to venture through pristine areas with minimal signs of civilization. You should have good land navigation skills evidenced by competent working knowledge and experience using a map and compass.

Game trails provide good routes when traveling off-trail and often lead to water. However, the destination of the game trail may be different from your intended destination. When following game trails, be aware that animals generally follow the path of least resistance, but that does not mean there will be no resistance. Off-trail travel is referred to as *bushwhacking* for a reason, and generally the bushes are doing the whacking. Spread the group out when walking off-trail to avoid being smacked by a branch pulled back by the person in front of you. Also be sure to minimize gear hanging from the outside of your pack; it can easily become tangled in low-hanging branches. If you must leave items outside the pack, secure them so they do not swing and so that they produce a minimal profile. In addition, be cautious of unseen hazards such as holes, rocks, or streams hidden by the underbrush.

By consulting your map, you can anticipate the terrain in a given area and locate streams and rivers. You can also check the map for heavily wooded areas that generally indicate mature trees and less underbrush, providing a less encumbered route.

When traveling off-trail along mountainsides, you are likely to encounter talus or scree, two different forms of loose rock. Talus is formed when sections of rock break off cliffs or peaks and can range in size from as small as a fist to the size of boulders (see figure 6.6). Talus consists of rock fragments, so it has sharp edges that can cause injury if you fall. Be especially careful when traveling downhill since your footing may be less certain due to the force of your momentum. Scree is much smaller rock that looks like gravel. Hiking is difficult, especially uphill, because the scree slips under your feet, requiring extra energy.

Figure 6.6 Making your way through a talus field involves closely watching your step.

Be aware of the danger of falling rocks as you travel through talus or scree. Keep the group close together so that rock will not have time to build up momentum, but stay out of each other's fall line. If you detect a rock beginning to fall, shout "Rock!" to warn other hikers who may be traveling in the path of loosened rocks.

Boulder Fields

Boulder fields provide a unique challenge to hikers and backpackers, requiring stamina and balance (see figure 6.7). Trekking poles can aid your balance and increase your stability through rocky terrain, but they can become a liability if you are traveling over boulders 6 feet (2 meters) or taller. On such boulders you will need to have your hands free to negotiate. Look two or three steps

Figure 6.7 Hiking Mahoosuc Notch Trail, possibly the hardest mile of the Appalachian Trail due to a maze of giant boulders.

ahead to locate your path. Larger boulders are heavier and less likely to shift. You should step on the center of a rock instead of the edges; stepping on the edges is more likely to cause the rock to shift.

Descending and Climbing

What seems like the edge of the world is really Hermit Trailhead at the South Rim of the Grand Canyon. You easily lose count of the switchbacks as your eyes travel down the work of art that took millions of years to form. The bright blue sky complements the colors of the inner walls. You take a big breath, put one foot in front of the other, and begin the descent to the great Colorado River. Descending and ascending takes controlled and strategic placement of each step. Accidents occur when hikers are not paying attention to their footing or the body is severely fatigued. Many hikers in the Grand Canyon briskly hike or run down the trail and do not realize that their muscles are getting tired and the ascent takes twice as long.

Hiking on trails with a lot of elevation gain or loss is very different than walking around the neighborhood park. On a trail with several hundred or thousand feet in elevation change, it is helpful to have trekking poles or a hiking stick for extra balance and support. Determine estimated elevation gain and loss before hiking the route. Muscles greatly fatigue on descents, significantly slowing the pace. When descending, muscles are eccentrically contracting; therefore they are still being used. An example of this is a biceps curl. When bringing the dumbbell closer to the chest, the muscle is contracting. At this point, you do not drop the weight to the floor; the biceps muscle is controlling the weight until it is at your side. This motion is called *eccentric contraction*. Leg muscles (calves and quadriceps) are similar in that they are stabilizing and controlling the next downward movement. Refer to chapter 2 to review ways to train your muscles for descending and ascending and reduce the chances of muscle, tendon, and joint injuries.

When ascending, the most important thing to consider is elevation gain. No matter what kind of training and conditioning you have done, everyone is affected by altitude to some degree. If you travel to an area significantly

TRAIL TIP

Here is a question to consider: What is the appropriate distance to maintain between hikers when descending? If a hiker falls when right next to the person in front, the accident may be more serious and affect more people. Space your group out at least 5 feet (1.5 meters) when traveling on level ground and 10 feet (3 meters) or more if traveling uphill or downhill.

Figure 6.8 The side step should be used when the terrain is too steep for a forward step.

above sea level for a week of backpacking, you will see a big difference in your breathing. As elevation increases, the amount of available oxygen decreases. It is wise to always acclimate to your surroundings before hitting the trail. When hiking in higher elevations, the average recommendation for ascending is no more than 1,000 feet (305 meters) in net elevation gain per day. Hydrating and camping at lower elevations reduces the chances of getting altitude sickness and high altitude pulmonary edema (HAPE).

If the terrain is too steep for a forward step, one effective method is the side step (see figure 6.8). To side step, face perpendicular to the trail and step from side to side uphill. Using trekking poles helps significantly. This method does require a little more balance, but it allows your legs to be used in a different stride.

TECHNIQUE TIP
Descend With Ease

- Tighten boot straps to prevent toes from hitting the toe box.
- Maintain controlled steps; do not let momentum cause slippage.
- Extend the length of trekking poles.
- Alternate the placement of trekking poles in front of feet to secure footing.
- Use side steps when hiking in steep grade.
- Yield to hikers ascending on the trail.
- Yield to horseback riders by stepping off the trail on the downhill side if possible.

TECHNIQUE TIP
Climb With Confidence

- Loosen the top lacing of your boots to reduce friction on the lower shin.
- Take small rest steps.
- Shorten the length of trekking poles.
- Alternate the placement of trekking poles in front of feet to create balance.
- Use side steps when hiking in steep grade.
- Yield to horseback riders by stepping off the trail on the downhill side if possible.

Crossing Streams and Rivers

Imagine your first morning on the trail. Your route leads you through a meadow blanketed with glistening dew. You pause a moment, enamored by the rich, deep blue of an indigo bunting as it sings a melody of loud, high-pitched notes. As the trail meanders through a stand of oaks, you feel a gentle breeze rustling the canopy of leaves. After hiking a couple of miles, you come upon the soothing sound of water passing over a mossy rock bed (figure 6.9). Though enjoying the picturesque view, there is a decision to be made: Will you cross the stream, find an alternative route, or retrace your steps back to the trailhead?

Crossing streams and rivers can add to the adventure and challenge of hiking and backpacking. Taking time to consider key concerns before crossing can help you avoid a misadventure or worse. Does it have to be crossed? This is the most important question you should ask yourself when arriving at a stream or river. Are alternative routes on the map? Have you hiked a sufficient amount of time and you're ready to return to the trailhead? If you decide to pursue the crossing, then an evaluation of the scene is necessary to reduce the probability of an accident or injury occurring. Table 6.1 is a guide for making sound decisions at the scene of a stream or river.

Recognizing Water Features

To ensure a safe crossing, a general knowledge of river features is important. Narrow passages of water typically have a swifter current than wide-open sections. If you cannot see the bottom of the riverbed, chances are it is too deep to safely wade across. The current is swift if the flow is high and the gradient is steep. Large obstacles in the water create rapids and swift currents. Eddies are typically calmer sections that are found downstream of a large boulder or a bend in the river. See figure 6.10 for various river features.

Figure 6.9 What decision will you make when faced with a river crossing?

Table 6.1   Questions to Ask Before Crossing a River

Question	Choices
What is the condition of the group or yourself?	Tired or energized
What is the strength of the group?	Weak or strong
What is the group's swimming capability?	Cannot swim or strong swimmers
What are you carrying?	Heavy pack or day pack
What does the remainder of the hike entail?	Additional miles or make camp
What is the air temperature?	Cool or warm
What is the weather forecast?	Storms or blue skies
What is the temperature of the water?	Snow melt or cool
What is the distance of the crossing?	Wide or narrow
What is the depth of the crossing?	Deep or shallow
What is the flow of the stream or river?	Swift or calm
What is the gradient of the stream or river?	Steep or gradual
What is on the bottom of the stream or river?	Large obstacles or fine sand

(continued)

Table 6.1 *(continued)*

Question	Choices
What is downstream of the crossing?	Strainers (sticks or logs in the middle of the stream or river that block the passage) or clear passage
What is on the other side?	Steep terrain or easy transition walk
Are there any other concerns?	

Note: The risks are too great if the majority of the answers are the first of the two choices.

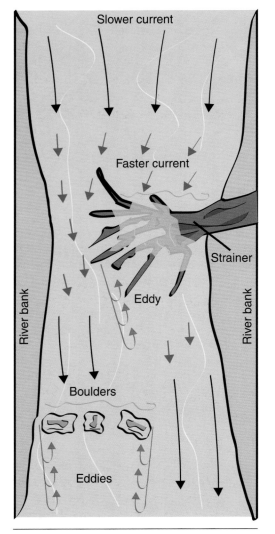

Figure 6.10 Various river features.

Evaluating Footwear

After you have assessed the features of the river and determined the ideal crossing, footwear and gear are the next items to evaluate. You should always wear closed-toed shoes (boots or tennis shoes) to cross any river or stream. Your feet are the most valuable things to protect when hiking. If you cross the stream or river barefooted and you get cut, the remainder of the hike will be compromised. Sandals are not recommended because they do not provide the appropriate ankle support and stability that boots or tennis shoes offer. It is always smart to bring additional pairs of socks to change into after crossing a body of water. If you do not have an extra pair of dry socks to change into, you may remove your socks before crossing and wear just your boots or tennis shoes. Gaiters can also be worn to reduce the amount of water that gets in your boots.

The size and weight of your pack are key variables when crossing a stream or river. If you have a small frame and are carrying a large pack, you will have a greater difficulty crossing; if you are carrying a lighter load or a small day pack, you will have more stability and an easier time wading across. Larger hikers and hikers who have long legs will have less difficulty crossing than short-legged, weaker hikers. The stronger and more experienced hikers in the group may want to help shuttle other hikers' packs across the river. Packs of any size can be a hindrance if you should lose your footing and have to swim. Always unbuckle your sternum strap and hip belt buckle, and loosen shoulder straps when crossing. If you end up taking a swim, it is easier to free yourself from your pack if you already have it loosened and not secured to your body. Make sure all things in the pack are secure and remove any items on your body that might cause entanglements if you should have to swim.

If your crossing point is a large, deep pool and there are no dangerous objects below the stream, you may consider floating your backpack and swimming across. This should not be your first option, and your swimming capabilities will determine if this is even a safe consideration. Weather, water temperature, and clothing need to be evaluated before deciding to swim across. If you do choose to cross by floating the pack and swimming, make sure the backpack is buoyant and contents are waterproofed. Remove the pack from your body, wrap it in a large trash bag with air left inside, and securely tie off the bag. Float the pack in front of you as you doggy paddle or use the freestyle stroke to swim across. Keep your head above water at all times so that you are always aware of your surroundings.

Solo or Group Crossings

As discussed, trekking poles or walking sticks are beneficial for your lower joints and overall stability, and they are also useful for river crossings. A pair of legs and a pole or stick creates an excellent tripod for balance when crossing. Select the strongest and most experienced hikers from the group and have them hike across without their packs while using trekking poles or hiking sticks. This will help determine if all members of the group will be able to cross. If you are

SAFETY TIP
Wading Across Water

- If you are hiking alone, you can generally cross water that is ankle to midcalf deep.
- If you are hiking with three or more people, you can generally cross water that is ankle to midthigh deep.
- If you are hiking with three or more people, it is generally too difficult to cross water that is midthigh to waist deep; find another route.

use the skills appropriately. For example, you may decide to stretch each time before you begin hiking because it has been recommended. After you have discovered through personal experience that the few moments spent preparing your muscles in this way really does help you hike more efficiently and with greater comfort, stretching is more likely to become a habit you embrace.

Always temper your skills and knowledge with judgment based on experience, whether you are deciding if you should cross a swift river or deciding on the wisdom of attempting to traverse a boulder field at dusk. The dynamics of the wilderness environment require not only well-honed skills, but sound, thoughtful judgment. As you establish a level of competency with basic hiking skills and an appropriate understanding of your strengths and personal growth areas, you will be prepared to learn and apply the advanced knowledge and skills presented in future chapters, enabling you to expand the scope of the outdoor adventures you can embark upon. Like Muir, you may find that in going outdoors, you are really going in.

CHAPTER 7

Hiking Adventures

I think that I cannot preserve my health and spirits, unless I spend four hours a day at least—and it is commonly more than that—sauntering through the woods and over the hills and fields, absolutely free from all worldly engagements.

Henry David Thoreau

There is something about a walk in the woods that both soothes and invigorates—it's a sure cure for what ails you. A walk in the woods can contribute greatly to our physical and emotional health, as well as to our spiritual well-being. A footpath winding through a grove of trees or a desert canyon, skirting the shoreline of an ocean or lake, or climbing a hill or a peak can provide many pleasures—the sounds of birds, the smell of the ocean, sweeping views from a mountain summit. At the very least, a long walk in the outdoors should be more satisfying than time on a treadmill at the local fitness center.

Day hiking is the easiest of all outdoor recreation activities—you need little other than comfortable clothing and footwear. As you become more involved, you can begin to accumulate more equipment and knowledge. Joining a hiking club or getting involved with a reputable outdoor program is a great way to gain experience and to learn from more seasoned hikers. When you become a seasoned hiker, you may find yourself sharing your knowledge and expertise with newcomers. As you become better conditioned, you may desire more challenging hikes. Time and again, most people stay within a couple of miles of the trailhead or the car. Within an hour or so, hikers have thinned out to the occasional encounter, and within two hours, there is rarely another soul around. If it is solitude you seek, hiking farther from the trailhead will reward you.

Many of the things that you need to consider before embarking on a day hike have been addressed elsewhere in this book. Chapter 2 addresses issues related to fitness and being physically ready for your hike. Chapter 3 discusses the basic equipment that you will need for your hike. Chapter 4 addresses issues related to planning yor hike. Chapter 5 addresses issues related to trail safety and how to handle emergency situations. Chapter 6 covers basic hiking techniques. This chapter addresses additional hiking considerations, including several kinds of day hiking adventures, the various types of terrain, and the seasons in which to hike. This chapter also covers social challenges that might arise while on the trail, hiking with dogs, and hiking with children.

Types of Hiking Adventures

Variety is the spice of life and hiking is no exception. There are several adventures for hikers to try. Following are some descriptions of a few of these adventures—just enough to get you started.

Trail Running

Other terms for this activity include *mountain running, adventure running,* or even *survival running.* No matter the name, this popular activity has existed nearly as long as the human passion for hiking or walking. The modern-day marathon (26.2 miles [42.2 kilometers]) celebrates the last achievement of ancient Greek messenger Pheidippides in his 25-mile (40.2-kilometer) sprint from the Marathon battlefield to Athens to bring news of the defeat of the Persians.

A trail runner running below the Rim Trail at Bryce Canyon National Park, Utah, USA.

Closer to home and nearly 50 years ago, the Tarahumara Indians (Raramuri) of Mexico hunted deer by patiently tracking them while jogging. Eventually the deer would collapse due to exhaustion. The Tarahumara still take great pride in their amazing physical endurance, holding numerous races of 50 to 100 miles (80-161 kilometers) annually to celebrate their culture and abilities.

Many runners run alone, including trail runners. Such runners need to be vigilant. Make sure that others know where you are going and when you plan to return. Carry identification and emergency information. If you have rescue medications, such as those for severe allergic reactions or asthma, always keep them on you. Decide which of the essentials are most important; most trail runners try to carry as little as possible and need to stabilize their pack to compensate for the bouncing that occurs. Some choose formfitting waist packs or low-riding backpacks as alternatives. Many articles of performance clothing, including shorts and shoes, also have zip pockets for essential items.

Trail runners may be more apt than other day hikers to carry hydration systems like those discussed in chapter 3. The external bags on these hydration systems also have small zip pockets for essential safety items.

Good footwear is needed for trail running, and this type of specialty footwear can be expensive. Many trail runners find that regular street running shoes with a tread that can grip various trail surfaces perform just fine. Regardless, it is essential that the running shoes fit comfortably and have enough cushioning to protect against protruding rocks and other obstacles. In addition, consider buying shoes a half size or full size larger than normal. Your feet will

CONSUMER TIP

Shoes can be purchased for running on snow and ice that have extra studs on the soles. A quick Internet search will also help you find instructions for embellishing your own shoes with extra-short machine screws in the treads for enhanced traction.

be continually forced into different directions as they encounter a variety of surfaces, and with the extra shoe space you can wear two pairs of socks and create even more cushioning.

Most trail runners invest in good trail-running shoes, which often have more lateral stability and deeper tread than regular running shoes but are much lower cut and lighter than light-hiking shoes. Several reputable companies have specialty lines of shoes for trail runners. As with hiking boots and shoes, it's helpful to seek the advice of a professional fitter. This will help you to understand your foot's shape and tendencies better and get a perfect, blister-free fit.

Another consideration in trail running is having to anticipate what is coming up, both in the short distance and farther ahead. Trail runners ideally want their feet to land on stable, flat ground. Immediate consideration is for what lies within the next 15 to 30 feet (6-9 meters). Unlike a day hiker who ambles through and can stop on a dime, trail runners must constantly be observing and making quick judgments: Should I shorten or lengthen my stride? Step right or left? Raise my foot to clear the rock or push off it? Some trail runners wear protective glasses to help with unseen branches and bugs in the eyes.

A longer-term consideration is being familiar with the terrain. Knowing the trail and what to expect is essential to having a well-paced and safe run. For example, if you are expecting a difficult section of the trail, pacing back so that you can hit it at full steam is helpful. You can also handle difficult climbs by walking. On inclines greater than 10%, trail runners save little time (and waste much energy) by keeping a running pace. Simply gear down to a hiking pace and keep your strides short and fast. Additionally, running downhill can be rougher than running uphill and more dangerous for twisting or compressing knees and ankles. At the very least, the large quadriceps muscles will be working hard just to keep you from falling forward.

Finally, don't expect to cover distances at the same pace you are accustomed to in your neighborhood. Rough terrain requires the use of more muscles, and safety demands a slower pace just to maintain your balance. Your arms are often used for counterbalancing to correct sudden weight shifts or to regain equilibrium rather than the traditional rhythmic arm swinging. As you become more accustomed to the specific trail, your ability and confidence to anticipate and negotiate these hazards will improve and your pace can increase.

SAFETY TIP

Good trail runners are always courteous and accept complete responsibility for their behavior. Your sudden appearance has the potential to surprise or frighten slow-moving hikers. Simply slow down a bit and communicate any additional runners behind you. On multi-use trails, regulations and etiquette state that mountain bikers must yield to all other trail users. However, consider letting mountain bikes pass by; it is often easier for you to step off the trail for a moment without losing too much momentum. Finally, as discussed earlier, all multi-use trail users yield to horses.

Endurance Hiking

In endurance hiking, or speed hiking, backpackers often carry ultralight packs, even chopping the handles off toothbrushes to save that 1/2 ounce (14 grams). In day hiking, you'll often see these folks moving at a fast pace or slow jog for hours. The goal is to gain as much distance as possible. Some people will, for example, try to hit more than one summit in a day, or make 100 miles (161 kilometers) in 24 hours.

Orienteering, Geocaching, and Letter Boxing

Orienteering is an old sport that uses a topographic map and magnetic compass to travel over the landscape, challenging both map-reading and compass skills. Some orienteering events are based on competitions wherein teams travel from point to point, collecting information that helps them to shoot their next bearing and proceed to the finish line. Other events are low key and emphasize team building and enjoyment of the outdoor experience.

Whichever way you decide to pursue orienteering, it is sure to sharpen your map and compass skills. Map and compass navigation in remote areas is an invaluable outdoor skill to possess and demands great attention to master. Despite the ever-improving GPS, outdoor enthusiasts and leaders should know the essentials of topographic map and magnetic compass navigation. Batteries and satellites sometimes burn out!

Geocaching has been gaining popularity over the past decade. Instead of using a map and compass, geocaching uses GPS to gather coordinates or way points. Participating in a cache hunt is a great way to enjoy the outdoors as well as learn about the capabilities of a GPS. Caches are established by individuals or groups all over the world and the locations are shared via various Internet sites. Cache seekers take the coordinates or way points and find the location.

CONSUMER TIP

As discussed in earlier chapters, GPS is an electronic, handheld device used to gain longitude and latitude points via satellite. Devices vary greatly in complexity (and price, from about $100 to $1,000), but even the most basic models will work for geocaching.

It sounds easy; however, knowing where an item is located based on the coordinates is only one aspect of this challenge. Many geocachers hide items under rocks, in tree holes, and so on to make the hunt more challenging.

A variety of items can be found inside geocaching boxes or buckets. The basic rules are, if you take something from the box, you also leave something. Geocaching etiquette requires that only appropriate and lawful items be left in a cache. Food is always a bad idea; most animals have a far greater sense of smell than humans and will chew through or destroy the cache. Also, there is almost always a notebook to write down comments, and the same rule applies—if you take information, you should give some back by writing in the log book.

Although the words *letterboxing* and *geocaching* are being used synonymously by many U.S. Forest Service districts and state park agencies, letterboxing is actually an older relative to the new geocaching phenomenon. With letterboxing, you receive a clue that contains both a description of the site and, like general orienteering, map and compass bearings to follow from given points. These clues are often based on a particular theme that may bear natural or cultural significance to the area, or may not.

Inside the letterbox is a notebook wherein you can stamp your insignia of choice. Some participants use one stamp that bears personal significance or represents a group to which they belong. For example, if you are a bird watcher, you might have a stamp that represents your favorite bird. Both handmade and commercial stamps are considered acceptable.

All three of these activities oblige us to once again remind you to consider the seven Leave No Trace principles, especially the principle of camping and traveling on durable surfaces. Seeking and locating caches demands the same vigilance and respect for the land. Both parties have an obligation to communicate problems with the location of a cache and seek to relocate it to a more appropriate spot to minimize human impact on the surrounding landscape. Currently, U.S. land management agencies are developing a policy for this outdoor adventure sport with a concern for excessive human effects on resources. If participants worldwide can embrace the principles of Leave No Trace and refrain from placing caches in illegal or inappropriate areas (federally designated wilderness, for example), there is no reason why this outdoor pursuit cannot be looked upon as a positive activity.

CONSUMER TIP

Are you interested in getting a great birding guide? The National Audubon Society's *The Sibley Guide to Birds* (Knopf, 2000) is a great pick and widely acclaimed.

Bird Watching and Other Nature Hikes

Birding has been one of the most popular outdoor recreation activities in the United States for nearly a century. Over 50 million U.S. citizens spend millions of dollars annually on all things bird related. This includes binoculars, field guides, hiking boots, bird feed and feeders, bird houses and nesting boxes, memberships to local and national clubs, contributions to various conservation groups, and traveling great distances across the country or internationally. Many birders have a lifelong passion for observing every bird in their chosen field guide. The beauty is that birds live outside, which usually requires you to get out of the car and take a hike to see them.

Hundreds of guidebooks and organizations are available that can help you begin to explore the world of birding. If you are taking off on your own, you might want to begin to learn the characteristics of a particular bird of interest. What type of habitat does it prefer? What is its favorite food source, and when does it feed? For example, scores

To get started with birding, you'll want some binoculars and a bird guide.

of heavy insect feeders will often be available at dusk. This information might help you to choose a hike location. Do you know the bird's call so that you can further locate it? Can you recognize its plumage?

Familiarity with nesting habits and tendencies is also important. Do they build nests in branches, or perhaps on the ground? Many birds can be very aggressive, flying close to your head or even pulling your hair, when it comes to defending their nesting areas. Birds might also have group nesting areas. Herons, for example, nest in groups, and these giant and extraordinary birds create quite a sight when they return to their nesting grounds each spring to hatch and raise their fledglings.

Most hikers enjoy observing local wildlife when hiking. However, it is important for both you and the animals to stay a safe distance apart.

Many hiking guides and maps include information on the local wildlife you may encounter, as well as important safety advice on how best to observe these animals. As discussed in chapter 5, avoid close interactions and do not feed wild animals. Over time, wildlife that has a regular source of human food becomes habituated and more aggressive towards hikers. Unfortunately, this unnatural behavior often results in the animal being captured or killed by land managers. Viewing wildlife from a distance reduces stress on the animal and allows for a more natural encounter. Two small turtles in a mating ritual, a mother deer nuzzling her fawn, or a shy coyote pouncing on field mice in an open meadow are experiences that can become indelibly etched in your hiking memories.

Historic Hikes and Walks

Numerous historic hiking trails can be found throughout North America and around the world. One example is the famed 33-mile (53-kilometer) Chilkoot Trail, which traverses the U.S.–Canadian border from Alaska to the Yukon Territory. The Chilkoot Trail was the gateway to the Yukon for prospectors during the Klondike Gold Rush. It is cooperatively managed by Parks Canada and the NPS.

Battlefields are another place where you might take a historical walk. Some battlefields allow you to trace the movement of troops during battle. Gettysburg and Richmond National Battlefield Park are two such sites. At many of these historic sites, there are often opportunities for guided walking tours.

A few historic hikes are quite extensive. The John Muir Trail, for example, is 210 miles (338 kilometers) long and celebrates the author and wilderness preservationist's love of the Sierra Nevada Mountains of California. In contrast, the Trail of Tears acknowledges a painful and somber event in American history: the relocation and death of thousands of Native Americans.

Long-Distance Hiking

As you become more enthusiastic about day hiking, you may gravitate toward overnight backpacking. In time, you will increase the number of days and nights away from home, perhaps up to several weeks. Having accomplished all this,

Long-distance hiking is one of many additional hiking adventures.

you then might consider taking several months to do a long-distance trail. Please refer to the next chapters for more information on planning a long-distance hiking trip and chapter 1 for specific places to hike.

Of course, many more people day hike on long-distance trails than through hike. Day hiking is not only an excellent way to get more physically and mentally in tune for hikes that happen over longer time spans, it is also a way to get experience on these trails. There is something out there called *trail magic*, and you don't have to be a through-hiker to participate in creating it. Hop on a long-distance trail and see what it's all about!

Hiking Environments and Seasons

Not only are there a great variety of hiking adventures, there are also many types of terrain to explore. Forests, alpine areas, deserts, prairies, and coastlines are the predominant environments to experience while hiking or backpacking. Within each of these, one has the opportunity to use designated trails and unimproved roads—or if you possess the navigation and Leave No Trace skills, to travel off-trail. See chapters 4 and 6 for more information on hiking environments.

Each kind of environment has its optimal seasons for hiking. Because hiking in the winter involves specialized travel techniques, this book will concentrate on hiking in the spring, summer, and fall. In general, summer is thought to be the optimal season for hiking: People find more time for hiking and backpacking because of vacations; the days are longer; the temperatures are comfortable; and it is the best time to enjoy blooming flowers, active wildlife, and green vegetation. The worst things that can happen in the summer include being caught in a thunderstorm (lightning can be deadly), getting lost, or sustaining an injury. These risks are also present in the spring and fall, but during those seasons, hikers may also have to contend with colder temperatures and even snow.

The seasons are indicated by the following symbols:

 summer

spring

fall

 **Forests**

For many, forests are the most accessible terrain for hiking. Woodlands vary according to location; each continent holds both coniferous and deciduous forests. Many maps in more populated regions will show a myriad of hiking trails and unimproved roads. Well-designed and -constructed hiking trails have a 6 to 10 percent grade. In contrast, you may find that older trails or social trails are far steeper. Another characteristic of well-designed trails is the use of switchbacks. Switchbacks zigzag up a mountain side or ridge. They are longer, but they reduce erosion and help hikers conserve energy. Hiking trails usually have a well-defined tread and are maintained, or cleared of obstacles like boulders and downed trees. If a trail is not maintained, expect to climb over (and sometimes crawl under) downed trees and to maneuver around other obstacles, like washed-out sections, and through thick brush. On all trails except those that have been paved, expect to walk over loose rocks, tree roots, and trail structures like water bars, which divert water off the trail to prevent erosion.

Some forests have a history of being logged or mined; thus there are places where hikers will walk on dirt or unimproved roads for some part of their journey. Some of these roads are no longer used and have become overgrown, looking like single walking paths. For some, it's fun to look for historical clues—rusted mining equipment or 100-year-old stumps from a logging operation. Other forest roads are still open to automobiles. A good map and guidebook will let you know whether a four-wheel drive vehicle is needed for access. It's almost always best to walk on the side of the road where you will be facing traffic, but use your judgment on blind curves.

Summer is the most popular season to explore forests, but don't discount fall and spring. In most areas, forests are great escapes from the heat of urban environments. To be prepared to hike or backpack in the summer, you need to avoid being on exposed ridges and peaks in thunderstorms, and you need to carry water and purification equipment to stay hydrated, food for energy, a warm layer, rain gear, a map and compass to stay oriented, and a first aid kit for emergencies. See chapter 3 for a complete list of essentials.

In the spring and fall, be prepared for colder temperatures and extreme changes in the weather. Hikers and backpackers must be prepared for precipitation in the form of rain, snow, or any combination that can turn the trail into a stream. Wear waterproof boots and gaiters and walk on the wet trails instead of creating new trails in the name of keeping your feet dry. Spring weather can deliver an array of challenges, so hikers need to be prepared for sun, rain, and snow in all extremes. Choose your clothing and equipment with the extremes in mind. Fall weather is more predictable.

An inviting trail in the Sitka National Forest of Alaska.

Often, it is drier than in spring, but it can also be cold and produce snowstorms that turn an easy day into a survival scenario. Again, choose your clothing and equipment with the worst-case scenario in mind. Once you're prepared for the weather, enjoy the fall. The changing color of the trees will leave a lasting impression, and the cool, crisp air is refreshing and perfect for hiking.

Desert Hiking

There is a reason that the desert environment is depicted in movies and on television as an inhospitable place. Water is scarce, distances are immense, and failure to plan and prepare well can be disastrous. However, these same obstacles can provide the hiker who possesses good judgment and experience with wonderful opportunities for solitude, complete silence, diverse terrain, and endless vistas. Previous chapters have addressed many universal safety precautions for hiking. Here are a few that are specific to desert travel.

Do not deviate from your route. In a desert environment, especially one with box canyons and small hillsides that do not show up on a topographic map, it is very easy to become lost or confused. If traveling off-trail, you need a good map, compass, and GPS skills.

Prepare very seriously for the weather. It is unrealistic to attempt summer hiking in low-elevation deserts, unless perhaps you are guaranteed shaded canyons and year-round water sources. Otherwise, it is just too hot. For example, Death Valley National Park in California has recorded a summertime air temperature of 134 degrees Fahrenheit (57 degrees Celsius) with a ground temperature reading of 201 degrees Fahrenheit (94 degrees Celsius)—a good place to fry eggs, but not to hike!

Furthermore, desert temperatures can vary wildly in the fall, winter, and spring. In the southwestern United States it is common to experience daytime conditions of 80 degrees Fahrenheit (27 degrees Celsius) in the months of December and January, but as the sun descends it can bring fierce winds that drop the air temperature below freezing. Windproof clothing is essential for desert travel. Many seasoned desert travelers often comment that the strong winds of the Himalayas are nothing compared with the winds generated in the Southwestern deserts of the United States

Be alert to flash floods, one of the most dangerous and awesome sights in the desert. Recognize if your hiking route follows a wash, arroyo, or natural drainage course. These low-lying, dry riverbeds or creek beds are swept clean by occasional torrential floods. A rainstorm that is miles away from where you are hiking can send a wall of mud, rocks, and water roaring like a freight train down your hiking path with little to no warning. In the event you are confronted with stormy weather, seek high ground and wait the storm out.

Don't overdo it. Desert terrain varies from durable, water-polished rock to soft sand. If you have ever walked a mile in soft sand, then you know the physical exertion as well as the toll it takes on your feet and legs. In addition, dry air is synonymous with the desert. Those from more humid environments often fail to realize how quickly they become dehydrated since they sweat very little. An average-sized person needs to consume a gallon (4 liters) of water per day along with quick-energy snacks and other food items. There's an old saying, "The best canteen is your stomach." Too many inexperienced desert travelers have been found facedown in the sand still clutching a half-filled water bottle because they were trying to ration their intake. Think like a camel and consume as much water as you can the night before your desert hike and once more at the trailhead. This ensures that you are well hydrated to start your hike, and the gallon in your pack should be more than enough for a full day on the trail. When spending multiple days hiking in the desert, it is a good idea to add powdered electrolyte solutions to drinking water.

Some other considerations include wearing loose-fitting, light-colored cloth-ing that offers protection from the sun. Long-sleeve shirts with high collars and wide-brimmed hats will protect your head, neck, and arms from the sun and complement the copious amounts of sunscreen you are continually applying. Sturdy hiking boots protect your feet and ankles against varying terrain, loose rock, and cactus spines. Lastly, in your first aid kit you should have a comb and

Always be prepared when hiking in the desert; the weather can change quickly.

tweezers. Cactus fragments inevitably leap onto unprotected legs or arms, and simply slipping the comb between the skin and spines allow you to flick the spines away. The tweezers are for the spines that don't easily brush off.

Edward Abbey, a prolific writer and advocate for desert protection, has said, "What draws us into the desert is the search for something intimate in the remote" (Abbey, 1973). Rock, sand, canyons, peaks, flats, cacti, oases, and enduring silence—the desert is a landscape reduced to its essence. Within this essence there is an intimate beauty that can only be discovered by those willing to spend a day on a desert trail, sliding their hand over polished stone, studying the intricacies of a blooming cactus, or following the footprints of a coyote.

Mountaineering

More than other types of hiking, many view mountaineering as trophy seeking. You may hear climbers boasting of the peaks they have bagged as though they have captured the ascent and carried the mountaintop home with them.

Beware, mountains are fierce competitors and their summits are rarely cheated. *Mountaineering: The Freedom of the Hills* (Graydon & Hanson, 1997) is considered one of the most instructive texts on mountaineering. It states, "Distant view of mountains may speak of adventure, but they seldom more than hint at the joys and hardships that await. If you want to climb mountains, be prepared for the totality of nature" (p. 15).

In previous chapters, elevation gain has been discussed as a challenge that alters the hiker's speed, energy, and endurance. In mountaineering, elevation gain also leads to high altitude. Altitude can pose a variety of challenges and risks, including shortness of breath at best, and altitude sickness at worst. Altitude sickness, or acute mountain sickness (AMS), is caused by climbing faster than the body can acclimate to the changes around it. Because of reduced atmospheric pressure at high altitudes, the body is unable to fully use oxygen in the air and begins to feel the effects of oxygen deprivation. If you are hiking to higher altitudes and start to feel poorly, stop! Symptoms such as headache, nausea, and fatigue are all related to AMS and may start as early as 8,000 feet (2,438 meters) above sea level, which is well below most of the peaks in the Rocky Mountains. Slowing down, spending the night, or moving to a lower elevation will help you to acclimate. If more severe symptoms occur, such as increased respiratory and cardiac rates or fluid in the lungs, immediate emergency medical assistance is needed. Descend the mountain as soon as possible.

Traveling on snow and ice requires special knowledge that should be taught by an instructor trained in mountaineering skills.

Mountaineering entails not only hiking, but often specialized equipment and climbing skills as well. In addition to consulting a text such as *The Freedom of the Hills,* those who plan to partake in adventures wherein climbing within a safety system is warranted are advised to gain instruction along with practicing these skills before their first ascent. These skills are best learned with professional instructors rather than by reading or trial and error.

Other knowledge that must be learned for mountaineering is how to travel on snow and ice. This includes not only learning

It's not the mountain we conquer, but ourselves.

Sir Edmund Hillary

about staying warm and dry in intense, exposed conditions, but also about using specialized equipment, such as crampons for your boots to keep you from slipping on ice and an ice axe to arrest your fall should you find yourself sliding uncontrollably down a snowy, icy slope. Learning how to recognize avalanche danger, knowing how to minimize the risk of being caught in an avalanche, and knowing proper rescue technique should you or one of your companions be caught in an avalanche is essential when hiking in mountain environments. Should you ever venture onto a glacier, there are additional skills that you will need in order to remain safe. A primary risk in glacier travel is falling into a crevasse, a deep fissure in the glacier. Learning to travel in rope teams and learning vertical rescue technique is essential to minimizing the risk of injury or death due to a mishap when traveling on glaciers.

Finally, the high alpine environment requires special Leave No Trace skills. These cold, rugged landscapes seem almost impermeable, and you have to marvel at the toughness of the plants and animals that inhabit these areas. However, alpine areas are really quite fragile, in that vegetation takes far longer to recover once damaged because of the short growing season. If hiking off-trail, routes on bare rock or snow are the most resilient. If this is not possible, groups should spread far apart to minimize heavy foot impact over meadows or plants.

As in wet areas in more temperate regions, it is better to cross through muddy areas (often caused by snowmelt) than to skirt them, keeping impact to a minimum. Do not randomly search for dry ground. In the alpine environments, dry areas are often covered by colonies of lichen. Many of these colonies have existed for hundreds of years, and they do not have root systems. Hence, trampling easily flakes them off rocks and damages their ability to regenerate

CONSUMER TIP

A number of reputable companies offer training in mountaineering skills. A few of these include the following:

- American Alpine Institute in Bellingham, Washington
- Alaska Mountain Guides and Climbing School in Haines, Alaska
- National Outdoor Leadership School (NOLS) in Lander, Wyoming
- Exum Mountain Guides in Moose, Wyoming, near Grand Teton National Park
- Colorado Mountain School based in Estes Park, Colorado

(which may take upward of 30 years), and it also damages the loose coverings of soil to which they cling.

Humans have been climbing to mountaintops for centuries to elevate their spirit. You may do so as well, but take great care for your safety and that of the surrounding environment.

Hiking in Coastal Areas

If you're looking for a hiking experience that's opposite to deserts and mountains, hiking on the coast can be a good option, and you can prepare for it in the same manner as for hiking in a forest. Coastal hiking and backpacking trails will take you in and out of lush forests and often through remote beaches or on the edges of cliffs overlooking an ocean. Instead of cryptobiotic soil, you will see rich, dark soil teaming with vegetation. You will also find yourself walking through sand, which can be a challenge. With every step there is a lot of give, so it almost feels like you lose half a step with every step forward. The best thing to do in sand is to walk near the shoreline, if possible; compacted sand is easier to walk on than loose, dry sand.

The other unique feature of coastal hiking and backpacking is crossing beaches in accordance with the tide. Review the route before leaving, take a tide chart, and know how to read it. You may have to plan each day in order to make certain crossings when the tide is out, for there will be places that are impassable if the tide is in. It is also advisable to camp well above the tide line if you are camping on a beach. If in doubt, camp off the beach so that you're not drenched suddenly in the middle of the night.

Coastal hiking and backpacking offers the experience of working with the tides and witnessing how the land and sea interact. Sand and trails through lush forests can be very durable, so you don't have to worry about erasing 100 years of growth with one footstep. Falling asleep in a remote area listening to the sound of waves is an experience that every backpacker needs to have at least once.

A backpacker hikes the coastal hiking trail, a 37-mile (60-kilometer) trail along the shore of Lake Superior in Pukaskwa National Park, Ontario, Canada—the only wilderness national park in Ontario. The trail traverses a rugged landscape of the Canadian Shield and the northern boreal forest.

Additional Considerations for Day Hiking

Some additional considerations for day hiking include social challenges that can arise while on the trail, hiking with small children, and hiking with dogs. This section provides information that will help you plan hiking experiences that reinforce—rather than test the bonds of—friendship while on the trail. It provides information that will help you exhibit socially and environmentally responsible behavior when hiking with dogs. This section also provides helpful tips for hiking with children.

Social Challenges

Listen to the stories of others' first hiking and backpacking trips and you are sure to be regaled with stories of clashing expectations among group members. However, most hikers learn early that you need to find out what each group member's expectations are and then honor them.

Some hikers are in it for the physical challenge—how many minutes does it take to cover the trail? This, of course, is going to be difficult for those who are more interested in looking at that interesting fungus or identifying songbirds. Even the best of friends can reach their limits when these two conflicting ideals are tested on the trail. Revisit the reason for your hike with your partner or group and make sure you are on the same page before heading off.

Not everyone prefers hiking in pairs. What size group are you comfortable with? Make sure that everyone has the same hiking goal in mind, and decide how to set a comfortable pace for the group. If you're hiking in a group of three or more, establish a lead person (ideally the slowest hiker; see chapter 6) and a sweep person, who hikes in the back of the line, making sure that the group remains intact and that no one leaves anything behind after rest breaks. This is not only a nice safety feature; it also reinforces the social norms that have been set.

There are a few considerations when day hiking in a group. The most popular trails attract the most people, and group size may not be your only consideration. Before selecting your group size, check with the land management agency regarding size limits. Many areas establish group size limits for those staying overnight or longer, especially in federally designated wilderness areas. These areas may limit group size to 8 or 10. Even if there is not a regulation set for day hiking, you should consider how your group size will affect the experiences of other visitors. An easy solution for a large hiking group is to divide up into smaller groups that depart from the trailhead at intervals of 15 to 20 minutes. You can also agree that you will limit meeting up on the trail or establish a durable place to meet off the trail and out of the hearing of others.

Many people seek the outdoors for quietness and solitude. Although general conversation is usually seen as acceptable, yelling up and down the trail is inconsiderate and upsetting to other visitors. Walk in a manner that does not trample vegetation or widen the trail, and be conscientious of the way in which your group affects the trail side during rest breaks. If others approach who are hiking faster, step to the side and let them pass.

Hiking With Your Dog

Many of us love our dogs. Is your Fido ready for the trail? Is the trail ready for your Fido? Here are a few things to think about.

First, is your dog suited to the trail? We often think of our dogs as ready to ramble, despite the terrain. After all, isn't that what dogs used to do? Maybe, but that doesn't mean your dog is ready to go on your hiking trip. For a minute, think of your dog as a human. Is he fit or is he a couch potato? Does her body shape and size allow her to cover the intended terrain? Will he be able to control his body temperature well enough?

We'll refer to a couple of dogs as examples in this section. The first is Levi, a Labrador retriever. The second is Willie, a rat terrier mutt.

Dog Etiquette

If your dog is suited for the trail, you must follow the proper etiquette. Levi was a great hiking dog when she was young. Her pace matched an adult's step for

Before heading out on the trail with your dog, you need to determine if your dog is suited for the trail.

step, and she was fit and strong. She was well trained and always under voice control. However, she had a problem on the trail: She was not very excited to meet others, whether they were human or canine. She was the epitome of a guard dog—no one could approach her owners. Therefore, it was critical that she be leashed and under voice control at all times. This is important for your pooch, too, even if he is the friendly sort—he could run into a dog like Levi who is not so friendly.

Proper dog etiquette also includes cleaning up after them—dog poop is not part of the natural ecosystem—and having your dog stick to the trails so as not to trample the vegetation. And you might want to consider leaving the noisy ones at home. Willie is a good example of a dog that others do not appreciate in the woods—he screams whenever he sees other animals, especially rodents. Now he stays home and patrols the yard when his owners go on day hikes. Others will appreciate your efforts when you make sure that your dog is a good hiking companion.

Planning Considerations

If you have determined that your dog is ready to hike and you are prepared to be a responsible companion, it's imperative that you learn about the area in which you'll be hiking. Are dogs allowed in that area? For example, most national parks do not allow dogs at all (and a stiff fine can be imposed for ignoring this rule). However, national forests and other areas are often open to dogs. Some rules require pets be under voice control, and others require leashes shorter than 3 feet (1 meter)—which can prove quite challenging if you're hiking with a large dog.

You also need to think of the wildlife that you may encounter. There were several occasions when we needed to have a good handle on our dog because of bears, wild boars, and once even a bull on the trail! Alligators are also a concern in certain areas. One hiker who was talking with a park ranger at a state park in southern Georgia said, "Surely my 90-pound [41-kilogram] dog isn't going to be considered easy prey," to which the ranger responded in his polite, Southern drawl, "It's just the smell of them, ma'am." She took his advice and kept her dog away from the lake.

Gear for Dogs

Two essential items for dogs are a harness and a leash. The harness provides easy hookup and great control in excitable situations. Most important, though, are your dog's tags. If your dog takes off in an unfamiliar area, you will want to make sure that he can make it back home safely.

Many amazing pieces of gear are available for dogs these days. Some dogs have their own packs and carry their own food and water. If you choose to have your dog carry a pack, be aware that it puts more strain on the joints, and you should pack it lightly, in accordance with the dog's weight. Other items to consider are dog sweaters and fleece for warmth, as well as paw covers. Some paw covers are insulated for warmth, and others serve as protective mittens in terrain that may be damaging to the pads (such as heat or ice). If you are in an area where your dog may be swimming, there are life jackets, and if you are in an area where there is hunting, you should strongly consider attaching blaze orange gear to your dog's harness.

You can even buy collapsible food and water bowls and fancy little bowls with water bottle attachments; but reused plastic containers also work just fine. Finally, you might consider bringing along some healthy treats for your pooch. Dogs need to take in calories more frequently when hiking, just as you do.

Hiking With Children

Children change everything in life, and hiking is no exception. Even if you have not heard the recently coined term *nature-deficit disorder,* it should not be a surprise that children are spending less time outdoors now than in years past. Family hiking can be a big part of the solution.

Children love being outside, whether it's the backyard, local playground, or beach. Including age-appropriate hiking adventures can promote and influence a lifetime of outdoor appreciation.

Planning Considerations

No two hikes are the same. You may be out for a few hours with little complaint from the kids, slowly exploring new terrain and talking about the surrounding natural world. Or you may find yourselves trying multiple times in one day to get up a nearby trail, only to make it less than 100 feet (30 meters) before giving up and once more retreating to the playground. The best advice is to be flexible with your plans.

Think about your planned hike and the terrain, and imagine all of the hills or rocks being twice as big and the distance being twice as long. Or, if you have toddlers or preschoolers that are about one-quarter of your size, quadruple the size of hills and rocks and the distance. That helps to put things in perspective when choosing a route. Many parents have found that it takes at least twice as long to cover the same trail with children than it does without.

Finding a destination that has interesting views at

Taking children on a hike can be rewarding for the entire family as long you plan ahead and are flexible.

3 feet (91 centimeters) and below as well as 5 feet (152 centimeters) and above (the smaller ones often ride in a pack) is helpful. Also, just finding a trail with a destination (something really cool to look at or a field to picnic in or rocks to scramble on) meets the goal-oriented needs of preschoolers. "Are we there yet?" is a phrase that is found not only on car trips, but on hikes as well.

Children's Gear

You can find all kinds of cool things in the way of children's gear. Some of it is meant to be parent friendly and some kid friendly, but all of it deserves a test run if possible.

When outfitting a child, try to follow the same principles that you follow for yourself. Cotton is generally not trail friendly unless you are in the desert. Well-fitting boots or trail shoes with appropriate wicking socks are a must. Children also need weather gear like fleece and rainwear. Check their layers frequently for temperature control, and check for blisters on rest breaks. Kids do not necessarily say they are in pain if they believe it will jeopardize their ability to keep doing what they want to do.

Transport devices for little ones come in all shapes and sizes. A heavy-duty pack that stands on its own when removed (perhaps with its own diaper deck and storage bag) and a jogging stroller that is meant to cover all terrain can pretty much get young kids anywhere you want to trek. There are several ways to determine which items are best for you. For example, will you be going on short jaunts or longer journeys? Will the weight distribution be kind to your back? Is your child a squirmer or a climber—who will hence continually want to exit the pack? What is the weight of the carrier and how much weight will it carry? It may say it holds 40 pounds (18 kilograms), but do you really want to carry or push your 40-pound child in it?

Overall, pack plenty of snacks and drinks, and plan lots of time to stop and smell the sassafras. Your efforts will be rewarded when your child says things like, "Mama, the moon is getting bigger this week!", "Listen, I hear a coyote," or even simply, "Let's go outside!"

Conclusion

Are you thinking, "There are so many options, I don't know where to begin?" It is as easy, literally, as taking your first step. You have a lifetime of discoveries to make, and many of them may be as close as the local park. With all of the physical and mental health benefits you will gain from your treks, chances are good that you'll have more years to try more adventures. Happy hiking!

CHAPTER 8

Basics of Backcountry Camping

Now I see the secret of making the best persons. It is to grow in the open air, and to eat and sleep with the earth.

Walt Whitman

A group of novice backpackers prepared for what they thought would be the best summer trip of their life. After everyone weighed in on their preference for a destination and activity, the group decided to try a 4-day overnight camping trip in a location that one of the group members had scouted earlier that spring. They spent lots of time researching the perfect clothing and equipment and even planned extravagant trail meals. They felt confident that they had made the right choice as they drove to the trailhead and listened to the weather forecast for the weekend, which called for clear skies and temperatures in the 80s (27-32 degrees Celsius), perfect weather for a backpacking trip.

The trip went just fine until they started down the trail. They soon found a large population of water moccasins and ticks that were not apparent when the location was scouted in the spring. To make matters worse, the group was prevented from crossing the river along their intended route due to high water from rainfall that occurred a few days earlier. In the end, the group cut the trip short because their route was impassible and they were overrun by ticks and water moccasins. The group was in good spirits, though, and could not wait for the opportunity to try their backcountry skills again—but with better preparation for the intended camping and hiking area.

A variety of tips and techniques for backcountry camping, including the reasons why certain principles and practices are followed, are presented in this chapter. Judgment and decision making are inherent to the leadership of a backcountry experience. These qualities are developed first and foremost by knowing what questions need to be asked and in what order.

This chapter covers the basics of backcountry camping, including how to evaluate a potential campsite, set up camp, cook, sleep, and break camp. The purpose of this chapter is to learn to ask questions and to develop skills that will transfer to a variety of natural settings. Whether camping overnight using a tarp, tent, bivy sac, or natural shelter, your competence as a camper will enhance your overnight experience.

Many organizations have adopted Leave No Trace principles as best practices for minimizing human impact while camping in the natural environment. Many of the guidelines presented in this chapter are based on Leave No Trace principles (see figure 1.1 on pages 10-11).

Before Camping

A good camping experience begins with planning and preparation. The more information you obtain prior to your experience, the better the decisions you will be able to make on the trail. One important item that should be considered during planning and preparation is regulations.

Planning and Preparation

When preparing for an overnight camping experience, consider the following:

1. Be sure you have the proper clothing and equipment for the location, terrain, climate, type of trip, and group size.

2. Know how to use all of the equipment before venturing out. Check your stove, tent or tarp, flashlight, and other essential equipment to make sure they are functioning properly.

3. Locate the nearest medical facility, evacuation route, and pay phone in case of emergency. Cell phone reception is limited in many backcountry areas. Be aware of the nearest potential help, such as a ranger's house or station. This information can be obtained by calling a ranger or a visitor center or doing an Internet search.

4. Check the weather forecast for the area where you will be camping.

5. Find out if there are any other special considerations or limitations regarding the area. For example, have there been any recent reports of animal attacks, rabies outbreaks, Lyme disease, or various crimes? Again, this information can be obtained by calling a ranger or a visitor center or by doing an Internet search.

Regulations

Permits are required for many areas and must be obtained beforehand since backcountry usage sometimes is limited (see chapter 4). If you are planning to camp in federal- or state-managed areas, contact your local ranger station or visitor center for more information before the start of your trip. Be sure to find out about any special regulations related to the area where you will be hiking and camping. Some regulations may vary seasonally or with environmental conditions. For example, fires often are prohibited in certain areas during dry or drought conditions and in other areas they may not be allowed at all; you might be required to store food in bear-proof containers in some areas; and it is illegal in many areas to camp close to the shoreline of lakes since erosion is an ongoing problem. Time spent on preparation is time well spent because it can enhance the experience greatly.

Selecting a Campsite

After arriving at the trailhead, we turn our attention to selecting an adequate campsite. When considering where to camp, ask key questions about the site. In essence, you should become a landscape detective looking for clues that will help you evaluate a potential campsite. For example, you should not locate your campsite in an obvious avalanche chute, which may be indicated by an absence of vegetation and vertical scarring on the slope above the site. Selecting an appropriate location takes time. Be sure to stop early enough in the day before everyone in the group becomes too exhausted or darkness inhibits your ability to scout the area. Tired campers usually place personal needs higher than environmentally sound campsite selection. Allow time and energy to find a proper site, and consider the following.

Site Safety

You should consider several factors when evaluating the safety of a potential campsite. These factors include storms, rocks, trees, floods, animals, and plants.

Storms

It is never a good idea to be the highest object in an area since lightning and thunderstorms pose potential threats. Camping on top of an exposed ridge, open flat, grassy bald, or heath bald (i.e., an exposed area dominated by shrubby plants such as azaleas, mountain laurel, rhododendron, and blueberries) can enhance the threat posed by bad weather. Look for lightning scars on nearby trees. Lightning that strikes trees often runs down the tree and through some of the roots. This provides another reason for not camping on roots. If a thunderstorm does come up, use the flash–bang method to calculate the distance and direction of the storm in relation to your present location. (See chapter 5 for a detailed description of this method.)

Rocks

You should not camp at the base of cliffs due to the danger of falling rocks. Physical and chemical weathering of the cliff face loosens rocks, producing frequent rock falls. Weathering is enhanced in areas that are subject to freeze–thaw action on a regular basis. Freeze–thaw action occurs when water expands in rock cracks as it freezes, thereby loosening and dislodging the rocks.

Trees

Closed canopies can act as windbreaks, provide some protection from precipitation, and help to hold in some heat. Open canopies allow more air circulation and more heat to escape.

The trees at a potential site may or may not be adequate for setting up a tarp. Be sure to check the trees before tying off to them. Dead trees, commonly called snags or widow makers, should not be used as anchors (see figure 8.1). The weight of the tarp in combination with strong winds could uproot the tree. The likelihood of this is increased when camping in areas with shallow soils, such as coniferous forests. Do not set up your tarp or tent near or beneath widow-maker trees and limbs.

Floods

Good campsites have relatively flat sleeping sites, but the surrounding topography should drain away from the tent or tarp. It is important to note where surface water would flow in case of a storm. Look for visual evidence, such as bent vegetation pointing downslope, to ascertain the most likely channels where water will flow.

You also should consider whether the area would be prone to flash flooding should you get caught in a major storm. Water levels can rise very quickly in

Figure 8.1 Dead snag. These types of trees should not be used as anchors, and you should not set up your tarp or tent near or beneath them.

narrow gorges and canyons with steep walls and little floodplain, and flash flooding can occur so quickly that campers may be swept away without even exiting their tents. It does not have to be raining in the immediate area for flash flooding to occur where you are camping; this kind of flooding depends more on precipitation and the topography upstream. Locate your site above the floodplain. Small floodplains can be identified by the presence of bent vegetation and debris trapped in trees and bushes, indicating high water levels in the area. High-water lines are often discolored on canyon walls, beaches, or rock faces. Be aware that glacier-fed rivers will rise due to daily ice melt. In all cases, be sure to camp above the high-water line of rivers, streams, and ocean tides.

The type of soil or lack of soil must also be considered. For example, camping close to the base of a steep slope increases the likelihood of getting wet should bad weather occur because steeper slopes usually favor more surface runoff. There have been cases of campers drowning in deserts because they located their campsites in dry streambeds and a heavy rain occurred in the evening. A layer of soil called caliche inhibits infiltration and increases surface runoff in deserts.

Animals

Avoid choosing a campsite that might negatively impact wildlife in the area. Survey the immediate surroundings. Look for scat (feces) or any other type of animal signs, such as gnawings, scratchings, rubbings, dams, nests, burrows, prints, hair, fur, animal trails, or gnarled limbs in the trees. These signs suggest that animals frequent the area.

Look for evidence of snake or rodent holes. Be aware that cold-blooded organisms such as snakes warm and cool themselves by lying on rocks or under vegetation depending on the time of day.

Uprooted or hollow, downed trees provide potential den sites for animals, and uprooted areas, or windthrows, can be home to multiple species. Animal trails are small but well-worn pathways usually leading to food or water. Camping in these areas can disrupt patterns of animal movement and may interfere with an animal's path.

Camping in areas frequented by wildlife can disrupt wildlife behavioral patterns and consequently negatively impact the welfare of those animals. Camping in an animal's vicinity may also place you at risk of having a negative encounter with it. These areas should be avoided when choosing a campsite. Refer to chapter 5 for further safety considerations related to wildlife.

Insects

Be aware that camping close to bodies of water can enhance the chances of problems with mosquitoes and other insects that breed there. Depending on the part of the world you are in, this may increase the possibility of contracting mosquito-borne illnesses, such as malaria and some forms of encephalitis.

Plants

Appropriate footwear and leg wear will help you avoid developing rashes or other skin irritations from plants such as poison ivy, poison oak, poison sumac, and stinging nettles. See chapter 5 for photos of these plants. The sap from jewelweed, or touch-me-not (see figure 8.2), can be used on these rashes to soothe the itch if no other remedy is available. When camping in desert areas, always wear appropriate footwear to avoid unpleasant encounters with various cacti.

Types of Campsites

The type of campsite that you select will depend on the type of trip you are taking and the type of area in which you are camping. The three basic types of campsites are established or high-impact sites, medium-impact sites, and pristine or low-impact sites.

Established Sites

Established or high-impact sites usually are designated by a land management agency or have received heavy use. These sites often have established fire rings, tent pads, food protection systems, and other amenities that help to

Figure 8.2 Jewelweed, also known as touch-me-not, can be used to soothe rashes.

An established camping site often has amenities such as picnic tables, tent pads, fire rings, and established trails.

concentrate the camper's impact on the environment. Use of established sites is often required in certain backcountry areas. Focusing impact in several readily accessible areas helps to protect more pristine areas.

Medium-Impact Sites

Medium-impact sites have been slightly used and show signs of impact but have not become established. Usually there is trampled vegetation, possible fire remnants, and other indications of use. With further use, these sites will become established, thus increasing the impact of humans in the area. Medium-impact sites should be avoided; when possible, consider taking a few minutes to help camouflage such sites so that others are not attracted to them.

Pristine Sites

Pristine or low-impact sites are those that show little or no sign of human use. A pristine site can be very rewarding for the backcountry camper because of its remoteness, which offers a greater sense of solitude and adventure. Use of pristine sites requires an increased level of competence in following Leave No Trace principles.

There are no words that can tell of the hidden spirit of the wilderness, that can reveal its mystery, its melancholy, and its charm.

Theodore Roosevelt

Ultimately, you make the choice each night where to sleep based on the purpose of your trip and the area. Do not camp in a site for more than 2 days unless it is an established site. Allow the process of ecological succession to help restore the campsite. Many plants are resilient and can recover in a relatively short period of time.

Additional Considerations

The level of impact in established, medium-impact, and pristine areas affects everything from the resources available to methods of waste disposal. Three additional factors should be considered before choosing a site: wood, water, and waste.

Wood

If you plan to cook on a fire, sufficient wood must be available to start and maintain the fire, so you need to consider whether there is an adequate supply of dead and downed wood to be burned. The areas around high-impact sites often are picked over, although you sometimes can buy wood at local kiosks or entrance stations. Wood is usually much more plentiful in low-impact sites.

Water

Be sure to check your maps before arriving at your destination site to make sure that the area has sufficient water sources for cooking and drinking. Also, check the maps to see what is upstream from the site. Established sites often have water available from spigots or pumps. A rule of thumb for pristine sites is to try to camp at least 200 feet (61 meters) from water sources, which prevents water from being polluted by dishwater, urine, or soil eroded from the riverbanks or stream banks. Do not use stagnant water for drinking water; stagnant water often has high bacteria counts and much decomposition. Another good rule of thumb is to move upstream and far away from shores to obtain water.

Waste

Two basic strategies are used to control pollution: concentrate and contain, and dilute and disperse. These strategies are important in campsite selection. Camping in pristine areas often favors diluting and dispersing substances, whereas high-impact areas favor concentrating and containing environmental impact.

The same two strategies can be applied to individual activities. For example, after brushing your teeth, you may spit into a cathole (see page 194) and cover it up (concentrate and contain) or spew it over a much larger area (dilute and disperse). Concentrating and containing attempts to minimize the space impacted by waste by confining it to a limited area. Diluting and dispersing is rooted in the belief that materials will degrade faster if they are broken down and spread out over a larger area. This maximizes the surface area for microorganisms and sunlight to break down the substances.

Off the Trail and Out of Sight

The campsite should be located well off the trail so that campers are not seen or heard. The goal is to prevent both noise and visual pollution. The visual impact of a brightly colored tent or tarp against a beautiful vista in a remote area is jarring, so choose colors wisely. Be quiet when camping in order to respect other campers and to avoid attracting attention.

If camping close to a lake, you may also want to consider how popular the water source is for recreating. Camping near the shoreline may decrease the aesthetic beauty of the area for others who are visiting and may limit your privacy. The best campsites are secluded.

Surface

The ground cover must be able to withstand the impact of the group. Durable surfaces, such as a large rock, gravel, sand, or coarse soil, are good for camping. Inspect groundcover to see what types of plants would be disturbed. When possible, confine activities to areas where there is little or no vegetation cover and try not to create new trails to and from areas surrounding the camp. Soil compaction increases runoff and creates root pressure problems for plants, leading to diminished cover. In high-impact areas, this process mimics desertification on a small scale.

Elevation and Latitude

The elevation of the area can play a role in both temperature and precipitation. Ordinarily, the temperature drops approximately 3 to 6 degrees Fahrenheit (2-3 degrees Celsius) for every 1,000 feet (305 meters) of elevation gained, depending on whether the air is dry or humid. This is known as the adiabatic lapse rate. Humid air resists temperature change because of the high specific heat of water, whereas dry air changes temperature faster. Due to the adiabatic lapse rate, camping at higher elevations usually means cooler nights. Mountain topography, however, sometimes exhibits a phenomenon known as thermal inversion in which colder air flows downslope at night and is trapped by a layer of warmer air above. Thermal inversions often show themselves as fog pockets since the moisture contained within condenses as it cools. This reversal of what you would ordinarily experience with respect to temperature and elevation means that you may be warmer camping a little higher on the mountain.

Another consideration is the side of the mountain on which you are camping. As air is forced up and over a mountain or range, it cools and the moisture within it condenses. This so-called orographic effect increases the chances of getting wet on the windward side of the mountain whereas the chances decrease when camping on the leeward side. Which side is the windward side? Between 30 and 60 degrees latitude, the predominant wind direction is west to east, making the west side more susceptible to precipitation. An extreme example of this effect is Mount Waialeale on the Hawaiian island of Kauai. The windward slope averages 486 inches (1,234 centimeters) of rainfall per year, while the leeward side, also called the rain shadow, receives only 20 inches (51 centimeters) of rain annually.

Considerations When Selecting a Campsite

- ☐ Check all regulations before going to the area.
- ☐ Make sure the site is relatively safe with respect to storms, falling rocks, dead trees, floods, dangerous animals, people, and noxious plants.
- ☐ Determine the appropriate type of campsite based on the area, the size of your group, and the types of shelters you are using.
- ☐ Consider the distance from water, drainage, path, and the amount and type of resources available.
- ☐ Consider your impact both on the site and on other campers nearby as you locate your camp.
- ☐ Think about the topography when choosing a site.

Factors Involved in Setting Up Camp

Once you have selected an appropriate site, it is time to set up camp. Many of the strategies described here vary greatly depending on group size, location, and type of shelter. Consider the basic principles presented here and adapt them as necessary to create a safe and functional campsite. An enjoyable campsite is a safe campsite, and camp safety is driven by each camper's awareness of potential hazards. There are some basic things to remember, but the best advice is to always ask what-if questions. For example, "What if I let my 9-year-old daughter go to the river bank by herself at dusk?" "What if I refill the fuel bottle too close to the fire?" "What if the only place to attach my tarp is to a dead tree?" The questions go on and on, but a prudent camper is always asking "What if?" in anticipation of potential human and natural hazards.

Wind Direction

The dominant wind direction should be considered when deciding how to orient your camp. The environment offers clues as to dominant wind direction, so survey the area. Do you notice any flag trees? These trees develop when windblown ice crystals blast new limbs as they grow, leaving branches extending out primarily on the protected side. Flag trees point to the direction that the wind blows toward (see figure 8.3), and this information can be useful when selecting a campsite and orienting your tarp. For example, if you are camping on a hot summer night, you may want to orient the more open ends in the direction of the wind to increase air circulation. When camping in cooler weather, you may want to orient your tarp perpendicular to the dominant

Figure 8.3   Flag trees indicating dominant wind direction.

wind direction, using it as a break to provide shelter from the wind. Be aware that saddles and gaps between mountain peaks often experience strong winds due to the Venturi effect, which is characterized by air flowing faster through constricted areas.

The environment offers other clues about wind direction. In the winter, ice tends to accumulate on the windward side of objects, indicating the direction the wind is blowing. In high alpine areas, plants often grow by spreading out low to the ground. This effect, called Krumholtz, indicates consistently strong winds in the area. The patterns of growth behind obstacles such as boulders also often indicate dominant wind direction. Since the leeward sides of the boulders are protected, certain plants can establish themselves more easily. Identifying these clues can help you determine where and how to set up camp.

Campsite Layout

Wind direction is also important when determining where to set up the camp components, including sites for cooking, sleeping, food storage, and waste disposal (see figure 8.4). You do not want the wind blowing your scent out in

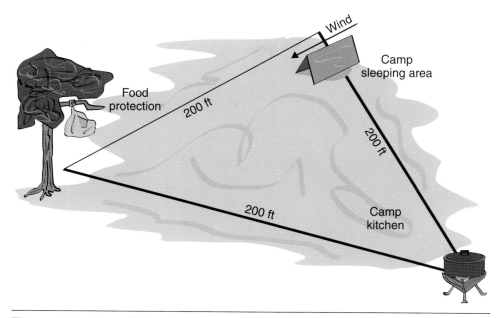

Figure 8.4 Campsite layout showing the suggested relationship between sleeping, cooking, and food storage locations.

front of you and advertising your presence to animals, especially bears, so it is important to locate cooking and food storage sites downwind of the sleeping site so that animals attracted to any food or food scraps will not be drawn to your tent. In bear country, campers sometimes bring clothes to wear only while cooking. Avoid using scented products, such as shampoo, toothpaste, and biodegradable soap, because they can also attract animals. Any scented products should be sealed tightly to prevent odors. When setting up camp in bear country, consider locating your sleeping, cooking, and food-protection areas in a triangle with approximately 200 feet (61 meters) between each location.

Shelters

You have already chosen an appropriate site based on the size of your group and the types of shelters you are using. Now, it is time to fine-tune your living quarters to create a comfortable and safe place to lay your head. If using tarps, consider the location of suitable trees that you can attach the tarps to or consider using an alternative method to pitch the tarps. Tarps usually are set up as an A-frame or a lean-to (see figure 8.5).

Freestanding tents can be pitched anywhere that is suitable for sleeping. Whether you are using a freestanding tent or tarp, consider its location relative to major traffic areas through camp so that you do not trip over guy lines when finding the bathroom or kitchen area.

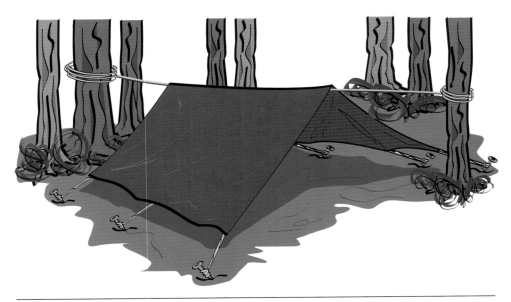

Figure 8.5 A typical A-frame tent set up using a ridgeline.

TECHNIQUE TIP

A useful exercise for tarp camping is to practice tying the requisite knots while blindfolded. This can prepare you for setting up in the dark when the flashlight isn't working properly—in other words, the worst-case scenario.

Minimizing Impact

Digging trenches around the tarp or tent is not recommended. Digging disrupts the ecology of the soil community and causes erosion by destroying some root systems while exposing others. Digging also disrupts mycorrizhae, a symbiotic relationship between fungi and plant roots. The fungi aid in water absorption while the roots provide stored food.

A good environmental practice is to try to leave every campsite a little better than you find it. This can involve anything from picking up trash to cleaning out a fire ring to helping restore an eroded bank. You can have a big effect on the vegetation in the area where you are camping just by walking to and from your sleeping area, kitchen, bathroom, and water source, so in pristine sites, be sure to not use the same pathways so that you disperse your impact. Also, if you are considering staying at the site for more than one night, be sure that the surface on which you are camping can withstand the use of your group. For example, a group of six people who hope to camp in a site for 3 days will want to choose an area where they can camp on sand, gravel, dry grasses, or snow.

Water Sources

Precautions should be taken to protect all water resources at the campsite. The campsite should be located at least 200 feet (61 meters) away from rivers, lakes, and streams. When getting water, cross downstream from the water station to avoid contaminating water sources with soil, organic debris, and anything that feeds on organic material, such as microorganisms. Look for pathways to the water source that will minimize erosion. Switchbacks minimize erosion and should never be bypassed for the sake of a shorter route. Cutting switchbacks can cause minor erosion, forming small depressions (rills) that enlarge over time into gullies and, eventually, wash out the trail and add sediment to streams.

Consider water sources carefully. Cleaner water tends to be clear, cold, and running (CCR). Cold water can slow the growth of pathogens, or disease-causing microorganisms. Clear water means there is less organic debris and algae on which these organisms feed. Running water is oxygenated, which kills many anaerobic bacteria and pathogens. Streams tend to alternate between two zones: riffles and pools. Oxygenation occurs in riffles as the water tumbles over rocks, whereas there is more decomposition in pools. The CCR method reduces but does not eliminate the chance of getting sick. Therefore, you should purify your water by filtering, boiling, or treating it with chemicals. Iodine and chlorine often are used, but their effectiveness decreases with colder water. See chapter 3 for more on water treatment.

Look for animal droppings around the stream. This could indicate the presence of *Giardia lamblia,* the organism that causes giardiasis, a disease affecting the gastrointestinal system. Although giardia has a 1- to 3-week incubation period, this protozoan can cause health problems for many months and even years after the trip is over. Parasites called entamoebas can cause diarrhea, nausea, and vomiting. In some cases, campers can become dehydrated due to

SAFETY TIP

Check the color of your urine to see if you are taking in enough water. Darker urine may indicate a fluid deficiency.

TRAIL TIP

In arid and semiarid areas, the presence of indicator plants, such as cotton-wood trees, can help you locate potential water sources from great distances. Cacti can be good sources of water in these regions since they store water. In emergency situations, your own urine can be filtered for water. This can be accomplished by heating the urine with sunlight and capturing the evaporating moisture by allowing it to condense on plastic and run into a larger catch basin. This technique is intended to extract or distill water from the urine.

losing so much fluid. Filtering or boiling water will help prevent illness from all of these organisms. Do not forget, however, to clean your water bottle frequently to eliminate mold, bacteria, and other pathogens.

Fires

If you are building a fire at the campsite, consider the following guidelines. First, know whether fires are allowed in the area where you are traveling. Second, consider the availability of wood to burn, as discussed earlier in this chapter. Your goal is to burn all the wood and coals to ash, which means you only want to use small, dead branches found on the ground. Use fire rings when they are available or build a pit fire or mound fire or use a fire pan (see Fire Site Selection and Construction later in this chapter). When camping near a river or by the ocean, consider creating a small pit in the sand or gravel below the high-water line. After the fire is out, scatter the ashes and fill in the pit. When the next high water arrives, it will wash away any fire remains.

Bathroom Use

Various methods have been devised for disposal of urine and fecal waste, including dispersing it, burying it, and packing it out. All of these methods work, but the appropriate one depends on where you are camping. It is accepted practice to bury feces in a cathole dug 6 to 8 inches (15-20 centimeters) in depth at least 200 feet (61 meters) from water, camp, and trails. When traveling with larger groups or using established campsites, consider the potential overuse of the area. Many high-impact areas have a pit toilet or ask campers to use an alternative method to pack out their waste. Toilet paper should be packed out. Leaves, needles, and even snow can be used in place of toilet paper. If using leaves, however, know what leaves you are using. Many campers have reached for leaves in the dark only later to find that they used poison ivy. Looking for a soft leaf? It's hard to beat mullein, a plant with large, velvety leaves. The only real way to prevent an impact on the environment, though, is to pack out feces. Used tampons should be placed in a container and packed out.

Urinating on rocks can have an adverse effect on lichens, mosses, and other vegetation growing on them. In areas with large rivers and certain soil types, urinating in the river is preferred over the soil. The amount of urine is inconsequential compared with the large volume of water, and the river can break down the waste. Rivers with higher flow (>2,000 cubic feet per second [>57 cubic meters per second]), more silt, and warmer temperatures will degrade waste faster.

Food Storage

Food should be stored safely and securely away from the tarp or tent each night. Consider the types of animals that are active in the area and then determine an appropriate method for protecting your food and food waste. There are various methods for protecting food, including hanging food from trees, using animal-proof canisters, using portable electric fencing, and setting up an alarm system using a perimeter rope with hanging pots and pans surrounding the food cache. When setting up camp, locate an area that is approximately 200 feet (61 meters) downwind from both the sleeping and cooking sites to store your food.

Some wilderness programs discourage hanging food. Instead, they recommend dealing with the ultimate cause of the problem, odors, by sealing all food items in pouches or double bagging them. The food is then stored well away from the sleep site as shown in the campsite layout diagram (figure 8.4 on page 191). In addition to food, some animals, such as porcupines, will also go after clothing, pack straps, or anything else that has a sweat residue in an attempt to obtain salt. Be sure to secure these items to prevent animals from chewing on them.

CONSUMER TIP

On a small scale, campsites face the same dilemmas as landfills. If you compact waste too tightly, it minimizes space, but it can also slow down the decomposition process. To maximize the decomposition rate, waste should be covered with soil and litter but not to the exclusion of sufficient oxygen. Air will help microorganisms break down the waste over time.

TRAIL TIP

As strange as it might sound, waxed dental floss is a very handy addition to an emergency kit. Apart from the obvious benefits to dental hygiene, it has multiple uses. It is very strong yet lightweight. It can be used for making loop snares and other animal-capture devices. The waxed version also burns easily and can help in getting a fire started.

Considerations When Setting Up Camp

☐ Take time to plan where to locate various camp components before beginning to set up, including orientation of the cook site, sleeping site, water sources, and food storage.

☐ Look for ways to reduce your impact on the environment as you determine how to dispose of waste, clean dishes, and use the bathroom.

☐ Take steps to ensure that water is suitable to drink by filtering it, boiling it, or treating it with chemicals such as iodine.

☐ Make sure that all food is stored properly.

Cooking

Once you have set up camp, attention often turns to preparing a meal. The methods used vary greatly depending on local regulations, the presence of firewood, and the goals for the group. For example, a group of 10 people who all want the opportunity to cook may wish to use a couple of backpacking stoves and cook in groups of 3 or 4. Consider the basic principles presented here and adapt them as necessary for cooking at your campsite.

Campsite Kitchen Layout

Preparing meals while camping can be a lot of fun when you are able to enjoy yourself. Allow enough time to safely prepare a tasty and nutritious meal. You want the cooking area located downwind from both the sleeping and food-protection locations. If cooking over a fire, prepare all of the ingredients far enough away from the fire so that dirt and ashes do not enter the food as people help keep the fire going. If cooking on a stove, locate an area away from the kitchen for refueling the stove. You also want to pick a spot that is

and a sense of adventure. Do not hesitate to try a new recipe when camping. Particularly if you are backpacking, don't forget to stoke your metabolic furnace between meals with healthy, high-energy snacks. Fat stores more energy per gram and releases it more slowly than either carbohydrate or protein. One gram of fat yields approximately 9.3 kilocalories of energy as opposed to 3.7 kilocalories per gram for carbohydrate and 3.1 kilocalories per gram for protein. Complex carbohydrates, such as pasta, burn more slowly than simple sugars, such as those found in fruits or candy bars. Here are a few suggestions to help you as you begin the art of cooking in the backcountry.

Considerations When Cooking in the Backcountry

☐ When backpacking, eat the heaviest food first in order to minimize weight as the days continue.

☐ Always wash your hands before and after handling food; not washing your hands is one of the quickest ways to transfer illness in the backcountry. Hand sanitizers can be used, although some studies have questioned their effectiveness.

☐ Keep the kitchen area and all cooking utensils and pots clean. Daily dunking of cooking and eating utensils in boiling water for 60 seconds or a bleach–water mixture (ratio of 1:10) can be helpful.

☐ Conserve fuel. Keep pots covered when trying to boil water, don't let stoves run without anything cooking on them, and create meals that can be cooked with one stove. Many stoves come with windscreens and heat reflectors, which can increase efficiency.

☐ Be aware that water takes longer to boil at higher altitudes. At 5,000 feet (1,524 meters), for example, it takes approximately twice as long to boil water than it does at sea level.

☐ Be careful when using knives. Always use a solid surface and cut away from yourself.

☐ Avoid burning food. On a stove or fire, stir food often, and try to keep the heat steady and low.

☐ Be sure to clean the dishes immediately after cooking to make it easier to remove the food residue. Heat a pot of water while you are eating so it is ready for cleaning when you are done with your meal.

Kitchen Cleanup

One of the arts of backcountry camping is to create tasty meals and enough food to satisfy everyone without wasting food. The ultimate goal in dealing with waste is to minimize your impact on the environment. When it comes time to clean the dishes, consider the following suggestions, but remember to make your own decisions based on what is best for the place where you are camping.

Considerations for Dish Cleanup

☐ Try to eat everything that you prepare, saving leftovers in sealed containers for future meals. Perhaps the leftover beans and rice from dinner could be tomorrow's lunch.

☐ If there is leftover food that you are not going to use, scrape it into a plastic bag and pack it out. It is a good idea to double bag or vacuum-seal the solid particles to prevent leakage and odors. Strain liquids to filter out solid particles. Scatter the liquid on the ground.

☐ Never throw food waste, including fish remains, into a river or stream. This causes bacterial populations to increase and oxygen levels in the water to decrease. It also can promote algal blooms and disease in aquatic life.

☐ Once your pots and personal cookware are free of all food particles, remove the food residue. Take your pots at least 200 feet (61 meters) away from any water source.

☐ You can use natural items like sand, snow, or leaves to clean dishes. Additionally, you might want to pack a small section of soft cloth to use as a dish cloth. Do not use abrasive items on nonstick cookware. Be wary of using scrubbies (scrubbers made of nylon net) since trapped food particles can support bacterial growth.

☐ Any water that has been used in the cleaning process can be scattered away from the camp as long as it is free of food particles.

As with any part of the camping experience, cooking is most enjoyable when you have planned ahead, make fun and nutritious meals, and allow enough time to cook. Even an expert chef cannot prepare a good meal without proper ingredients, appropriate kitchen utensils, and enough time. Have fun cooking and get others involved in the process.

Sleeping

After eating a good meal, it is time for bed. Sleeping in the backcountry can be a wonderful experience if you are prepared. Survey the scene before setting up for the evening. Avoid sleeping on rocks and roots that can create an uncomfortable night's sleep and are much easier to avoid before your shelter is pitched. Much of the details on site selection have already been covered in this chapter, so this section will focus on a few basics to remember when sleeping outdoors. While moving about camp, especially at night, appropriate footwear and leg wear can help you avoid getting a rash from poisonous plants such as poison ivy, poison sumac, and poison oak.

Preparing the Sleep Site

You should become familiar with your immediate surroundings during the day so you can safely move about in the dark. Use a groundsheet and a ground pad or mattress to increase your comfort and to decrease the loss of body heat into the ground. Make sure that the groundsheet does not extend out from under your shelter since moisture can run underneath it. When sleeping under a tarp, close the top of the sleeping bag tightly to prevent spiders, snakes, scorpions, or other animals from crawling into the bag. Also secure shoes and boots for the night to prevent these types of animals from crawling into them, and always inspect shoes and boots the next morning before putting them on.

When selecting a sleeping location, your head should be even with your feet or slightly higher. Remember to place a flashlight in a convenient place in your bag, under your pillow, or just outside your bag so you can get to it in a hurry should you need it. As discussed earlier, any food or scented items should be stored away from the sleep site and protected against animals. This location should be downwind of the sleeping area. Time spent choosing and preparing a good sleeping site is time well spent.

Preparing for Bed

Before going to sleep for the night, ensure that the entire campsite is secure. Imagine a storm coming through during the night. It is much easier to put things away now than to chase them in the middle of a rainstorm. Personal items should be secure inside your pack and your food and all other equipment should be secure in the event of strong winds, rain, snow, or any other unexpected condition.

Next, take care of yourself. Using the restroom before you go to sleep is a good habit to cultivate. Be sure to change into dry clothes and let your body recuperate from the day. Do a quick head and body check for ticks before crawling into your sleeping bag. If you get cold easily, you may want to do a few jumping jacks just before crawling into your sleeping bag to warm yourself by elevating your metabolism. After all, it is your body that produces the heat that you will need to stay warm during the night; the sleeping bag simply helps to hold it in. In cooler climates, be sure to wear a stocking hat or have one close by in case you get cold. If you are sleeping in a mummy bag, draw the hood up over your head and around your face to stay warm. Finally, if you have been active during the day, use this time to let your body air out, especially your feet. Oftentimes, it is only when backpackers sleep that they are not wearing their socks and boots. A little sanitizer can provide welcome relief from foot odor. Furthermore, going to bed with clean, dry feet can help to prevent the growth of fungi, such as athlete's foot.

First Night Out: Things That Go Bump in the Night

Campers often have trouble sleeping soundly during the first night out for a variety of reasons. The best outdoor mattress may not compare favorably with the well-worn mattress back home. Campers also are bombarded with many sounds and smells that they are unaccustomed to. Perhaps you have had the experience of waking up suddenly when animals come close to your tent or tarp. Your brain's reticular activation system constantly filters incoming stimuli while you sleep and wakes you up when something out of the ordinary occurs. Most campers acclimate to the sounds and smells associated with sleeping outdoors within a few nights, so give it some time. Following the guidelines here will enhance the chances of getting a good night's sleep.

Considerations for Backcountry Sleeping

- [ ] Check your sleeping site to ensure that it is relatively free of roots, rocks, poison ivy, poison oak, poison sumac, and snake holes.

- [ ] Store scented items such as toothpaste and shampoo with your food.

- [ ] Know the types of wildlife that frequent the area so that you can plan an appropriate place to sleep.

- [ ] Be sure to take care of essentials, using the bathroom and brushing your teeth, before crawling into bed.

- [ ] Check your body for ticks. Don't forget to feel behind your ears and over your scalp and check other areas that might be good hiding places.

- [ ] Check your shelter and personal attire to make sure that you will stay dry and warm or cool enough for the night.

Breaking Camp

After a good night's sleep, it is time to break camp and prepare to move to the next destination. The way in which you leave your camp makes a statement to the next people who use it and provides an opportunity to improve the environment where you have camped. Participants often rush to get to the next campsite or pack the car to head home and neglect their responsibility to leave their campsite better than they found it. Following are a few things to consider when deciding how and when to leave your campsite.

Plan ahead for breaking camp so you have time to leave the campsite better than you found it.

TECHNIQUE TIP

If you have multiple groups following each other in sequence from one campsite to another, challenge each group to do two things. First, they should leave their present camp with no evidence that anyone camped there. Second, upon arriving at their next campsite, they should scour the area to see if they can find any evidence of the previous group. Each group can compile a list of clues at each site.

Departure Time

Your decision about when to break camp and any chores that need to be done should be guided by when you hope to be on the trail, river, lake, or roadway, headed to your next destination. Just as it is not recommended to get into camp late at night when it is dark and you are tired, we do not recommend rushing out of camp because you inevitably will forget something or will not have taken the time needed to leave the site better than you found it. So, first determine when you want to leave and then think about what you need to do to get to that point.

Leaving Pristine Versus Established Sites

The golden rule for breaking camp is to always leave your site better than you found it. Many established sites get high use and are dependent on the campers who use them to take care of them. If there is a fire ring, consider stacking your leftover firewood neatly for the next campers, cleaning up the fire, and scattering any excess ashes that may not be contained. Consider carrying out trash that has accumulated around sites that get heavier use. This is a great thing to do on your last night out when you can carry the trash directly to a garbage can.

When leaving a pristine site, follow the Leave No Trace guidelines and pretend a team of campsite detectives is following you. Your role is to preserve the natural landscape and disguise your presence as much as possible. Once you have taken down your shelters and packed up your camp, place all belongings on the edge of the site and walk through the camp looking for evidence that you have been there. You will want to fluff the duff (i.e., rustle the leaves and vegetation with sticks and your hands and feet), especially in the areas where you have slept, cooked, and walked. Even in just one night, you will be amazed at how trampled the vegetation

Following Leave No Trace principles means removing all evidence that you have been there.

can become. Have some fun and turn the breaking-camp process into a game to see who can disguise their presence the best. Groups will sometimes appoint a sweep person to make sure that all items belonging to the group have been collected.

As always, every situation is different. Know your group, the area in which you are camping, and the things to be aware of when breaking camp. Here are a few helpful reminders as you pack up your camp.

Considerations for Breaking Camp

☐ Check all areas for items you may have left behind or traces of your visit. Areas to check include the pathways surrounding the camp, water sources, bathroom areas, kitchen, food storage, and sleeping areas.

☐ Check for any clothes or equipment that may have been drying on clotheslines, bushes, or trees.

☐ Check the sleeping area closely for stakes and cord that may be left after packing the shelter. Shake out your sleeping bag in case you placed any items inside.

☐ Scour the kitchen area closely for food remnants, small pieces of trash, important utensils, and anything else that may have been overlooked because it was under a leaf or behind a rock.

☐ Once you are sure that you have collected all of your belongings, do one final walkthrough of the camp and try to disguise your presence. Always leave the site better than you found it.

Conclusion

Backcountry camping can be a wonderful experience. The key to any camping experience is to know the purpose of your trip and then to assess all other decisions through that lens. This may seem like common sense, but we have seen many trips end in disappointment because one person expected a laidback weekend camping in large tents and sleeping on cots while someone prepared all the meals only to find out that they were part of a group that expected them to participate in every phase of the camping process. Camping can be a great way to introduce young people to the wonders of the natural world and an ideal setting for families, intact groups (e.g., church youth groups, scouting groups, school classes), and others to further expand their own potential and that of the group. Do not underestimate the power of a night spent sleeping under the stars or weathering a storm under a tarp or tent.

Preparation and planning will go a long way toward helping you enjoy a quality camping experience. Use this guide and the many resources available in print and online to help you plan your trip before you set foot into the backcountry. Most important of all, learn to ask the key questions related to backcountry camping, because the answers to those questions will enable you to make better decisions. Camping is a learning experience. The only way to get better at what to take, where to camp, and how to cook is by botching it a few times! So, get out and explore your local state or national park, national forest, or wilderness area and enjoy the unparalleled experience of camping.

Key Questions to Consider

Selecting a Campsite

☐ Are you aware of all regulations for the area?

☐ Is the area safe?

☐ What type of campsite is appropriate for the purpose of the trip and the area (i.e., established, medium impact, pristine)?

☐ Is the campsite secluded? Is it off the trail?

☐ Does it have the necessary natural resources to aid in cooking meals (e.g., adequate wood for a fire, water for drinking)?

☐ Is the campsite sufficiently distant from water sources? Is it far enough away from the shoreline, stream bank, or riverbank?

☐ How will the water drain if it rains?

☐ Are the trees adequate for setting up a tarp?

☐ Is there any evidence that animals frequent the area?

☐ Is the site above a floodplain in case a flash flood occurs?

☐ Does the site provide shelter against the wind?

Setting Up Camp

☐ How should the camp be oriented with respect to the dominant wind direction?

☐ Where should the camp kitchen and food storage be located in relation to the sleeping station?

☐ What style of shelter is most appropriate?

☐ How can you minimize your impact on the site?

☐ What precautions should you take to protect water sources? Should the water be filtered, chemically treated, or boiled?

☐ With respect to urine and fecal matter, should you bury it, smear it, or pack it out?

☐ How do you plan to protect food and food waste from animals?

Cooking

☐ How does the type of camping trip affect the amount and type of food you are taking? (For example, a group who is backpacking is going to be much more conscious of food weight than a family choosing to car camp for the weekend.)

☐ Should you use a fire, stove, or both for cooking? Have you checked the land management agency's regulations for fires? What type of fire should you build?

☐ Do you have appropriate cooking pots and utensils?

☐ If using a stove, has it been tested? Do you have a backup plan in case it fails?

☐ Have you packed spare stove parts, extra matches, and so on?

☐ What should you do with leftover food, food waste, and dishwater?

Sleeping

☐ Is the ground relatively flat and free of roots, rocks, poison ivy, poison oak, poison sumac, and snake holes?

☐ What precautions should you take when preparing the sleep site?

☐ Where and how should you store food and scented items in relation to where you plan to sleep?

☐ What should you do if you encounter wildlife?

☐ What should you do to stay warm while sleeping?

Breaking Camp

- [ ] When do you want to be on the way traveling to the next campsite or heading home?

- [ ] How should you leave a pristine site versus an established site after spending the night?

- [ ] What else should you be thinking of before moving on from the camp?

CHAPTER 9

Planning Your Backpacking Experience

I have always found that plans are useless, but planning is indispensable.

Dwight D. Eisenhower

Each season of the year you can pick up the regional newspaper near a wilderness area and read about someone who died while participating in some form of outdoor recreation. In the spring, we read about novice white-water paddlers drowning either because they didn't take personal floatation devices (life preservers) or they paddled a river that was clearly beyond their skill level. In the summer, we read about hikers getting lost because they didn't bring a map and compass. In the fall, hikers make headlines by dying of hypothermia because they didn't bring the proper clothing, and of course winter provides its own headlines due to the cold, avalanches, and other dangers that travelers don't plan for. The key word here is *plan*. Each of these examples goes back to trip planning. At the very least, poor planning leads to discomfort, going hungry, or perhaps not getting along with your companions. At the very worst it leads to injury or death. We should no more go on a weekend outing without planning than we would attempt to travel around the world without planning.

The purpose of this chapter is to describe how to plan safe, enjoyable, and environmentally sound wilderness trips of various lengths. Good wilderness travelers also need to be good wilderness planners in order to anticipate potential problems, be good stewards of the environment, and ensure that they have fun.

Thinking Through the Planning Process

Whether planning a weekend outing or an extended expedition to remote parts of the world, the planning fundamentals remain the same. The WEA lists 16 considerations in planning their expeditions. Most campers can modify this list to meet their specific needs. We have decided to focus on 14 of the considerations here. For our purposes we will combine consideration 15, risk management, with emergency planning. Although important for commercial adventures, consideration 16, public relations, has no practical value for personal trips, so we'll leave that one out also. The crucial thing is to give some thought to all 14 considerations before the start of the trip.

As you start planning, it is important to get organized. Using some sort of organizational structure that describes who is going to do what and who is responsible for what not only ensures that you don't forget the matches, it also allows participants to understand their role and obligations as a team member. This frequently minimizes problems and personal conflicts. Be a list maker.

Most veteran wilderness leaders grab a clipboard, or perhaps their laptop computer, and start by anticipating what questions they have to ask, such as, "What do I have to do, who is going to do it, who is going to pay for it, and when does it have to be done by?" Possible lists include the following:

- Tasks to be done and who will do them
- Shopping list

A successful trip starts before you hit the trail. Anticipate what might happen and plan for it.

- Equipment and clothing list
- Food list

Try to anticipate what will happen, what might happen, and how you might react. Anticipation includes having contingency plans for a variety of scenarios. What will you do if it rains the entire trip? What will you do if someone sprains an ankle? What will you do if you and your camping companion have a fight? Anticipation does a couple of things. First, it frequently prevents bad things from happening because you have anticipated them and taken steps to keep them from happening. Second, it allows you to deal with surprises more effectively because you have anticipated them. You'll see the word *anticipation* frequently sprinkled throughout this chapter.

Trip Planning and Length

Whether your trip is a weekend, 2 weeks long, or a major expedition, the fundamentals of trip planning are the same. Here are some things to think about regarding the length of trips.

- **Short trips (2-7 days):** The biggest thing to remember on short trips is that most of the planning considerations are just as important as for expeditions.

WEA instructors make it a habit to go through their lists just as thoroughly for a weekend as they do for longer trips. The decisions to be made are frequently less complex on shorter trips, but they need to be made nonetheless. The biggest difference is that shorter trips are usually in less remote areas so that might be taken into consideration when preparing a first aid kit, for example. In a less remote area a simpler first aid kit might be adequate.

- **Longer trips (7-14 days):** Longer trips may involve rerationing and more complex transportation requirements that require more complex decision making.
- **Expeditions (14 days or longer):** The longer and more remote the trip, the more complex the planning becomes; however, the considerations remain the same. Getting your party and all their gear to base camp in the Himalayas is certainly more complex than getting to New Hampshire's Mount Washington, but the questions that you need to ask remain the same.

Planning Considerations

Let's take a look at each of WEA's planning considerations and see how they might relate to your trip. Don't let the length of the trip dictate your planning process. Ask the same questions; just take more time to address the issues as they become more complex. Within each of the considerations, we will address three types of trip length: short trips, longer trips, and extended expeditions.

Purpose

Why are you going in the outdoors? What do you hope to get out of the experience? These questions seem simple—so simple, in fact, that you may not even give them any thought. Most people travel in the outdoors to have a good time, and frequently that outcome is good enough. However, some people come back from their trips having had a miserable time because their goal or purpose was not met. Perhaps you have had the same experience. You wanted to hike a mountain but because your friend was so out of shape you never made it out of camp. Perhaps you just wanted to sit on the shore of the lake and read a book but your companion wanted to climb three peaks. Having a common understanding of the trip purpose increases the chances of everyone getting along and having a vested interest in the success of the trip.

Short Trips

Considering the purpose or objective of short trips is generally not as critical as it is for longer trips and usually is implied if not explicitly stated. We recommend that at the very least there be a discussion about why people want to go on the trip. If there are wildly conflicting reasons, they can be addressed and everyone can feel that their goals have been met. Most people can tolerate a weekend even if the objective isn't consistent with their own.

Longer Trips

It is critical that the objectives be discussed thoroughly for longer trips. Would you want to go on a trip where your friend wants to hike long distances while you were hoping to spend time on the shore of a remote pond working on your fly-fishing technique? Having clear agreement on what you are going to do and why you are going to do it is vital. Conflict and disappointment await those who don't.

Extended Expeditions

Can you imagine spending 14 days or more with people who have a different goal for the expedition than you? A colleague of ours has, and she assures us that it wasn't much fun. After graduating from college, she and a group of five friends and relatives decided to spend 3 months traveling across Europe. They were all thinking it would be fun, but they never talked about which countries they wanted to spend the most time in, they never talked about why they were going in the first place, and they never talked about how they were going to resolve problems as they arose. Within 2 weeks, problems came up, and by the end of the first month, they started splitting up and going different directions. Although the trip wasn't an entire disaster, all of the group members wished they had done a better job clarifying the trip objectives.

In contrast to this example is the story told by a veteran instructor of an ascent of Denali (Mount McKinley) early in his career. Before signing on to the expedition, the trip objectives were explained to all those invited. Everyone knew that the objectives were prioritized so that the first one was most important and the last was least important. The objectives were to have a recreational experience where friendships would be made and maintained, to test equipment donated by manufacturers, and, if conditions permitted, to reach the summit. When the team was at 19,500 feet (5,944 meters), less than 1,000 feet (305 meters) from the summit, and they had to turn back because of deteriorating weather conditions and the health of one of the group members, there was disappointment but not anger or despair. They knew that they had been successful in their first two objectives and were able to let go of the third.

Leadership

When friends or family members get together for a camping trip, little thought is ever given to leadership. Frequently that works out fine, but occasionally it doesn't. Often the person who comes up with the idea for the trip is the de facto leader. Perhaps the person who has the most experience is the leader. We would encourage you to ask the following questions regarding leadership:

- Do you trust your leader?
- Do you feel that your leader will provide a safe and comfortable experience?
- Do you believe that the designated leader will be able to make appropriate decisions if an emergency occurs?

If you answer no to any of these questions, you need to have a discussion with the group about the group's leadership.

Short Trips

Sometimes leadership is implicit, especially on short trips. If your parents are planning the trip, then they are the leaders and you are probably the follower. If your buddy is a veteran camper and this is your first trip, you will probably defer to him regarding leadership. Many shorter trips use consensus-based leadership. If a decision needs to be made, all group members put their heads together and make a decision. This system works fairly well for decisions that don't need to be made quickly. At the very least, however, consider who will take charge if something goes wrong.

Longer Trips

The longer the trip and the higher risk the activities, the clearer the need for definitive leadership. If you are rock climbing, white-water paddling, or out for more than a few days, you need a plan for leadership. What are you going to do to make sure everyone is comfortable with the risk level? How are you going to communicate and check in to see how people are doing? Who's going to make the decision to turn back or change the itinerary? These questions all center on leadership.

How does consensus leadership work on trips of moderate length? One WEA instructor tells of canoeing on the San Juan River in Utah with a group of seven friends. The three most experienced group members took different leadership roles. The most experienced paddler made all decisions about whether to run the rapids or line the boats through them. The most experienced expedition camper took the lead on basic campsite and camping decisions. The person who had taken the lead in organizing the trip took the lead in most logistical decisions. Generally this system worked pretty well, but because the river levels were way up, the paddling was more challenging than expected, and a couple of family members who felt the paddling was over their head informed the rest of the group that they were abandoning the expedition halfway through. Perhaps if there had been a clear leader, different options for the family members could have been explored more thoroughly and instead of abandoning the trip they could have come up with a better solution. Perhaps they could have rented some play boats and stowed their open canoes. Perhaps they could have rented a raft. Perhaps there was an option that would have allowed them to stay on the trip and still feel safe, but because there was no clear leader, the problem wasn't even discussed.

Extended Expeditions

On extended expeditions there is virtually always a clear leader. On some major climbs the leader isn't even part of the summit team. The leader is the person who makes sure everything happens. This person is sort of a super-logistician who not only coordinates logistics but makes or helps make all major decisions regarding the expedition.

Itinerary

Where are you going to go? How far are you going to hike each day? Does the plan mesh well with the purpose of the trip and the physical abilities of the group members? Are there permit restrictions or Leave No Trace considerations that will influence your itinerary?

We generally recommend less mileage, not more. We have never had people come up to us and say, "Wow, I really wish that we had planned to hike more miles. We really underestimated how fast and far we could travel in a day." On the other hand, we frequently hear comments like, "Oh boy, we bit off more than we could chew!", "I felt like all we ever did is travel. We never got to explore the area we were traveling through," and "We made it and I've got blisters all over my feet to prove it. I'll never do that again!" Good itinerary planning encourages fewer miles with more time to explore and rest.

Short Trips

The itinerary needs to be closely linked to the purpose of the trip. Since shorter trips are usually based on recreation, that makes the job simpler. It usually comes down to how hard you want to work. Our advice for short trips is to keep it simple. Get experience under your belt, then be more creative and stretch yourself.

The most basic consideration is, are you going to start and finish at the same trailhead or are you going to finish someplace else? Obviously if you finish someplace else you have to plan your transportation accordingly. See chapter 4 for more details on planning for this consideration.

Longer Trips

Trips up to 2 weeks long permit considerable flexibility and creativity in itinerary planning. You can cover a considerable amount of territory without exhausting yourselves. Again, experience makes the job of itinerary planning much easier. For example, a group of friends planned a 12-day trip down a portion of the Green River in Utah a number of years ago. They all agreed they had a great trip and it was one of the highlights of their camping career. Six years later with numerous trips in between, they decided to go back to the Green River. This time when they planned the itinerary they decided to start 15 miles (24 kilometers) downstream. Even though they had the same number of days, they wanted to shorten the canoe mileage so they could spend more time exploring some of the hiking trails. Without their previous experience they wouldn't have been able to make that decision, and the trip turned out even better than the first one.

Extended Expeditions

On extended expeditions the sky is the limit: Whatever you can think of, you can do. You just have to figure out how you are going to transport food and gear. For example, most people can travel between 1 and 2 miles (1.5 and 3 kilometers) per hour when hiking over the long term and need about 2 pounds

(2 kilograms) of food and approximately 1/3 of a pound (136 grams) of fuel for each day. We also estimate that one person needs between 25 and 30 pounds (11 and 14 kilograms) of clothing and equipment. With that knowledge you can decide the maximum amount of weight you want to carry (we suggest no more than 60 pounds [27 kilograms]) and how many hours a day you want to hike.

Let's say our maximum load is 60 pounds (27 kilograms) and we don't want to hike more than 6 hours a day. That means we can hike between 6 and 12 miles (10 and 19 kilometers) in a day and that we can carry food for approximately 13 days before we need a reration (30 pounds divided by 2.33, the 2 pounds of food plus 1/3 pound of fuel needed per day). Now you can plan the itinerary accordingly. Like all the considerations in planning, they are interdependent. Planning a more complex itinerary will affect rationing and resupplies, frequently called *food drops,* as well as emergency planning and possible evacuation routes.

Emergency Planning

What are you going to do in anticipation of something bad happening? It could be as minor as a severe cold or as major as a traumatic injury. Where would you come out if your trip had to end prematurely because of illness or injury? Who's going to worry about you and perhaps contact the authorities if you don't arrive home when expected? When should they contact the authorities? Whom should they contact and how should they contact them?

This is a serious part of trip planning that is frequently left to chance. We recommend that you designate someone as your emergency contact person, perhaps a neighbor or a parent. That person has a written copy of your itinerary, a list of the group members, your expected return time, and the emergency telephone numbers of authorities to call at a predesignated time. For example, perhaps you plan to return home by 5:00 p.m. in the afternoon, so you might designate 9:00 p.m. as your emergency contact time. If you don't show up by that time, your contact person is to call the authorities (usually the local forest ranger in the area where you are hiking). See chapter 4 for more on emergency planning.

Short Trips

Generally speaking, the shorter the trip, the less remote it is and as a result the less complex the emergency plan is. Although the basics as described previously are the same, the overall plan is simpler. There are WEA instructors who frequently travel to the same area six or more times a year. As a result they have standardized information that they always keep in their pack. Local rescue squad telephone numbers, forest rangers' numbers, and so on are always in the backpack so that these authorities can be readily contacted in an emergency. They also have a standard emergency card that they leave at home with someone so that if they don't return at the expected time, action is taken (see figure 9.1).

front

EMERGENCY CONTACT CARD		
Leader	Contact tel. #	❏ Home ❏ Work ❏ Cell
		— — —-— — — -— — — —

Trip members	Contact #	Expected return time/date
		Emergency call time/date
		This is the time to call the emergency contact if we don't return!

Emergency contact:

Call this person/office if we don't return by the emergency call time/date.

Leave this completed card with a friend or relative. Your life could depend on it!

back

Trip location	Starting trailhead parking lot location
Tentative itinerary	Finish trailhead parking lot location
	Miscellaneous information

Figure 9.1 A sample emergency contact card.

Longer Trips and Extended Expeditions

Longer trips into more remote areas require a more complex plan, although in the most extreme cases the expeditions are so remote and rescue options so limited that the plans actually become simpler. Let's look at two different examples. On Mount McKinley, the highest mountain in North America, you would need a very thorough emergency plan. The park service demands it, and because there is such a comprehensive network of rescue services, you would want to take advantage of that network should an emergency arise. In contrast, a group of WEA instructors took a trip to a remote portion of northeastern Siberia a number of years ago and the area was so remote that support services were nonexistent. In this case the emergency plan focused only on what they could do to help themselves and did not depend on outside support.

The determining factors in developing good emergency plans are knowing where you can access help, letting people know when you should return, and instructions of what do to if you don't return when expected.

Land Management Rules and Regulations

What are the rules and regulations in the area you are traveling? Are fires legal? Are there limitations on group size? Do you have to camp in certain areas? Do you need a hiking or camping permit? These are the types of questions you need to anticipate as you consider the rules and regulations in the area where you are traveling. They differ from location to location depending on the management agency and the management plans that govern the specific area. You will want to contact the management agency and learn about the regulations in the area.

The length of trip has little to do with rules and regulations. Some simple weekend trips to heavily used areas require more regulations than many remote expedition locations. On the other hand, some extended expeditions may require permits that cost thousands of dollars. There is no consistent rule of thumb.

Food and Nutrition

How will you decide what food to bring? Who will purchase and pack it? Who's going to cook? Bringing and eating delicious and nutritious food is one of the many fun aspects of outdoor travel. Generally speaking, we can eat as much as we want and not worry about gaining weight when traveling in the outdoors. Answering these questions will ensure that you bring foods that taste good, are relatively easy to prepare, and meet basic nutrition needs.

Food Drops

On longer trips, food drops are inevitable. *Food drop* is a term for any time your group has to have food and equipment delivered or picked up during your trip. Food drops are frequently made by mail, motor vehicle, horseback, airplane, or boat. No matter how you get your food, we have found the following things to be invaluable.

Careful packing and planning ensures you have the food and equipment needed for your expedition.

- Have a written food-drop plan that includes
  - the exact date and time of the food drop, and
  - the exact location of the food drop with an accompanying map (including *X* marking the spot).

- If possible, have a food-drop orientation with the assigned personnel so that all the procedures can be reviewed and questions answered before you venture into the wilderness.

- Make sure that the trip leader has a copy of the food-drop plan as does each person actually making the drop.

- Food should be packaged in appropriate containers (plastic-lined heavy-duty cardboard or varmint-proof material if necessary) and clearly marked with the who, where, and when of the food drop.

- If you are mailing your food, the USPS recommends that you not ship glass, liquor, or perishable items and that you waterproof everything. Use a sturdy box or container that is taped well with the address clearly marked. It is also recommended that you include the address inside any package that is mailed.

Short Trips

Food planning for short trips is relatively simple. Things like spoilage, weight, nutritional balance, and perhaps even cost are less of a factor for a weekend trip. What is important is that you have plenty of food items that you like and that will stoke the body's furnace and that you take into account environmental concerns such as packaging materials when selecting the food to bring on your trip. Even for the shortest of trips, we repackage most food into environment-friendly weatherproof containers. We leave the glass, cans, aluminum foil, and cardboard packaging at home and use plastic bags and plastic screw-top containers exclusively. That reduces weight and, more importantly, reduces the amount of garbage to pack out.

Longer Trips

As the length of trip increases, more factors are added to the list of considerations. When trips are longer than a few days, factors such as spoilage (better leave the hamburger at home), weight, and bulk (cheese may be heavy but it provides lots of calories per pound whereas cereal may be light but has relatively few calories and takes up a lot of space) become much more important.

Extended Expeditions

For trips longer than 2 weeks, the factors discussed previously become even more important, and other factors are added, such as nutritional balance—health concerns like scurvy and other vitamin deficiencies aren't just old pirates' tales. Ease of preparation is also important; you don't want to spend 2 hours cooking barley and long-grain rice after a 15-mile (24-kilometer) day. Finally, don't forget about variety. Any kind of food gets old if you've had it every day for the past 30 days!

Equipment and Clothing

How are you going to make sure that all group members are dressed properly and have the clothing and equipment that will ensure their safety and comfort? This is not something to take lightly. Every year search and rescues take place because campers did not anticipate changes in the weather and were not dressed or equipped properly. We recommend using clothing and equipment lists to make sure you don't forget anything. Sometimes it is also a good idea to have an understanding of who will be responsible if a piece of equipment such as a tent or stove is damaged. See chapter 3, pages 80-83, for sample lists.

Short Trips

For all trips the key is to make sure you have a safe, fun experience and take care of the environment. As the trips get longer, it gets harder to meet those criteria. For short trips where weight is less of a factor, making sure you have the proper equipment and clothing should be no problem. In general, the clothing you need for a weekend is the same clothing you need for a month-long expedition. We hear of too many deaths due to hypothermia that could easily have been prevented if the victims had worn proper clothing. See chapter 3 for more information on proper clothing.

Longer Trips

For trips up to 2 weeks in length, things don't change too much. You need spare parts and repair kits because you are more dependent on your equipment, and you need to be able to repair it when necessary. Clothing layers are the same, with perhaps a few extra pairs of socks and an extra pair of underwear thrown in.

Extended Expeditions

For trips longer than 2 weeks, you frequently want backup equipment. What if the stove dies and can't be repaired in the treeless northern tundra? One of the reasons we like to cook and tent in small groups is because it builds in redundancy. If a cook group's stove dies, they can go cook with another group. If for some reason their tent is shredded, they can split up and tent with others.

Clothing doesn't change much between 2-week and longer expeditions. You may want more buttons in your sewing kit, but your clothing doesn't change. Some people will exclaim that they need more underwear, but you can only wear one pair of underwear at a time. If you bring two extra pairs (one more than most WEA instructors bring on month-long expeditions), that allows you to wear the original pair, have one pair drying on the line, and have one pair in your pack ready to change into. Socks fall into the same category, except they are even more important than underwear. After all, you depend on your feet to get you to your destination. We try to have four complete pairs of socks for longer expeditions. The rest of your clothing is the same that you would pack for a weekend trip.

Skills and Knowledge

Many people think that camping safely, enjoyably, and with little damage to the environment is an innate skill that we inherited from our pioneer ancestors. Unfortunately, that is not true, and camper ignorance results in damage to the environment, search and rescues, and memories of discomfort and misery that we yearn to forget rather than cherish.

In the planning process you will want to think about skills that you would like to acquire or improve upon. The most common ones are covered in this book, including map and compass use, cooking, and first aid, among others. You will want to determine if there are any skills areas you would like to improve upon before you head out on a trip.

Short Trips

Although the basic camping skill sets are the same no matter how long the trip, certain skill sets become even more important on longer trips. For shorter trips, the knowledge and skills necessary to have a fun, safe, and environmentally sound trip are first and foremost. Basic skills in navigation, Leave No Trace, cooking, campsite selection, and first aid are essential.

Longer Trips

As trips get longer, the list of necessary skills does as well. Basic first aid skills need to be expanded to wilderness first aid or Wilderness First Responder skills. Knowledge of good expedition behavior and skills becomes valuable and leadership and decision-making skills become more critical.

Extended Expeditions

For extended expeditions, knowledge of expedition behavior becomes essential. In the remote backcountry, expertise in navigation skills is a prerequisite, as are good leadership skills.

The bottom line is that knowledge and skills are an essential component in trip planning. What do you need to know and be able to do to have an enjoyable, safe, and low-impact wilderness experience, and what are you going to do to make sure that happens? Of course, that's probably why you're reading this book, right?

Expedition Behavior

What can you do to make sure group members get along? Wilderness education pioneer and WEA founder Paul Petzoldt characterized poor expedition behavior as "a breakdown in human relations caused by selfishness, rationalization, ignorance of personal faults, dodging blame or responsibility, physical weakness, and, in extreme cases, not being able to risk one's own survival to insure that of a companion." He described good expedition behavior as an awareness of the different interrelationships of people "plus the motivation and character to be as concerned for others in every respect as one is for oneself" (Petzoldt, 1984, p. 220).

The key to good expedition behavior is anticipating the stresses of getting along in the outdoors and providing ways to deal with those stresses. Setting a positive tone before the trip by setting expectations goes a long way in ensuring good expedition behavior. We encourage a frank discussion of expedition behavior before the trip and providing opportunities for participants to openly discuss their concerns on a regular basis. In addition, giving people opportunities for personal reflection, privacy, and downtime all can go a long way in helping people get along.

Short Trips

We joke that good expedition behavior isn't important on shorter trips. Who cares if people don't get along and hate each other by the end of the weekend? It's only a weekend. The point is that people getting along for 48 hours or a few days isn't nearly as critical as the need for people to work productively for 2 weeks or a month.

Longer Trips

Many WEA instructors lead trips with friends and families as well as formal educational expeditions. For these trips, which are frequently in the 10-day to 2-week range, we always have some sort of planning session that orients group members to the trip purpose and addresses expedition behavior. We find these trips to be much more fun and enjoyable than trips that were conducted without the benefit of an orientation session.

Extended Expeditions

For trips longer than 2 weeks, having a plan for how the group is going to get along, what you are going to do to promote good expedition behavior, and how you are going to deal with problems when they arise is essential. Paul Petzoldt used to love to tell stories about how well-educated people would treat each other so poorly that they would attack each other with ice axes. Today, knowledge of expedition behavior, group dynamics, and individual and group behavior suggests that with good planning, groups should be able to play and work side by side in a much more productive manner than ever before.

Water Sources

Is potable water available? How will you treat water to make sure it is safe for consumption? We take for granted that water is always available, but in this day and age this is still not assured. You must have a plan for making sure water is safe for consumption.

Short Trips

No matter what the length of trip, you have to have plenty of water. On average you need at least 1 gallon (4 liters) per person per day. Short trips are among

Coming together
is a beginning;
keeping together
is a process;
working together
is success.

Henry Ford

the easiest because in a pinch you can carry needed drinking water. Cooking water is rarely an issue because, in North America, by bringing water to a boil, it becomes safe to consume.

Longer Trips

For trips up to 2 weeks long, it is unreasonable to expect campers to carry their water, so some sort of purification system is necessary. Any water treatment system should work for that time period.

Extended Expeditions

For longer trips the challenge is to have a durable, long-lasting system that will hold up to the rigors of expedition use and treat the volume of water necessary on a long expedition. Over the years WEA instructors have used just about every system available. In general, simpler is better. Boiling water and crystalline iodination are two of the simplest yet effective methods that work in most environments. See chapter 3 for more on water treatment.

Weather

It is amazing how many groups run into trouble because they didn't anticipate possible changes in the weather. Information is readily available on the Internet regarding historical weather patterns as well as short- and long-term weather forecasts. Not taking advantage of this information is foolhardy.

Short Trips

Keep it simple, check the weather forecast, and plan accordingly. If you are going to an area where you haven't been before, you can find historical weather information for the United States at www.noaa.gov/pastweather.html. That information will help you determine how hot or cold it gets or what the odds of rain are in a given month.

Longer Trips and Extended Expeditions

For a trip of 10 days to a month, the weather forecast isn't going to be much help, but knowing the historical weather patterns can be. Knowing what the average daily highs and lows are, what the average precipitation is, and what the record highs and lows are can help you be prepared and have a safe trip.

Resources

In planning your trip are there any resources from which you could learn things that would help make the trip a success? Is there anyone who has been to the area before and can provide firsthand information (e.g., friends, rangers, locals, guides)? Are books, brochures, magazine articles, maps, or other materials available about the area? Have you done an Internet search on the area to see if information is readily available that might be helpful in planning your trip? All of these things will help make your trip safer and more enjoyable as well as help protect the environment.

Short Trips

What is the consequence of not doing your homework on a short trip? You waste a weekend and you don't have much fun. The longer the trip, the greater the consequences of not using available resources.

Longer Trips and Extended Expeditions

Imagine you are leaving your home in California for a 3-week backpacking trip in the Gallatin National Forest in Wyoming and you haven't done any research. You arrive to find that the forest is closed due to forest fires in the region. You will have to pay a considerable price in time and energy for a trip that doesn't pan out. Some might argue that these unexpected events just add to the adventure of the trip. However, we feel that you get plenty of unanticipated adventures even when you do plan, so you don't need additional problems that you could have prevented.

Finances

How much are things going to cost and who is going to pay for them? How will incidental expenses along the trip be handled? Having a plan for these expenses will go a long way in reducing stress and maintaining good expedition behavior.

Short Trips

Short trips have limited costs, so they are fairly simple to anticipate and deal with. But even short trips have expenses that need to be considered. Whose car are you going to use and who's going to pay for the gas? Who is paying for the food? Did you have to purchase group equipment specifically for this trip? Who is going to pay for that, and who gets to keep it once the trip is over?

Longer Trips

Trips up to 2 weeks that involve considerable travel to and from the trailhead require a financial plan that everyone agrees to beforehand. As an example, on a winter cross-country ski trip through Yellowstone National Park, a group member provided his car for traveling over 1,000 miles (621 kilometers) to the trailhead. However, he never told the other group members he wasn't planning to pay for gas, since he had provided the car. His expectation wasn't unreasonable, but he should have shared his plan and the reasons behind it with his camping partners. Coming to an agreement beforehand about how you are going to cover expenses is essential, and then having a treasurer or designated person to keep track of expenses is indispensable. Using a computer with a spreadsheet program is one easy way to keep track of trip finances.

Extended Expeditions

Longer trips frequently can cost thousands of dollars and benefit from having a treasurer or financial officer who is responsible for carrying out the financial plan that everyone has agreed on. For extended expeditions, it isn't unusual for fund-raising to be part of the responsibility.

Transportation

Who is going to provide transportation? Who will pay for gas? Who is responsible for the maintenance of the vehicle? Where can you safely park your vehicle? How will you get a vehicle to the finish point? Transportation can be a major expense, and not planning for it can create major problems.

Shuttles and Parking

In areas that frequently have wilderness travelers, a number of shuttle services are usually available. Outfitters and shuttle services will pick you up and deliver you to the trailhead or move your car to your finish point. In more remote areas you may have to ask around the community to find someone willing to shuttle you or your vehicle. Even in more remote parts of the world we have rarely had problems trusting local people to shuttle vehicles. They frequently are willing to do it for little or no pay, but we recommend that you pay them generously.

Consult with the local authorities about the legality and safety of parking your car long term in trailhead parking lots. We rarely hear of problems, but there is the story of a camper who parked her older Volkswagen Beetle at a trailhead within 100 miles (161 kilometers) of a large metropolitan area and after her camping trip returned to find her car turned upside down and ransacked in the middle of the parking lot!

One colleague was worried about his car battery being dead at the end of his month-long winter expedition, so he asked a Wyoming rancher to store his car and battery while ski touring through Yellowstone National Park. He came out a month later and the rancher had kept the battery on a trickle charger and his car started up like he had only left it for the day. The rancher was pleasantly surprised when the backpacker gave him a quart of Jack Daniels as a thank-you for taking such good care of his car and battery. See chapter 4 for more on transportation considerations.

Short Trips

Transportation needs for short trips rarely have too many complications unless you are relying on public transportation or someone to drop you off and pick you up. If that is the case, it helps to make sure your pickup person knows exactly where to pick you up. It is frustrating to be waiting at one location while your pickup person is waiting someplace else with no cell phone service.

Longer Trips

Will your car be parked in a safe place? How will you get from the airport to the trailhead? As trips get longer, these questions and many others start to crop up. It is not unusual to need multiple forms of transportation. Wilderness travel in northern Canada, for example, might involve driving to Winnipeg, taking the train north for a couple of days, and then perhaps flying in to a remote lake where you start your trip. That's three different modes of transportation and you haven't even started the trip yet!

Extended Expeditions

As you can imagine, longer trips frequently get even more complicated. It is not unusual to have border crossings and language barriers that make transportation even more complex. Good organization skills and anticipating what you need will go a long way in making the trip go smoothly.

Posttrip

Where will you be able to shower and clean up? How will leftover food and equipment be split up? Who has what responsibilities after the trip is over? The trip is not finished when you get back to civilization. You still need to wrap up all the loose ends before it is really over.

Short Trips

Finish the trip, go home, and take a shower. You've only been gone a few days so you aren't too dirty, and cleaning up is no big deal. Just make sure that you do indeed wrap up the loose ends of the trip. Nothing strains friendships like debts unpaid or equipment not returned.

Longer Trips

Trips longer than a week start to get a little more complicated. You are definitely dirty and will most likely stink. A shower takes on greater importance as do the logistical chores of cleaning up gear and taking care of any loose ends.

Extended Expeditions

At the end of a month-long trip, coming back to reality (or perhaps reality is the wilderness and you are coming back to unreality) gives you a glassy-eyed stare as you drive into town and encounter civilization. Everything seems a bit surreal. We have a talk with our students about adjusting to civilization. Keep in mind that with your unruly hair, dirty clothes, and so-called bouquet de wilderness odor, it is best to avoid the glassy-eyed stare when you stop at the convenience store, and perhaps it is better to have just one person go in and do the ice cream purchase for the entire group. Make a plan for slowly integrating back into civilization, cleaning equipment, paying bills, and returning items to their rightful owners.

Special Considerations

Backpacking with children and dogs presents special challenges. See chapter 7 for more on these considerations.

Backpacking With Children

Many books have been written about camping with kids, and it is difficult to do the topic justice in the space we have here. However, here are the key things to keep in mind when camping with children.

- Camping is possible with every age group from infants on up. Each age group has its own pluses and minuses. For example, infants are easier than you might think because they aren't mobile; when you set them down, they stay there. You just need to make sure you have plenty of diapers and diaper wipes and that you pack them out. Food grinders for grinding adult food into infant-friendly mush work well, but not as well as mother's milk.

- Camping with toddlers becomes more challenging because they can get into trouble in countless ways. Bring plenty of extra clothes and a couple of books. It helps if you are camped near a pond or lake. The job of monitoring your children isn't any easier, but most kids love to wade and play in the water.

- Keep it light. Let them come along for the ride while the adults carry most of their gear and food, though they should carry very light loads so that they feel they are contributing their share. As they get stronger, let them carry more. Remember, by the time they're 18 you'll be ancient and they will be able to carry stuff for you.

- Keep the distances short and let them get longer as the days and years go by. Fewer miles and more exploring around camp will keep children's interest high.

- Plan for the kids, not you. As they get older, start planning the trips around their interests, not yours. You'll be surprised how far they can hike if it is something that they find fun and interesting.

- Plan for the car ride. Most camping involves traveling by car. Plan accordingly and bring books and their favorite music. Take frequent breaks and remember, this is supposed to be a vacation. If it stops being fun, make a change.

- Avoid mixing children and pets. They require considerable work on their own, but bringing both requires an exponential amount of work. We recommending bringing one or the other but not both until the children are old enough to care for themselves.

Backpacking With Dogs

The general rule is, if in doubt, leave your dog at home. Not all wilderness travelers are dog lovers, and dogs can have an incredibly negative impact, particularly when they bark and chase wildlife. Okay, your dog is a mild-mannered, nonbarking, non-wildlife-chasing version of man's best friend that has learned to poop at least 200 feet (61 meters) from the nearest trail and water source. If we can't convince you to leave the dog home, then here are some guidelines to remember when traveling with dogs.

- Is the dog allowed? Check the rules and regulations and make sure dogs are allowed in the area where you are going. Dogs are not allowed in national parks.

- Make sure your dog's vaccinations are up to date; not to do so is illegal in most places and unfair to your dog. Also make sure your dog has been licensed and has its license and identification on its collar. A data microchip is a good idea, and an improvised tag with an abbreviated version of your itinerary and your campsites is extremely helpful.

• Keep the dog leashed. It may seem a form of cruel and unusual doggy punishment to keep your dog leashed, but it isn't as cruel as seeing the remnants of a dog-killed deer left to rot. In many wilderness areas it is the law to have dogs leashed, and it just makes good sense. A wilderness instructor tells the story of encountering a dog and owner along the trail. The dog barked furiously at the instructor, who had grown up with dogs but was terrified by this ferocious-looking dog that wasn't on a leash. The owner assured the instructor that the dog was harmless, but trust us, the dog will look a lot more harmless when it's on a leash.

• Know your dog. Know what excites your dog and learn how to keep it under control. Obedience school is highly recommended for both the dog and its owner.

• Keep your dog's barking under control, and if you can't, then leave the dog at home. One grizzled old WEA instructor tells of his love for dogs; he owns two but rarely takes them into the wilderness. "My yellow lab gives a protective yet harmless bark whenever anyone approaches," he says. "It would be unfair of me to inflict that noise on people in a wilderness area. I take my dogs on hikes in areas where I don't have to worry about ruining someone's wilderness experience."

• Pick up after your dog. Carry extra plastic bags and be sure to pick up after it poops around campsites, near the water, and along the trail. Dispose of the poop appropriately.

• Be prepared. Bringing a muzzle is highly recommended. Even if your dog is not aggressive and doesn't bark, it might become aggressive and start barking in a new environment. Also, a can of pepper spray can be handy. Get the pepper spray that postal workers use on aggressive dogs. You'll probably never need to use it on your dogs, but you may want it in case other dogs attack yours.

• If your dog can't sleep on the ground, then you may want to bring a dog bed. You can't improvise a bed with native materials. Make sure your bed is made of synthetic materials so that you don't introduce nonnative plant species by bringing straw or other so-called natural bedding materials.

Conclusion

For many, trip planning is not the most exciting part of the experience. Nonetheless, it is a critical part that will go a long way in determining the success of the trip. One wise old instructor once said, "There are three things that determine the success or failure of a wilderness trip: leadership, expedition behavior, and trip planning. All others pale in comparison. The funny thing is that, by and large, the three are all determined before you leave home."

Web Resources

General Interest Sites

American Hiking Society (AHS)
www.americanhiking.org
A national network of over 150 hiking and trail clubs, contact this society to find the affiliated club nearest to you. This site has resources for trail advocacy, volunteer opportunities, local hiking clubs, and gear manufacturer sites.

Appalachian Mountain Club (AMC)
www.outdoors.org
In the eastern United States, the AMC offers outdoor leadership and skills-training opportunities for adults and teenagers, with special programs for youth workers and teachers.

American Mountain Guides Association (AMGA)
www.amga.com

Appalachian Trail Conservancy (ATC)
www.appalachiantrail.org
Along with a great deal of historical and statistical information about the Appalachian Trail itself, you can get started on planning hikes or learning how to volunteer to protect this valuable natural resource.

The Backpacker
www.thebackpacker.com
This site offers a message board, a guide to trails and places, articles on adventure, information for beginners, information on gear, and a gallery of pictures.

Backpacker Magazine
www.backpacker.com
This site links you to information on gear, destinations, technique, a training center, and a backpacking community. It has also a forum where users can pose questions to a larger audience.

Great Outdoors Recreation Pages (GORP)
http://gorp.away.com/index.html
A comprehensive outdoor recreation and adventure site with thousands of pages of content, GORP includes an activity guide, information on national parks, a city guide for urban hiking, an active vacation planner, and a gear guide.

Hiking and Backpacking
http://hikingandbackpacking.com
This site provides information on trails, hiking tips, lots of links, and a great list of clubs in each U.S. state and organizations in the United States and Canada. It also has advice on gear and recommendations for best gear sites.

Leave No Trace (LNT)
www.lnt.org
This site will help you to learn more about the basic LNT principles, as well as their history and ways to become an educator on the subject. You can also become a member of the association and be part of a community group.

National Outdoor Leadership School (NOLS)
www.nols.edu
This organization provides educational trips so that you can hone your skills on the trail. Trips vary in length from 7 days to more than 69 days.

Outside Magazine
http://outside.away.com/index.html
This is a great site for travel, gear, fitness, and outdoor recreation culture.

Outward Bound
www.outwardbound.org
Outward Bound provides educational trips to allow you to hone your skills on the trail. Trips vary in length from 7 days to more than 69 days.

Pacific Crest Trail (PCT) Association
www.pcta.org
Similar to the ATC Web site, the PCT Association Web site lists ways to plan your trip, learn more about the trail, and help to conserve it.

The Trail Database
www.traildatabase.org
This site provides information on trails throughout the world, including Europe, North America, Latin America, Africa, Asia, and the Pacific.

Trails.com
www.trails.com
This site will help you find hiking and backpacking trails near you.

Wilderness Education Association (WEA)
www.weainfo.org
The WEA promotes professionalism of outdoor leadership, thereby improving the safety of outdoor trips and enhancing conservation. It also provides educational trips to allow you to hone your skills on the trail. Trips vary in length from 7 days to more than 69 days.

Fitness

American Alliance for Health, Physical Education, Recreation and Dance (AAHPERD)

www.aahperd.org

A professional organization, AAHPERD offers consumer news, career links, graduate program lists, research, and a link to the *International Electronic Journal of Health Education.*

American Council on Exercise (ACE)

www.acefitness.org

This comprehensive site offers Fit Facts information sheets, whole-body workouts, daily fitness tips, a question-and-answer page, discussion boards, newsletters, and information on ACE. Both the general public and fitness professionals will find this site useful.

Body Composition Laboratory

www.bcm.edu/bodycomplab

This informative Web site, sponsored by the Body Composition Laboratory at the Children's Nutrition Research Center in Houston, explains high-precision techniques to measure body composition, including bioelectrical impedance analysis.

Medline Plus

http://medlineplus.gov

Supported by the National Library of Medicine and the National Institutes of Health, this site provides health information and interactive tutorials.

Shape Up America!

www.shapeup.org

This site helps you assess your physical readiness for activity. After entering your personal data (weight, height, age, gender), you can perform some physical fitness assessments, including activity level, strength, flexibility, and aerobic fitness.

Sparkpeople

www.sparkpeople.com

This is a large site with health information, exercise demonstrations, a free e-newsletter, fitness and dietary planning, recipes, and a community section with message boards and support teams.

Weight-Control Information Network (WIN)

http://win.niddk.nih.gov/index.htm

WIN provides the general public, health professionals, the media, and Congress with up-to-date, science-based information on weight control, obesity, physical activity, and related nutritional concerns.

Gear

Campmor
www.campmor.com
This is a retail site that often provides closeouts on last year's items that you can get for a reduced cost. It also offers new equipment.

Hiking and Backpacking
http://hikingandbackpacking.com
This site provides information on trails, hiking tips, lots of links, and a list of clubs in each U.S. state and organizations in the United States and Canada. It also has advice on gear and recommendations for best gear sites.

Recreational Equipment Incorporated (REI)
www.rei.com
This retail site has most items needed to start backpacking. It allows you to see side-by-side gear comparisons to allow you to make an informed decision.

Government Agencies

Bureau of Land Management
www.blm.gov
The Bureau of Land Management manages 258 million acres of grasslands, forests, high mountain arctic tundra, and desert landscapes located predominantly in the western United States.

Mountain Rescue Association (MRA)
www.mra.org
Established in 1958, the MRA is the oldest search and rescue association in the United States. One of the best ways to learn about trail safety and survival is to learn about wilderness search and rescue. Explore this site to discover how to become involved in the search and rescue team in your area and to learn about training opportunities.

National Park Service
www.nps.gov
The National Park Service is charged with preserving almost 400 natural, cultural, and recreation sites in the United States. The Web site links you to all the sites and is a great resource for hiking and backpacking the nation's treasured places.

National Recreation Reservation System
www.recreation.gov
This is the site for finding and reserving federal recreation opportunities.

U.S. Fish and Wildlife Service (USFWS)
www.fws.gov

The USFWS is responsible for conserving fish and wildlife resources in the United States and their habitats. Visit this site for information on various forms of wildlife that you are likely to encounter in your area.

U.S. Forest Service National Avalanche Center

www.avalanche.org/~nac

This site will link you to regional avalanche centers that give updates on snow conditions and avalanche dangers in your area. It also provides basic information on avalanche safety as well as opportunities for education on avalanche safety and rescue.

USDA Forest Service

www.fs.fed.us

The Forest Service manages 193 million acres of forests and grasslands throughout the United States. The variety of hiking and backpacking opportunities on Forest Service lands is impressive.

Hikers With Disabilities

National Center on Physical Activity and Disability (NCPAD)

www.ncpad.org/fun/fact_sheet.php?PHPSESSID=d9dc9e321b0b41ee1e3004 e5e1ada3c9&sheet=75

This site is an excellent resource for outdoor travel for people with disabilities.

Several organizations specifically organize trips that accommodate people with disabilities. Power to Be (www.powertobe.ca), On the Tip of the Toes Foundation (www.pointe-des-pieds.com/nousen.asp), and Wilderness Inquiry (www.wildernessinquiry.org) are examples.

Hiking Adventures

American Trail Running Association (ATRA)

www.trailrunner.com

The mission of this organization is to "represent and promote trail and mountain running." They have news and events, race information, and membership information as well as state and international trail listings.

Audubon International

www.audubon.org

This site offers information about birds and science, as well as international issues on which you can take action to save bird populations. There are also links to states, centers, and chapters.

Geocaching

www.geocaching.com

You can learn how to hide and seek a cache on this site, as well as search for caches all over the world.

Letterboxing North America

www.letterboxing.org

In addition to information on how to get started and clues for letterboxes around North America, this site hosts a section specifically for kids.

U.S. Orienteering Federation

www.us.orienteering.org

This site gives an in-depth look at orienteering as a sport, as well as information about clubs and team events and results.

Nutrition

Cyber Kitchen

www.nhlbi.nih.gov/chd/Tipsheets/cyberkit.htm

This interactive site can help you plan a healthy, delicious diet.

Nutrition Analysis Tool and System (NATS)

http://nat.crgq.com

This site features a free interactive program that provides a nutrient analysis of your diet, calculating the calories, carbohydrate, protein, fat, vitamins, minerals, and fiber in the foods you eat.

USDA Center for Nutrition Policy and Promotion

www.cnpp.usda.gov

This U.S. government site provides dietary assessment, dietary guidelines, and healthy recipes.

Weather Information

U.S. National Weather Service (NWS)

www.nws.noaa.gov

Visit this site for up-to-date weather conditions, weather forecasts, and historical weather trends in the area in which you plan to hike or backpack.

A variety of sites, such as www.infoplease.com/ipa/A0004587.html, can give you valuable weather information for other parts of the world. A quick Internet search will readily turn up weather information that will help you plan your trip.

Wilderness First Aid Training

SOLO Wilderness Medicine

www.soloschools.com

SOLO provides training in wilderness medicine, beginning with basic wilderness first aid training and progressing to wilderness emergency medical technician (WEMT) training.

Wilderness Medical Associates (WMA)

www.wildmed.com

The WMA provides training in wilderness medicine, beginning with basic wilderness first aid training and progressing to WEMT training.

Wilderness Medicine Institute (WMI)

www.nols.edu/wmi

The WMI is a subsidiary of NOLS. It provides training in wilderness medicine, beginning with basic wilderness first aid training and progressing to WEMT training.

Wilderness Medicine Training Center (WMTC)

www.wildmedcenter.com/home.html

The Wilderness Medicine Training Center provides training in wilderness medicine, beginning with basic wilderness first aid training and progressing to WEMT training.

Success Checks

Chapter 1

1. You can hike in city parks.

    a. true

    b. false

2. Backpacking is a _____ hiking trip.

    a. multiday

    b. car camping

    c. higher elevation

    d. multi-agency

Match the trail to its description (see questions 3-6).

    a. Appalachian Trail

    b. Continental Divide Trail

    c. National Hiking Trail

    d. Bicentennial National Trail

3. _____ From Queensland to Victoria, this is the longest marked multi-use trail in the world (3,312 miles, or 5,330 kilometers).

4. _____ Goes from the Mexican border to the Canadian border (3,000+ miles [4,828+ kilometers]).

5. _____ Goes from Georgia to Maine (2,175 miles [3,500 kilometers]).

6. _____ Goes from Ontario to western Nova Scotia (6,214 miles [10,000 kilometers]).

7. In your own words, list the seven principles of Leave No Trace.

8. Fall has less predictable weather than spring for hiking and backpacking.

    a. true

    b. false

9. Alpine environments are

    a. abundant with wildlife

    b. easily accessed

    c. above the tree line

    d. accessible only in the spring

10. The most popular season to explore forests is
    a. spring
    b. fall
    c. summer
    d. winter

Match the hiking or backpacking scenario to the most likely setting for it (see questions 11-15).
    a. city park
    b. county park or open space
    c. state park
    d. national forest
    e. national park

11. _____ Half-day hike on a well-marked trail

12. _____ Half-hour nature break

13. _____ Peak ascent that takes a full day in a wilderness area

14. _____ Multiday trip where you need to obtain a permit

15. _____ Car camping trip with a variety of day-use trails

16. Cryptobiotic soils are alive.
    a. true
    b. false

Chapter 2

1. Most people can become fit enough to backpack.
    a. true
    b. false

2. You can start hiking at almost any level of fitness as long as you plan your hike in relation to your fitness.
    a. true
    b. false

3. People who are diabetic or have other special needs should not hike or backpack.
    a. true
    b. false

4. Making safe decisions on the trail is easier and more likely if you are fit.
    a. true
    b. false

5. If you are in a hurry to start your workout, don't bother with a warm-up period.
   a. true
   b. false

6. Contact with nature is correlated with living longer and decreased stress levels.
   a. true
   b. false

7. The adage "No pain, no gain" is not true and actually can be dangerous, both on and off the trail. Start slowly and progress with manageable increases in workout intensity, ussually increasing intensity or duration not more than 10 percent per week.
   a. true
   b. false

8. Cardiorespiratory endurance
   a. is set for each person and exercise will not change our endurance
   b. is the measure of a muscle's ability to generate force over and over again
   c. increases joint mobility
   d. sometimes called *aerobic fitness*, measures the heart's ability to pump oxygen-rich blood to working muscles

9. The 1.5-mile (2.5-kilometer) run test
   a. should be done without practice
   b. should be used by extremely overweight people
   c. works well for college students and other young adults who are in fairly good shape, and is a useful measure to be evaluated with other fitness indicators
   d. tests flexibility and strength

10. The general purposes of a warm-up and a cool-down include
    a. raising your core body temperature a few degrees
    b. reducing strain to the heart imposed by rapidly engaging in heavy exercise
    c. creating nutrient-rich, warm blood and lubricating the joints
    d. all of the above

Chapter 3

1. One advantage of synthetic fillings is that they fill a smaller area; thus a sleeping bag made with synthetics will take up less space in your pack than a down sleeping bag.

    a. true

    b. false

2. It is usually wise to wear a cotton T-shirt when hiking to help wick away perspiration from the skin.

    a. true

    b. false

3. Most food for backpacking is hard to find and must be bought at specialty shops like sporting good stores, mountaineering stores, and so on.

    a. true

    b. false

4. How well clothing ventilates is an important consideration in selecting outdoor clothing.

    a. true

    b. false

5. External-frame packs are generally more expensive than internal-frame packs.

    a. true

    b. false

6. Getting blisters are a function of the type of boot you have and little can be done to prevent them.

    a. true

    b. false

7. If you clean your gear after each trip, it will shorten its life span.

    a. true

    b. false

8. All backpacking stoves use the same type of fuel.

    a. true

    b. false

9. When at camp, you should wear open-toed shoes to allow your feet to breathe.

    a. true

    b. false

10. After purchasing your boots, you are ready to start hiking in them right away.

    a. true

    b. false

11. Of the reasons for wearing two pairs of socks, which is the most important during moderate weather?

    a. to help prevent blisters

    b. to keep your feet warm

    c. to help your boots fit

    d. to keep your feet from perspiring

12. The least effective fabric for all-purpose use in the outdoors is

    a. wool

    b. nylon

    c. polypropylene

    d. cotton

13. One characteristic of both wool and fleece is

    a. they retain their warmth when wet

    b. they are poor insulators

    c. they are waterproof

    d. they are petroleum based

14. The most important aspect of a pack is that it should be

    a. external

    b. internal

    c. expensive

    d. comfortable

15. A sleeping pad provides which of the following?

    a. comfort

    b. reduction of body heat loss to the ground

    c. both a and b

    d. none of the above

16. Clothing should *not*

    a. be sturdy

    b. be expensive

    c. have multiple uses

    d. be roomy and comfortable

17. The three layers of clothing in the outdoors include the

    a. base layer, insulating layer, and wind and rain layer

    b. bottom layer, middle layer, and top layer

    c. synthetic layer, wool layer, and Gore-Tex layer

18. What items should be placed for easiest access in your pack?

    a. rain jacket and stove

    b. rain gear and first aid kit

    c. rain gear and sleeping pad

    d. fuel bottle and tent

19. When packing your pack, you should use the CBS method, which stands for
    a. completely bottom stacked
    b. containers bags and sacks
    c. cannot bust seams
    d. conveniently balanced system

20. What is the most effective method of treating water in the backcountry?
    a. boiling
    b. filtering
    c. chemical treating
    d. no treatment necessary

Chapter 4

1. It is important to consider the desires of others in your group before planning a route.
   a. true
   b. false

2. The history of an area's seasonal weather should be considered when planning a trip.
   a. true
   b. false

3. GPS is a substitute for using a map and compass.
   a. true
   b. false

4. The magnetic needle on a compass points to true north.
   a. true
   b. false

5. A USGS quadrangle is an example of a large-scale map.
   a. true
   b. false

6. Which is the best navigation system to use for trip planning?
   a. maps
   b. compass
   c. GPS
   d. a combination of maps, compass, and GPS

7. Using copied maps or maps downloaded from the Internet are not always useful for land navigation because

    a. you have to tape many parts of maps together

    b. the colors come out wrong

    c. the image may become slightly distorted

    d. it violates copyrights

Match the following parts of the compass to those shown on the diagram.

8. compass base plate

9. orienteering arrow

10. direction-of-travel arrow

11. magnetic needle

12. compass housing

Chapter 5

1. To determine how far a lightning strike is from your present location, count the number of seconds between the flash of lightning and ensuing thunder and divide by

    a. 3

    b. 5

    c. 7

    d. 10

2. You are hiking with three companions along a ridge line when a thunderstorm suddenly closes in on you. What should you do?

    a. Find shelter beneath the nearest rock overhang.

    b. Continue hiking along your route.

    c. Descend from the ridgeline as quickly as possible, spreading out and moving away from tall trees or pinnacles.

    d. Find the nearest puddle of water and stand in it.

3. If you find yourself in a survival situation with food but no water, you should refrain from eating.

    a. true

    b. false

4. The first thing you should do in a survival situation is build a fire for warmth.

    a. true

    b. false

5. Which of the following conditions calls for immediate advanced medical care?

    a. early stage hypothermia, characterized by shivering, apathy, mumbling, and stumbling

    b. when you experience headaches, dizziness, loss of balance, or difficulty focusing

    c. when a blister bursts and becomes infected

    d. when your flesh freezes and turns black or ashen

6. You are hiking down a trail when suddenly you are confronted by a mountain lion. What should you do?

    a. Approach the mountain lion to get a closer look.

    b. Immediately turn and run away from the mountain lion.

    c. Offer the mountain lion food.

    d. Speak to the mountain lion in a deep, low voice and slowly back away.

    e. Smile at the mountain lion, showing your teeth.

7. An appropriate time to call for rescue in the backcountry would be when

    a. you underestimated the amount of time needed for your hike and realize that you will not get back to the trailhead before dark

    b. one of your hiking companions slipped and fell from a rock, breaking her leg

    c. one of your companions is feeling totally fatigued and insists that he can go no farther

    d. one of your companions was swept away by the current during a stream crossing, and you can find no sign of her

8. The first step to survival is

    a. conducting an inventory of the resources available in the situation

    b. finding suitable shelter to stay warm

    c. recognition of the fact that you are in a survival situation

    d. panicking and calling for help

9. How many liters of water, on average, should hikers and backpackers consume each day to remain well hydrated?

    a. 0-2 liters

    b. 2-4 liters

    c. 4-6 liters

    d. 6-8 liters

10. Who yields to whom when their paths cross in the backcountry?

   a. hikers yield to mountain bikers

   b. equestrians yield to hikers

   c. equestrians yield to mountain bikers

   d. hikers yield to equestrians

Chapter 6

1. Appropriate stretching focuses on smooth movement and avoids bouncing.

   a. true

   b. false

2. Slow, deep breaths will draw more oxygen into your lungs with

   a. less effort

   b. greater effort

   c. labored effort

   d. none of the above

3. The rest step is a technique that will help you to maintain your pace when traveling on

   a. steep trails

   b. snow-covered trails

   c. high-elevation trails

   d. all of the above

4. Drinking a quart (1 liter) of water in the morning before you begin hiking is not recommended to compensate for loss of body fluids overnight.

   a. true

   b. false

5. The recommended length of a rest stop to minimize buildup of lactic acid in the body is

   a. 2 minutes

   b. 5 minutes

   c. 10 minutes

   d. 15 minutes

6. Repeated shortcuts across switchbacks can promote

   a. erosion

   b. scarring of the natural setting

   c. rival trails

   d. all of the above

7. You should have good land navigation skills evidenced by competent working knowledge and experience using a map and compass before traveling off-trail.

    a. true

    b. false

8. You should space your group out at least _____ feet when traveling on level ground and _____ feet or more if traveling uphill or downhill.

    a. 2 feet (.5 meter); 4 feet (1 meter)

    b. 5 feet (1.5 meters); 10 feet (3 meters)

    c. 8 feet (2.5 meters); 16 feet (5 meters)

    d. none of the above

9. Suggestions when climbing are to

    a. tighten boot straps to reduce toes hitting the toe box of the boot

    b. loosen the top lacing of the boots to reduce friction on the lower shin

    c. extend the length of trekking poles

    d. use the side step when hiking on a steep grade

10. Using manmade stone walkways to cross streams or rivers is an acceptable practice because use of such bridges never results in serious injuries.

    a. true

    b. false

Chapter 7

1. If your group size is large and in an area meant for solitude, you may want to

    a. break into smaller groups

    b. have smaller groups leave the trailhead at 15-20 minute intervals

    c. choose a different area

    d. all of the above

2. These are all instances in which you should step aside and let others pass you on the trail: others hiking faster than you; horses or other large pack animals; mountain bikers, if feasible.

    a. true

    b. false

3. There is no need to remove dog poop from hiking areas because it will biodegrade naturally.

    a. true

    b. false

4. Gear for pets, such as harnesses, paw covers, and specialty backpacks, are expensive and unnecessary.

   a. true

   b. false

5. Which of the following is not a consideration discussed with regard to hiking with children?

   a. terrain

   b. the height of the views

   c. goal-oriented destinations

   d. patience

   e. all of the above are considerations

6. Trail running is a relatively new phenomenon pushed mainly by the gear industry.

   a. true

   b. false

7. Which of the following uses a map and compass as an integral part of the hiking adventure?

   a. orienteering

   b. geocaching

   c. letterboxing

   d. birdwatching

   e. a and c

   f. all of the above

8. When observing wildlife, it is best to set out food for them so they will come near.

   a. true

   b. false

9. As deserts and mountaintops are especially challenging environments, one should

   a. sharpen map, compass, and GPS skills

   b. never plan to stay overnight in these environments

   c. learn about flash flood and avalanche patterns

   d. a and c

   e. all of the above

10. Desert and mountain environments appear extraordinarily rugged, but they are actually very fragile and require special precautions to maintain their integrity.

   a. true

   b. false

Chapter 8

1. Describe one thing to consider in each of the following categories related to campsite selection.
   a. storms
   b. rocks
   c. trees
   d. floods
   e. animals
   f. wood
   g. water
   h. location to other campers
   i. elevation

2. List and describe the three basic campsite types and when you would choose to use each type.

3. You should locate your cooking and food storage areas downwind of your sleeping area.
   a. true
   b. false

4. Digging trenches around your tarp to drain water away is a recommended practice.
   a. true
   b. false

5. The campsite should be located at least 200 feet (61 meters) away from rivers, lakes, and streams.
   a. true
   b. false

6. Cutting switchbacks is acceptable because it allows faster access to your destination.
   a. true
   b. false

7. CCR stands for cold, clear, and running.
   a. true
   b. false

8. Food-protection systems include hanging food from trees, using animal-proof canisters, using electrically charged fencing, and using various alarm systems.
   a. true
   b. false

9. List and describe the four methods of campfire construction discussed. In what type of site (pristine or established) would each one be used?

Define the following terms:

10. adiabatic lapse rate

11. orographic effect

12. widow makers

13. flag trees

14. thermal inversion

15. *Giardia lamblia*

16. List three ways to treat water and one pro and con for each.

17. Diagram how the campsite components should be located in relation to one another. Be sure to include the cooking site, sleeping site, water sources, food storage, wind direction, and topography.

18. List four ways of dealing with human waste.

Chapter 9

A nonprofit camping organization in your area has hired your outfitting business to submit a proposal for a 10-day trip in the coming summer season for some of their members. The group is a mix of six males and four females ranging from 16 to 28 years of age. All are in reasonably good health and none are physically challenged. Two of the males are overweight and one of the women is a vegetarian. A few of them have their own packs and sleeping bags. One of the males has had some NOLS training, and the rest indicate that they have had some camping experience with family and friends. They have expressed an interest in learning the skills of backcountry living, overland navigation, elementary rock climbing, fishing, and plant identification. They want you to give them a fairly detailed understanding of what the experience will be like if they accept your proposed plans.

Your task: Create an informative, clear, and concise trip proposal for this group. A major feature of your proposal should be a clear breakdown of the 14 trip planning considerations and how you have incorporated them in your proposal. In addition, they would like an annotated time line that charts in reasonable detail what will happen from the time the group members start preparing for the trip until the closing activity at the end of the trip. As you put together your proposal and design your time line, please address the following:

- What are the key questions your participants will want answered by your proposal and time line? How will you answer them?

- What opportunities will there be on the trip for participants to pursue the interests that they have mentioned?

- How have you taken into account the 14 trip considerations in planning this experience?
- How will you ensure that the trip is safe, environmentally responsible, and enjoyable for all the participants?

Answers

Chapter 1: 1. a; 2. a; 3. d; 4. b; 5. a; 6. c; 7. plan ahead and prepare, camp and travel on durable surfaces, dispose of waste properly, leave what you find, minimize campfire impacts, respect wildlife, be considerate of other visitors; 8. b; 9. c; 10. c; 11. b; 12. a; 13. d; 14. e; 15. c; 16. a

Chapter 2: 1. a; 2. a; 3. b; 4. a; 5. b; 6. a; 7. a; 8. d; 9. c; 10. d

Chapter 3: 1. b; 2. b; 3. b; 4. a; 5. b; 6. b; 7. b; 8. b; 9. b; 10. b; 11. a; 12. c; 13. a; 14. d; 15. c; 16. b; 17. a; 18. b; 19.d; 20. a

Chapter 4: 1. a; 2. a; 3. b; 4. b; 5. b; 6. d; 7. c; 8 through 12, see figure 4.3 on page 94

Chapter 5: 1. b; 2. c; 3. a; 4. b; 5. d; 6. d; 7. d; 8. c; 9. b; 10. d

Chapter 6: 1. a; 2. a; 3. d; 4. b; 5. b; 6. d; 7. a; 8. c; 9. b; 10. b

Chapter 7: 1. d; 2. a; 3. b; 4. b; 5. e; 6. b; 7. e; 8. b; 9. d; 10. a

Chapter 8: a. See examples in chapter 8; 2. pristine campsite, medium-impact campsite, established campsite; 3. a; 4. b; 5. a; 6. b; 7. a; 8. a; 9. mound fire (pristine), pan fire (pristine), pit fire (pristine), fire ring (established); 10. the temperature drops 3 to 6 degrees Fahrenheit (2 to 3 degrees Celsius) for every 1,000 feet of elevation gained; 11. air approaching a mountain is forced up and over the peak, then the moisture in the air condenses, causing more clouds and precipitation on the windward slope; 12. dead trees that may uproot easily due to wind or the pull from a tarpline; 13. trees with branches growing primarily on one side, indicating dominant wind direction; 14. occurs when cold dense air flows downslope at night and collects in the valleys and drainages—a layer of warmer, less dense air lays above the cold air; 15. the organism that causes giardia, also known as giardiasis; 16. boiling (cheaper but time consuming); chemical (lightweight but affects taste); filtration (immediate potable water but adds weight and cost); 17. see figure 8.4 on page 191; 18. dispersing, burying, packing out

Photo Credits

Courtesy of Marni Goldenberg Pages 7, 54, 55, 90, 142, 143, 163, 165, 206, 221

Courtesy of Jennifer Hazelrigs Page 151

Courtesy of Tim Kidd Page 145 (left)

© Human Kinetics Pages 9, 17, 21, 51, 30, 54, 57, 60, 62, 69, 73, 75 (top), 94, 97, 98, 100, 133, 135, 138, 145 (right), 175, 185 (bottom), 186, 205, 213

Luminous World Photography Pages 1, 6, 57, 73, 129, 131, 170
inquiries@luminousphotos.com
Telephone: 303-912-4495

Jerry and Marcy Monkman Page 147

© PhotoDisc Pages 5, 21, 40, 169, 171

Courtesy of Jon Sachs Graphics Page 111 (bottom)

Jim West Page 173

Courtesy of Wilderness Education Association Pages 43, 137, 149

References

Chapter 1

Bureau of Land Management. (2007). BLM mission. Retrieved from www.blm.gov/nhp/facts/index.htm.

Martin, B., Cashel, C., Wagstaff, M., & Breunig, M. (2006). *Outdoor leadership: Theory and practice*. Champaign IL: Human Kinetics.

National Park Service. (2007). The National Park System: Caring for the American legacy. Retrieved from www.nps.gov/legacy/mission.html.

Chapter 2

American College of Sports Medicine (ACSM). *ACSM resource manual for guidelines for exercise testing and prescription* (3rd ed.). Retrieved from www2.gsu.edu/~wwwfit/physicalactivity.html.

Conners, C. (2004). *Lipsmackin' vegetarian backpackin': Lightweight, trail-tested vegetarian recipes for backcountry trips*. Guilford, CT: Three Forks.

Frumkin, H. (2001). Beyond toxicity human: Health and the natural environment. *American Journal of Preventive Medicine, 20*(3), 234-240.

Glanz, K., Lewis, F., & Rimer, B. (2002). *Health behavior and health education: Theory, research, and practice* (3rd ed.). San Francisco: Jossey-Bass.

Glaros, N.M., & Janelle, C.M. (2001). Varying the mode of cardiovascular exercise to increase adherence. *Journal of Sport Behavior, 24*(1), 42-62.

Howley, M. (2002). *2002 NOLS nutrition field guide*. Lander, WY: National Outdoor Leadership School.

Kreider, R., Fry, A., & O'Toole, M. (1998). *Overtraining in sport*. Champaign, IL: Human Kinetics.

Prochaska, J.O., Norcross, J.C., & DiClemente, C.C. (1994). *Changing for good*. New York: Morrow.

Sanders, C., Yankou, D., & Andrusyszyn, M.A. (2005). Attention and restoration in post-RN students. *Journal of Continuing Education in Nursing, 36*(5), 218-225.

U.S. Department of Health and Human Services. (1996). *Physical activity and health: A report of the Surgeon General*. Atlanta, GA: U.S. Department of Health and Human Services, Centers for Disease Control and Prevention, National Center for Chronic Disease Prevention and Health Promotion.

Chapter 3

Drury, J.K., & Bonney, B.F. (1992). *The backcountry classroom: Lesson plans for teaching in the wilderness*. Merrillville, IN: ICS Books.

Drury, J.K., Bonney, B.F., Berman, D., & Wagstaff, M.C. (2005). *The backcountry classroom: Lesson, tools, and activities for teaching outdoor leaders* (2nd ed.). Helena, MT: Falcon.

Drury, J.K., Bonney, B.F., & Cockrell, D. (1991). Basic wilderness skills. In D. Cockrell (Ed.), *The wilderness educator: The wilderness education association curriculum guide*. Merrillville, IN: ICS Books.

Drury, J., & Holmlund, E. (1997). *The camper's guide to outdoor pursuits*. Champaign, IL: Sagamore.

Graydon, D. & Hanson, K. (Eds.). (1997). *Mountaineering: The freedom of the hills* (6th ed.). Seattle: Mountaineers.

Nicolazzo, Paul. (1997). *The art and technique of wilderness medicine*. Mazama, WA: Wilderness Medicine Training Center.

Pearson, C. (Ed.). (2004). *NOLS cookery* (5th ed.). Mechanicsburg, PA: Stackpole Books.

Chapter 5

Brown, T. (1983). *Tom Brown's field guide: Wilderness survival*. New York: Berkeley Books.

Devoto, B. (Ed.). (1953). *The journals of Lewis and Clark*. Boston: Riverside Press.

Graydon, D., & Hanson, K. (1997). *Mountaineering: Freedom of the hills* (6th ed.). Seattle: Mountaineers.

Hale, A. (1984). *Safety management for outdoor program leaders*. Unpublished manuscript.

Isaac, J., & Goth, P. (1991). *The Outward Bound wilderness first-aid handbook*. New York: Lyons & Burford.

Jensen, S.C. (Ed.). (1998). *Beating the odds on the North Pacific: A guide to fishing safety* (3rd ed.). Sitka, AK: Alaska Marine Safety Education Association.

Kauffman, R.B., & Carlson, C. (1992). The rescue curve: A race against time. *American Canoeist*, March: 10-13.

Lundin, C. (2003). *98.6 degrees: The art of keeping your ass alive*. Layton, UT: Gibbs Smith.

Martin, B., Cashel, C., Wagstaff, M., & Breunig, M. (2006). *Outdoor leadership: Theory and practice*. Champaign, IL: Human Kinetics.

Morrissey, J. (2000). *Wilderness Medical Associates field guide for wilderness travelers, outdoor professionals, and rescue specialists* (3rd ed.). Bryant Pond, ME: Wilderness Medical Associates.

Petzoldt, P. (1984). *The new wilderness handbook* (2nd ed.). New York: Norton.

Priest, S., & Gass, M. (2005). *Effective leadership in adventure programming* (2nd ed.). Champaign, IL: Human Kinetics.

Chapter 6

Drury, J.K., Bonney, B.F., Berman, D., & Wagstaff, M.C. (2005). *The backcountry classroom: Lesson, tools, and activities for teaching outdoor leaders* (2nd ed.). Helena, MT: Falcon.

Fletcher, C., & Rawlings, C. (2002). *The complete walker IV.* New York: Knopf.

Graydon, D. & Hanson, K. (Eds.). (1997). *Mountaineering: The freedom of the hills* (6th ed.). Seattle: Mountaineers.

Guillion, L. (1987). *Canoeing and kayaking instruction manual.* Birmingham, AL: Menasha Ridge Press.

National Outdoor Leadership School (NOLS). (1999). *NOLS wilderness educator notebook.* Lander, WY: NOLS.

Petzoldt, P. (1984). *The new wilderness handbook* (2nd ed.). New York: Norton.

Wolfe, L.M. (Ed.). (1979). *John of the mountains: The unpublished journals of John Muir.* Madison, WI: University of Wisconsin Press.

Chapter 7

Abbey, E. (1973). *Cactus country: The American wilderness.* New York: Time-Life.

Graydon, D., & Hanson, K. (eds.). (1997). *Mountaineering: The freedom of the hills* (6th ed.). Seattle: Mountaineers.

Hampton, B., & Cole, D. (1986). *Soft paths* (3rd ed.). Mechanicsburg, PA: National Outdoor Leadership School.

Louv, R. (2005). *Last child in the woods: Saving our children from nature-deficit disorder.* Chapel Hill, NC: Algonquin Books.

Manning, H. (1975). *Backpacking: One step at a time.* New York: Vintage Books.

Morrissey, J., & Johnson, D. (2005). *The field guide of wilderness and rescue medicine* (3rd ed.). Portland, ME: Wilderness Medical Associates.

Petzoldt, P. (1984). *The new wilderness handbook* (2nd ed.). New York: Norton.

Schad, J. (2004). *Trail runner's guide: San Diego.* Berkeley, CA: Wilderness Press.

Chapter 9

Coyote Communications. *Camping with your dog.* Retrieved from www.coyotecom.com/dogcamp.html#participate.

Drury, J.K., Bonney, B.F., Berman, D., & Wagstaff, M.C. (2005) *The backcountry classroom: Lesson, tools, and activities for teaching outdoor leaders* (2nd ed.). Helena, MT: Falcon.

Drury, J., & Holmlund, E. (1997). *The camper's guide to outdoor pursuits.* Champaign, IL: Sagamore.

Hampton, B., & Cole, D. (1986). *Soft paths* (3rd ed.). Mechanicsburg, PA: National Outdoor Leadership School.

Moab Information Site. *Canyon country: Minimum impact practices.* Retrieved from www.moab-utah.com/rack/minimpac.html.

Petzoldt, P. (1984). *The new wilderness handbook* (2nd ed.). New York: Norton.

Wilderness Education Association (WEA). (2000). *Affiliate handbook* (6th ed.). Bloomington, IN: Wilderness Education Association.

About the Editors

Marni Goldenberg, PhD, assistant professor in the recreation, parks, and tourism administration department at California Polytechnic, San Luis Obispo, coauthored chapter 1. She is a WEA-certified instructor, a Leave No Trace master educator, and an instructor for Outward Bound. She has been hiking and backpacking for over 15 years.

Bruce Martin, PhD, assistant professor in the school of recreation and sport sciences at Ohio University, coauthored chapter 5. He has been hiking and backpacking throughout the United States and Canada for over 20 years. He is an American Canoe Association instructor trainer, a WEA instructor, a Leave No Trace master educator, and has taught outdoor leadership at the college and university level for a number of years.

About the Contributors

Andrew J. Bobilya, PhD, assistant professor of outdoor education at Montreat College, coauthored chapter 8. He also trains outdoor leaders through multiweek expeditions using the WEA's curriculum and looks for opportunities to paddle or backpack with his family, including a recent trip on the Colorado River through the Grand Canyon and backpacking in the mountains of western North Carolina.

Christine Cashel, EdD, retired professor from Oklahoma State University, coauthored chapter 4. She was an educator for 34 years and an outdoor leader and instructor for 27 years. She has planned and participated in more than 50 trips, ranging from weekend to 35-day expeditions, in the United States and abroad.

Jerel Cowan, MS, instructor at University of Central Oklahoma, coauthored chapter 3. He is a Leave No Trace master educator, WEA professional short course participant, backpacking instructor, climbing instructor, outdoor adventure trip leader, and former adventure camp director. He is an active backpacker and climber in the western and northwestern United States.

Brad Daniel, PhD, professor of environmental studies and outdoor education at Montreat College, coauthored chapter 8. He has course experience as a participant with Outward Bound, NOLS, and WEA. He has been lead instructor on many extended wilderness expeditions (longer than 20 days) and numerous shorter trips.

Jack Drury, co-owner of Leading EDGE, a professional development organization, has taught WEA courses since 1979, coauthored chapter 9. He is past president of WEA, a veteran of numerous National Outdoor Leadership School courses and has led adventures throughout North America, Central America, Europe, and Siberia.

Briget Tyson Eastep, PhD, assistant professor and director of outdoor recreation in parks and tourism at Southern Utah University, coauthored chapters 1 and 7. She has hiked and backpacked throughout New Mexico, Colorado, Utah, and Idaho with family and friends—from weekend trips to completing the 500-mile Colorado Trail in seven weeks.

Hugh Gibson, EdD, assistant professor in charge of the outdoor recreation curriculum at Missouri State University, coauthored chapter 3. He has led trips in the Northeast, Southeast, Midwest, and Colorado. He is an ACA instructor and Leave No Trace trainer.

Jennifer Marie Hazelrigs, ME, outdoor director of campus recreation at the University of Arkansas, coauthored chapter 6. She leads a majority of the outdoor educational trips, trains student leaders, and developed the trip leading program at the University of Arkansas. She has led backpacking trips in Arkansas, Florida, North Carolina, Arizona, and Tennessee.

Jennifer L. Hinton, PhD, assistant professor in the school of recreation and sport sciences and coordinator of the recreation studies program at Ohio University, coauthored chapter 7. In addition to her education and teaching experiences, she has been day hiking for much of her life and continues to do so with her husband and children.

Scott Jordan, MS, adjunct professor at the school of education and coordinator of outdoor adventure at Oklahoma State University, coauthored chapter 4. He is a certified instructor for the WEA and a Leave No Trace master educator. He coordinates the logistics for about 10 backpacking trips each year.

Timothy W. Kidd, PhD, associate professor of outdoor leadership at John Brown University, coauthored chapter 6. Over the past 25 years he has led backpacking trips for college students and other groups from the Smokies to the Rockies and from the Ozarks to the Northwoods. He is a WEA-certified instructor and a Leave No Trace master educator.

Jim Lustig, MS, outdoor programs coordinator and adjunct professor at San Diego State University, coauthored chapter 7. He has been leading and guiding hiking and backpacking trips professionally since 1984 and through-hiked the entire 2,100-mile Appalachian Trail in 1982.

Denise Mitten, PhD, associate professor at Ferris State University, authored chapter 2. She has taught rock climbing, skiing, and whitewater canoeing. A widely experienced adventure guide, she has led climbs on Mt. McKinley, in the Swiss Alps, and in the Himalayas. She has guided raft and kayak trips down the Colorado, Green, and Rio Grande rivers and bicycle trips in Europe and New Zealand.

Scott A. Robertshaw, MS, coauthored chapter 5. He is director of the experiential learning center at Colorado State University at Pueblo. He has been teaching for 10 years in camps, schools, and a wilderness program and has been hiking and backpacking for over 15 years.

Need more adventure?

Want to go canoeing, kayaking, hiking and backpacking, or rock climbing? Start today with the Outdoor Adventures series. This practical series provides you with the essential information to get ready and go. The Outdoor Adventures series is designed to prepare you with instruction in the basic techniques and skills so you can be on your way to an adventure in no time.

Hiking and Backpacking
by the Wilderness Education Association

Canoeing
by the American Canoe Association

Kayaking
by the American Canoe Association

Rock Climbing
by the Wilderness Education Association

To learn more about the books in this series, visit the Outdoor Adventures series website at
www.HumanKinetics.com/OutdoorAdventures.

For a complete description or to order
Call **1-800-747-4457**
In Canada, call **1-800-465-7301**
In Europe, call **44 (0) 113-255-5665**
In Australia, call **08-8277-1555**
In New Zealand, call **09-448-1207**

HUMAN KINETICS
The Information Leader in Physical Activity